From Happy Homemaker
to Desperate Housewives

From Happy Homemaker to Desperate Housewives

Motherhood and Popular Television

Rebecca Feasey

ANTHEM PRESS
LONDON · NEW YORK · DELHI

Anthem Press
An imprint of Wimbledon Publishing Company
www.anthempress.com

This edition first published in UK and USA 2012
by ANTHEM PRESS
75-76 Blackfriars Road, London SE1 8HA, UK
or PO Box 9779, London SW19 7ZG, UK
and
244 Madison Ave. #116, New York, NY 10016, USA

Copyright © Rebecca Feasey 2012

The author asserts the moral right to be identified as the author of this work.

Cover image © Splash News/Corbis

All rights reserved. Without limiting the rights under copyright reserved above,
no part of this publication may be reproduced, stored or introduced into
a retrieval system, or transmitted, in any form or by any means
(electronic, mechanical, photocopying, recording or otherwise),
without the prior written permission of both the copyright
owner and the above publisher of this book.

British Library Cataloguing-in-Publication Data
A catalogue record for this book is available from the British Library.

Library of Congress Cataloging-in-Publication Data
Feasey, Rebecca.
From happy homemaker to desperate housewives : motherhood and
popular television / Rebecca Feasey.
p. cm.
Includes bibliographical references and index.
ISBN 978-0-85728-561-4 (pbk. :alk. paper)
1. Mothers on television. 2. Television programs–Great Britain. 3.
Television programs–United States. I. Title.
PN1992.8.M58F43 2012
791.450941–dc23
2012032982

ISBN-13: 978 0 85728 561 4
ISBN-10: 0 85728 561 0

This title is also available as an eBook.

For Poppy

CONTENTS

Chapter 1	Introduction: Theorising Motherhood on the Small Screen	1
Chapter 2	Soap Opera: Challenging the 'Good' Mother Stereotype	13
Chapter 3	Situation Comedy: the (Un)Funny Mummy Wars	29
Chapter 4	Teen Drama: Absent, Inept and Intoxicated Mothers	53
Chapter 5	Dramedy: Struggling, Sexual and Sisterly Single Mothers	71
Chapter 6	Reality Parenting Programming: Fragile, Failing and Ineffectual Mothers	97
Chapter 7	Celebrity Reality Television: Maintaining the 'Yummy Mummy' Profile	121
Chapter 8	Factual Television: Pregnancy, Delivery and the New Mother	147
Chapter 9	Conclusion	177
Bibliography		185
Index		203

Chapter 1

INTRODUCTION: THEORISING MOTHERHOOD ON THE SMALL SCREEN

Women make up 52 per cent of the world's population (Gallagher et al., 2005, 18), and yet, recent research reveals that men continue to outnumber women on the ostensibly domestic and hence feminine medium of television by two to one (Thorpe 2010). However, even though women are seldom seen on television – and even less so in positions of power, authority, experience or maturity – extant literature from within the fields of feminist television criticism, media studies and women's studies deem it crucial to explore those representations that do exist on the small screen.

Recent feminist scholarship examines, unmasks and interrogates a myriad of female representations, including the depiction of the doting good woman in the hospital drama (Philips 2000), the powerful matriarch in the primetime soap opera (Madill and Goldmeier 2003), the single thirty-something woman in the situation comedy (Arthurs 2003), the domestic goddess in lifestyle television (Hollows 2003), the exhibitionistic woman in reality programming (Pozner 2004), the objectified female in television advertising (Gill 2006), the adolescent girl in the teenage text (Hains 2007), the smart women in the political drama (Berila 2007) and the abrasive female detective in the cop show (Jermyn 2010). However, although much work to date seeks to investigate the depiction of women on television, little exists to account for the depiction of mothering, motherhood and the maternal role in contemporary popular programming.

Likewise, although there is a burgeoning interest in work that critically engages with the lived experience of pregnancy and motherhood from within the fields of audience research (Miller 2005), social action (Thomson et al., 2008), social and economic research (Martens 2009), self-help literature (Vieten 2009), literary criticism (Podnieks and O'Reilly 2010), social history (Plant 2010), art history (González 2010), social issues research (The Social Issues Research Centre 2011) and citizenship (Jensen and Tyler 2011), there is little to account for the range of mothers and mothering practices seen on the small screen and no defining text that is dedicated to outlining and examining such representations. And even though motherhood has developed as a central issue in feminist scholarship, with a wealth of texts committed to exploring mothering practices in relation to sexuality (Ferguson 1983), peace (Ruddick 2007), disability (Thomas 2007), globalisation (Cheng 2007), work (Gatrell 2008) and health (Clark 2008), these texts do little to account for the portrayals of mothering and motherwork presented on television. The maternal figure is portrayed in a wide range of television genres, texts and schedules, and as such, it is crucially important that we consider the significance of these representations in a broader consideration of motherhood, motherwork and the maternal role.

More than 700,000 new babies were born in Britain last year, and over 4 million born in America. The average age of a first-time mother, or 'primigravida', has risen to 27.4 years in Britain and 25 in America, with growing numbers of women conceiving for the first time in their 30s or 40s (Office for National Statistics 2009; CDC's National Vital Statistics Reports: Births, 2009). The social construction of motherhood has changed in recent years due to the availability of contraception, advances in medical technology, changing attitudes towards sexual behaviour and challenges to the traditional institution of marriage. The number of births outside of marriage continues to rise in both Britain and America, and the numbers of working mothers continues to follow this same trajectory in both countries. Women today are given increased choices about whether, when and how to mother, and as such, they are mothering in a broad and diverse range of social, sexual, financial and political circumstances. However, these same women are being judged on their age, fertility and family choices and scrutinised in relation to their mothering practices and maternal behaviours. Such scrutiny is in relation to those issues surrounding what is perceived to be the 'correct' and 'appropriate' path to motherhood, so that those lone, working, teen, mature, lesbian or feminist mothers who do not fit the idealised image of the white, heterosexual, self-sacrificing, middle-class, 'good' mother or perform in line with the ideology of intensive mothering, tend to be judged, ranked and found wanting within and beyond the media environment.

The 'good' mother is a woman who, even during pregnancy, adheres to appropriate codes of style, appearance, attractiveness, selflessness and serenity (Pitt 2008). And later, when the child is born, this mother adheres to the ideology of intensive mothering whereby she takes sole care and responsibility for her children's emotional development and intellectual growth, is devoted to them and their needs rather than her own, and never has any negative feelings towards them, only unfailing unconditional love (Green 2004, 33).

Most importantly, however, she is a full-time mother who is always present in the lives of her children, young and old; she remains home to cook for them after school and if she works outside of the home, she organises such responsibilities around the needs of her children (Chase and Rogers 2001, 30). Deborah Borisoff tells us that in order for mothers to conform to the idealised image of the 'good' mother and adhere to the ideology of intensive mothering, mothers, and only mothers, must supervise each childhood activity, lovingly prepare nutritious meals, review and reward every school assignment and seek out educationally and culturally appropriate entertainment, whilst maintaining a beautiful home and a successful marriage (Borisoff 2005, 7). The 'good' mother finds this intensive maternal role to be natural, satisfying, fulfilling and meaningful and feels no sense of loss or sacrifice at her own lack of freedom, friendships, financial independence or intellectual stimulation (Green 2004, 33). Anthropologist Sheila Kitzinger informs us that 'once a woman has produced a child she bonds with it in utter devotion, forgets her own wishes, and sacrifices herself for her baby' (Kitzinger cited in Wolf 2002, 50). And yet, although it has been suggested that intensive mothering isolates both children and parents from society, and in so doing creates frustration and alienation for both parties involved (hooks 2007, 152), there is a sense that if the woman 'does not slip easily into this role, she risks the accusation of being a bad mother' (Kitzinger cited in Wolf 2002: 50).

The contemporary media environment is saturated by romanticised, idealised and indeed conservative images of selfless and satisfied 'good' mothers who conform to the ideology of intensive mothering. Susan Douglas informs us that the media landscape 'is crammed with impossible expectations [...] dominated by images of upper-middle-class moms, both real and fictional, who "have it all" with little sacrifice, counterposed by upper-middle-class women who have fled the fast track for the comforts of domesticity' (Douglas 1995, 285). More recently, Douglas and Meredith Michaels tell us that a range of media texts, from films and television, radio and advertising to print and broadcast news, the magazine sector and advice literature, raise 'the bar, year by year, of the standards of good motherhood while singling out and condemning those we were supposed to see as dreadful mothers' (Douglas and Michaels 2005, 14). These authors tell us that the 'good' mother who saturates popular media culture is selfless, serene, slim and spontaneous and above all else, satisfied by her maternal role (ibid., 110–39). So too, Kitzinger makes the point that media texts 'bombard' women with advice about how to construct and maintain socially appropriate motherhood practices, be it tips on health, relationships, surface appearances or maternal practices (Kitzinger cited in Maushart 2007, 464). Child-rearing manuals play a part in constructing and circulating the 'good' mother myth due to the fact that the women in these texts are asked to 'serve as a constant comforting presence, to consider the child's every need, to create a stimulating environment exactly suited to each development stage, and to tolerate any regression and deflect all conflict' (Thurer 2007, 336). Moreover, constructions of acceptable mothering demand that mothers conform to traditional gender rules, with cooking, cleaning and domestic chores being 'embraced' by the 'good' mother (Kinnick 2009, 12). Katherine Kinnick goes on to say that:

> the media idealize and glamorize motherhood as the one path to fulfillment for women, painting a rosy, Hallmark-card picture that ignores or minimizes the very real challenges that come along with parenthood [...] Media narratives often cast motherhood in moral terms, juxtaposing the "good mother" with the "bad mother", who frequently is a working mom, a lower-income mom, or someone who does not conform to traditional gender roles of behaviour, ambition, or sexual orientation. (Ibid., 3)

When the entertainment and news media present motherhood in moral terms by contrasting what they deem to be the socially acceptable 'good' mother with what they believe to be the reprehensible 'bad' mother, they are 'both prescribing and proscribing norms for maternal behaviour' (ibid., 9). With this in mind, Douglas and Michaels make the important point that the 'media have been and are the major dispenser of the ideals and norms surrounding motherhood [seeking] to advise mothers, flatter them, warn them and, above all, sell to them, they collaborated in constructing, magnifying, and reinforcing the new momism', or what I will throughout this book refer to as the 'good' mother myth (Douglas and Michaels 2005, 11).

Mumsnet, Britain's most popular website for parents, receives 570,000 site visits and over 30 million page views each month, with over 25,000 posts each day (Google Analytics 2011). And although the site gives parents the space for peer-to-peer support, there is a sense in which these forums adhere to a rather limited and privileged notion of the 'good' mother. The website was set up by two media professionals turned stay-at-home mothers and even a cursory glance at the site gives the impression of an upper-middle-class maternal environment. Under a banner entitled 'Money Matters' there is little here about tax credits, child benefits or school meal entitlements, rather, a helpful list that tells mothers 'Why you should save, 10 ways to save on family fun, 10 ways to save on family travel, Ethical savings, How to give to charity and Mortgage calculators' (Mumsnet 2012a). Moreover, the style and beauty pages give tips on 'Hair care, Skin problems, Botox and filler, Home pedicures and Fake tans' (Mumsnet 2012b). Under the title 'Lunchbox Tips and Ideas' we are reminded that 'what you pack is open to scrutiny – not just by other kids but by other mums. So if your child's going to a friend's house after school, make sure that's not the day you give in to Fruit Shoots and Greggs sausage rolls. Stick a few stray aduki beans/arugula leaves/seaweed sachets in the lunchbox' (Mumsnet 2012c). When the topic is education, the forums are peppered with conversations about the differences between private and state schooling (Mumsnet 2012d). Savings, family holidays, charitable donations, home pedicures, seaweed sachets and private education speak for and about a privileged notion of contemporary family life that appears in keeping with a socially acceptable, culturally appropriate and romanticised image of motherhood. Mumsnet, like existing media experiences, is keen to uphold the notion of the slim, serene, spontaneous and satisfied mother, with mothers themselves contributing to and circulating rather than critiquing the ideology of intensive mothering.

At a time when the British government is offering initiatives and support to encourage mothers to return to the workplace as soon as possible after the birth of a child (McRobbie cited in Skeggs, Thumim and Wood 2008a, 14), the media are keen to remind us that 'women remain the best primary caretakers of children, and that to be a remotely decent mother, a woman has to devote her entire physical, psychological, emotional, and intellectual being, 24/7, to her children' (Douglas and Michaels 2005, 4). And yet, even though this impossible, implausible and unattainable image of motherhood is far removed from the lived experience of many women in society, this idealised figure continues to be presented in the popular media environment as the epitome of perfect mothering that we should all aspire to and strive for. Indeed, we are told that the 'good' mother acts as 'the "legitimate" standard to which mothers are compared [...]. She becomes an ideal to believe in, and one that people both expect and internalize' (Green 2004, 33). Shari Thurer echoes this point when she states that '[m]edia images of happy, fulfilled mothers, and the onslaught of advice from experts, have only added to mothers' feelings of inadequacy, guilt, and anxiety. Mothers today cling to an ideal that can never be reached but somehow cannot be discarded' (Thurer 2007, 340). The theorist continues by commenting that

> the current standards for good mothering are so formidable, self-denying, elusive, changeable, and contradictory that they are unattainable [...] The current Western version is so pervasive that, like air, it is unnoticeable. Yet it influences our domestic arrangements, what we think is best for our children, how we want them to be raised, and whom we hold accountable. (Ibid., 334)

One might look to question why it is that mothers who themselves might be struggling to uphold the ideology of intensive mothering put on a mask of 'good' motherhood or speak with an appropriate yet inauthentic maternal voice. Douglas and Michaels make this point when they say that as mothers we 'learn to put on the masquerade of the doting, self-sacrificing mother and wear it at all times' to save maternal shame or humiliation (Douglas and Michaels 2005, 6). Patriarchal society remains the chief beneficiary of the 'good' mother myth, as the ideology of intensive mothering presents mothers as effective consumers whilst giving them the sole responsibility of childcare without financial recompense for their labours.

The problem here of course is that mothers are not capable of upholding the impossible, improbable and unachievable image of the 'good' mother in line with the ideology of serene, selfless and satisfied intensive mothering. Indeed, working mothers are automatically deemed 'poor' or 'bad' caregivers due to the time spent away from their children. The ideology of intensive mothering 'takes a toll on working mothers by asserting that this population is not doing – and can never do – enough to raise their children properly' (Borisoff 2005, 8). Stay-at-home mothers are also struggling to conform to the image of appropriate motherhood due to the exhausting physical labour and constant emotional intensity demanded of this ideal (Held 1983, 11). Susan Maushart makes the point that the 'gap between image and reality, between what we show and what we feel, has resulted in a peculiar cultural schizophrenia about motherhood' (Maushart 1999, 7). After all, even though mothers know that the ideology of intensive mothering is unachievable and that the figure of the 'good' mother is merely an unrealistic and unattainable myth, 'the ideal of motherhood we carry in our heads is so compelling that even though we can't fulfil it and know that we probably shouldn't even try, we berate ourselves for falling short of succeeding' (Warner 2007, 721). It has been suggested that the 'ideology of natural-intensive mothering [...] has become the official and only meaning of motherhood, marginalizing and rendering illegitimate alternative practices of mothering. In so doing, this normative discourse of mothering polices *all* women's mothering and results in the pathologizing of those women who do not or can not practice intensive mothering' (O'Reilly 2004a, 7; italics in original). The fact that many mothers are unable to mother within the ideology of intensive motherhood does not seem to lessen the power of this maternal model; rather, it means that many expecting, new and existing mothers present what Susan Maushart refers to as a 'mask' of appropriate motherwork which goes further to reinforce the dominance of the 'good' mother myth (Maushart 1999).

Although the 'good' mother myth might encourage us to assume that the ideology of intensive mothering is somehow fixed, stable or natural, or that women have always taken sole responsibility for their children's emotional, physical, intellectual and social growth, it is worth noting that 'motherhood is primarily *not* a natural or biological function; rather, it is specifically and fundamentally a cultural practice that is continuously redesigned in response to changing economic and societal factors. As a cultural construction, its meaning varies with time and place' (O'Reilly 2004b, 5; italics in original). There is no natural, universal or essential experience of motherhood, and a brief look at the history of mothering and motherwork demonstrates a number of broad shifts in what has been understood as appropriate mothering practices (Badinter 1980; Dally 1982; Thurer 1994; and Plant 2010).

In pre-industrialised societies, men and women, fathers and mothers worked on the land with their children, and both acted as physical provider and emotional caretaker for them. However, with industrialisation and a move away from family farming to factory work in the cities, men were employed away from the family home and had little hand in domestic chores, leaving women in the private domestic role to look after the house and their children in line with what we now understand to be the traditional nuclear family unit (Horwitz 2004, 43). Women and mothers were encouraged to return to the workforce during World War II, government funded nurseries were set up and women were reminded that they were capable of more than motherwork, and yet during the postwar period there 'was a concerted [...] shift to return women to the home' and the ideal mother was once again a stay-at-home figure (Bassin, Honey and Kaplan 1994, 6). However, we find that children would not necessarily be spending time with their mother, but rather, playing with other children in the local neighbourhood (O'Reilly 2004b, 8). It is only since the 1980s and the emergence of the ideology of intensive mothering that mothers were encouraged to be both at home and attuned to the physical, emotional, psychological and intellectual needs of her children (ibid., 7). The practice of intensive mothering 'is an historical aberration of twentieth-century industrialized life' (Maushart 1999, xx) because although 'the post-war discourse of good motherhood demanded that mothers be at home full time with their children, it did not necessitate the intensive mothering expected of mothers today' (O'Reilly 2004b, 7).

Douglas and Michaels make the point that the ideology of intensive mothering reduces a mother's identity to her relationship with her children, derides working mothers and presents stay-at-home mothers with improbable and impossible ideals (Douglas and Michaels 2005, 22–3). With this in mind, it has been suggested that the 'good' mother myth 'emerged in response to women's increased social and economic independence: increased labour participation, entry into traditionally male areas of work, rise in female-initiated divorces, growth in female-headed households, and improved education' (O'Reilly 2004b, 10). In short, while women were making social, sexual, financial and political progress in the post-feminist period, this maternal backlash developed to ensure that 'women would forever feel inadequate as mothers, and that work and motherhood would be forever seen as in conflict and incompatible' (ibid., 10).

The terms 'mother', 'mothering', 'motherwork' and the institution of motherhood are used liberally throughout this book, and to clarify it is worth briefly noting that I use the term 'mother' to refer to biological mothers unless otherwise stated, 'mothering' to refer to day-to-day childcare practices and 'motherwork' to foreground those wider domestic chores that are heavily intertwined with mothering. While I use the terms 'mother', 'mothering' and 'motherhood' to refer to the individual and personal experiences of women taking care of and being responsible for their children, I use phrases such as 'the institution of motherhood' and 'the ideology of mothering' to signal where and when I am referring to the patriarchal 'context in which mothering takes place and is experienced' (Miller 2005, 3). Andrea O'Reilly tells us that while the patriarchal institution of motherhood 'is male-defined and controlled and [...] deeply oppressive to women', a mother's personal experiences of motherwork 'are female-defined and centered and potentially empowering to women' (O'Reilly 2008, 3). The point here is that 'while motherhood, as an institution, is a male-defined site of oppression, women's own experiences of mothering can nonetheless be a source of power' (ibid., 3). The distinction between personal mothering practices and the patriarchal institution of motherhood is crucial, and has been the cornerstone of much second-wave and post-feminist debate concerning the role, representations and responsibilities of women as mothers in society.

Second-wave feminists have been accused of being 'anti-motherhood' or 'anti-family' due to the fact that the women's movement of the period declared the nuclear family oppressive to women and the housewife role as a key source of maternal isolation, depression and stress, not to mention exclusion from career opportunities (Bassin, Honey and Kaplan 1994, 6). However, many of these women were not anti-motherhood; rather, as already suggested, they were critical of the patriarchal institution of motherhood. Second-wave feminists campaigned for reforms on issues such as reproductive rights (Kinser 2010, 3), paid maternity leave, education (Friedan 1963, 323–6), and family-friendly policies in the work-place (Kinnick 2009, 2) in order to release women from the burden of domesticity and allow them a choice over their maternal role and motherwork practices (Ehrensaft 1983, 41). Amber Kinser reminds us that the women's movement did not set out to undermine the role of mothers nor to dismiss the importance of motherwork, but rather, it sought to challenge the notion of the nuclear family that 'requires a breadwinning, decision-making father and a nurturing, submissive at-home mother' (Kinser 2010, 96). An anthology of writing from the period informed us that 'we are not against love, against men and women living together, against having children. What we are against is the role women play once they become wives and mothers" (Babcox and Belkin cited in Tuttle Hansen 2007, 434). The movement has campaigned for equal opportunities for women, including mothers, and demanded that women have the power to decide whether, when and how to have children, or to remain childless, without social stigma or cultural critique (Kinser 2010, 96).

Women today are struggling to live up to an improbable and impossible image of the 'good' mother that dominates the cultural landscape, and as such, it is necessary to look at the representations of motherhood in contemporary television programming, and consider the ways in which popular genre texts either adhere to the unrealisable image of intensive mothering or negotiate such motherhood practices in favour of a more attainable depiction of 'good enough' mothering. I hope to trace the social, cultural and moral contours of contemporary motherhood before examining the depiction of mothers and the maternal role in a wide range of popular television genres. I seek to illustrate how motherhood is being constructed, circulated and interrogated in contemporary fictional and factual programming and point to the ways in which such images can be seen to challenge or conform to the romanticised yet demanding ideology of intensive mothering. This analysis is crucial, not because such representations are an accurate reflection of reality but because they have the power and scope to foreground culturally accepted familial relations, define sexual norms and provide 'common sense' understandings about motherhood and maternal behaviour for the contemporary audience. Katherine Kinnick makes this point when she tells us that what popular television programmes choose 'to emphasize and valorize', as well as what they overlook and ignore plays a profoundly important role in constructing societal norms and circulating popular cultural expectations for expectant, new and existing mothers (Kinnick 2009, 2). In this way, television should not be dismissed as mere entertainment, escapism or distraction; rather, it must be examined as 'a site of struggle over meaning and values' in general and a site over meaning and values concerning motherhood and the maternal role in particular (Valdivia 1998, 277).

Each chapter will present a clear and comprehensive account of the representation of motherhood and the maternal role in a particular television genre, paying attention to the ways in which specific case studies can be understood in relation to a wider consideration of motherhood, both on and off screen. In this way, readers are encouraged to acknowledge significant changes in both the lived reality of motherhood and the representations of the maternal role, with Chapters 2 to 5 seeking to unmask depictions of motherhood in a diverse range of popular fictional genres and Chapters 6 to 8 seeking to uncover popular depictions of maternity in a number of factual and 'infotainment' texts, concluding that contemporary programming forms a consensus as it investigates, negotiates and challenges the romanticised image of the 'good' mother.

The fictional genres point to the ways in which the maternal role is being scripted and depicted in a range of long-running and more recent popular television texts and the ways in which these genres might be seen to negotiate the 'good' mother myth via a number of anxious, anti-social and abhorrent maternal figures, be they for the viewing pleasures of the family, youth or a more mature female audience. Chapter 2 examines the construction of motherhood in the ostensibly female genre of soap opera, considering the ways in which a number of mothers are demanding social and sexual fulfilment outside of their maternal role in the popular *EastEnders* (1985–); Chapter 3 looks at the depiction of the mother as housewife in the domestic situation comedy, focusing on the relationship between non-mothers, stay-at-home mothers and working mothers in the humorous *Outnumbered* (2007–). Chapter 4 explores the portrayal of deviant, desiring and delinquent motherwork in the teen drama, paying particular attention to the absent, incapable and intoxicated mothers of the glossy *90210* (2008–); Chapter 5 then goes on to look at the depiction of the single working mother in the contemporary comedy drama, considering the sisterly mother-daughter dynamic in the critically and commercially successful *Gilmore Girls* (2000–2007).

The factual genres point to the ways in which pregnancy, birth and the maternal role are being experienced by 'ordinary' members of the public and more exhibitionistic examples of contemporary celebrity, and the ways in which such motherhood meanings and practices are being edited and in some cases re-enacted for the woman in the audience in accordance with the 'good' mother myth and the mask of appropriate mothering. Chapter 6 explores the representations of motherhood in reality parenting television, only to conclude that mothers are routinely presented as fragile, failing and ineffectual in the commercially successful *Supernanny UK* (2004–10), and *Supernanny USA* (2005–10); Chapter 7 examines the way in which the celebrity motherhood profile demands an improbable, impossible and unachievable image of serene, selfless and fulfilled motherhood in celebrity reality television, even when the sexually assertive, seemingly selfish and single mothers might ostensibly be seen to challenge the 'good' mother myth in titles such as *Glamour Models, Mum and Me* (2010), *Kerry Katona: The Next Chapter* (2010–) and *Katie* (2009–). Chapter 8 examines the depiction of pregnancy, delivery and the new mother in reality pregnancy and childbirth television, focusing on the ways in which programmes such as *One Born Every Minute UK* (2010–) and *One Born Every*

Minute USA (2011–) gives expectant and new mothers a voice seldom heard elsewhere in popular media culture.

The concluding chapter reminds us that although existing representations of mothers in contemporary popular programming are unable to achieve the ideals, norms and practices of the idealised 'good' mother, these sexual, sisterly and struggling depictions of expectant, new and existing mothers should be applauded for debunking the ideology of ideal motherhood and negotiating the unattainable myth in favour of what is more realistically seen as 'good enough' or achievable mothering. That said, even though both fictional and more factual representations of motherhood on the small screen continue to break through the mask of 'good' motherhood and what must be deemed improbable motherwork practices, these genres continue to do so while simultaneously upholding this romanticised maternal ideal. Fictional scripted characters, 'ordinary' members of the public and candid celebrity mothers appear to form a televisual consensus in that their authentic motherhood experiences and sincere maternal practices simultaneously condemn and condone the ideology of appropriate motherhood.

Although this books aims to cover a number of popular television genres and programme titles, readers will no doubt question the inclusion of some texts and the exclusion of others, and I hope to justify my choice of case studies by stating that they are those shows that were airing on free channels, that proved and continue to prove popular with audiences and which are archived and accessible. I have included a number of both British and American programmes, and where appropriate pointed to both versions of the same title due to the fact that both countries 'share a common language, cultural heritage and advanced economic state' and because many of the shows being presented here have created a powerful impact on audiences on both sides of the Atlantic (Feasey 2008, 6). No single book can ever hope to cover each and every significant case study as it pertains to an examination of motherhood and popular television, and as such, it is my hope that the programmes presented here will act as the first point of entry for a reader who will then look to unmask the ways in which those themes, theories and representations are also in evidence in a broader range of genre texts, be they UK or US, daytime or primetime, long-running or pilot programmes, with my argument being that the 'good' mother myth continues to dominate the wider televisual landscape. And it is to the representations of motherhood in my chosen popular texts that the discussion must now turn.

Chapter 2

SOAP OPERA: CHALLENGING THE 'GOOD' MOTHER STEREOTYPE

Introduction

Soap opera was originally conceived as a drama that would appeal to women, with a focus on mothers, matriarchs, family settings and personal relationships, and these elements are understood as the mainstay of the genre. Although soap operas have in recent years tried to extend their audience by bringing in a broader range of male characters as a way to attract the man in the audience and a wider range of television advertisers (Hobson 2003, 97–100; Feasey 2008, 7–19), soap opera continues to be understood as a woman's genre, in part because of its representation of the maternal role. With this in mind, this chapter will look at a number of independent mothers, other-mothers and teen mothers in the long-running *EastEnders* (1985–) and consider the ways in which these images of women confront and confound the 'good' mother archetype that dominates the current cultural climate.

History of the Genre

Soap opera emerged on commercial American radio in the 1930s, and since that time the genre has been interested in the domestic trials, everyday tribulations and seemingly ordinary emotions associated with motherhood, friendship and personal relationships. As such, the genre proved popular with female listeners, and remained popular with the female viewer when it moved to the small screen in the 1950s. Since that time, soap opera has become and remained a popular, prevalent and persistent part of both daytime and primetime schedules on both sides of the Atlantic. And although the genre has, since its inception, been dismissed and derided by a range of cultural critics and feminist commentators as low-budget, low-brow sentimentalism (Plant 2010, 42), it has routinely articulated social change and embodied 'the issues which are of personal and public concern' in different historical and political periods (Hobson 2003, 161). Tania Modleski tells us that soap opera has presented more references to social problems than any other fictional television genre (Modleski 2008, 31), and even though these shows should not be seen to mirror reality, they do tend to be '*based on fictional realism*' and the presentation of contemporary social concerns such as AIDS, euthanasia, immigration and changing gender roles (Hobson 2003, 35; italics in original). Indeed, it has been suggested that the genre acts as a 'social barometer' for the wider romantic, sexual, familial and domestic concerns of society (Salmon cited in Hobson 2003, 50), because these popular texts 'send messages about appropriate or expected behaviour' in any given period (Anger 1999, 110). Dorothy Hobson makes this point when she tells us that the soap opera has 'been at the forefront of reflecting the changes which have occurred in family life throughout the periods of their existence' (Hobson 2003, 118).

Although I will be mapping out various representations of motherhood as they are seen in the long-running *EastEnders*, I ask readers to consider my propositions against a wider range of both British and American texts. After all, even though there are obvious variations in the genre, even between British primetime titles, these domestic dramas do tend to share certain formal elements. The term soap opera denotes a popular, long-running, open-ended serial that resists narrative closure. These programmes are set in the present, located in the domestic sphere and based on the personal, and on occasion, the professional lives of a core set of characters in a small number of everyday locations. The domestic dramas are transmitted for 52 weeks of the year, with multiple storylines that create 'the illusion that life continues in the fictional world even when viewers are not watching' (ibid., 35). Although the sheer frequency and volume of soap opera narratives means that there is no single defining text or series to study, I encourage the reader to examine my propositions against the most recent depictions of motherhood and the maternal role as they are presented in the genre and see my case studies as evidence of broader maternal trends and motherwork narratives. After all, those pregnancies, birth stories, paternity mysteries and maternal experiences that are outlined here are replicated time and again in the genre, with regular characters moving in and through motherhood over the course of a show's history.

Women and Soap Opera

In the late 1960s the second-wave feminist movement believed that women's oppression stemmed from their position as housewives and mothers in the domestic sphere (O'Reilly and Porter 2005, 2). Feminist television theorists thus became interested in examining the representation of women in soap opera precisely because the genre was committed to the private arena, personal relationships and the family unit (Brown 1994, 48–9). Indeed, even though the slogan 'the personal is political' (Hollows 2000, 4) has become synonymous with second-wave feminism, it might also be seen to speak for the domestic drama (Brunsdon 1997, 38–40). We are long used to the division of public and private spheres whereby men dominate the world of work and women occupy the domestic environment, however, as I have suggested elsewhere, the soap opera blurs such distinctions by seeking to claim the public sphere as a personal realm (Feasey 2008, 13–17). Women in soap opera not only dominate the domestic world, but their presence, dialogue and emotions are also seen to unfold in the public realm, which goes some way towards breaking down rigid social distinctions and gender-specific expectations in the genre.

The centrality of female characters (Brown 1994, 49), the representation of strong women (Brunsdon 2000, 69) and the authority of the matriarch (Geraghty 1999, 74–83) are all sites of potential pleasure for the female viewer, and possible frustration for the feminist television critic. And although the strong woman 'must withstand repeated buffetings of fate [due to] the formal demands of the genre', seeing these women live through crisis after crisis does not detract from audience interest in and investment in such figures (Brunsdon 2000, 69). After all, by 'featuring powerful matriarchs, soap operas provide for women a fictional position only rarely available in the mass media' (Brown 1994, 51). Moreover, the genre depicts a variety of women in terms of 'different ages, class and personality types' and in so doing, offers numerous points of identification and empathy for the woman in the audience (Hobson 1982, 33). The fact that these roles are not stereotypes, but rather, fully rounded and psychologically believable characters goes further to explain female investment in the genre (Hobson 2003, 83–4).

In terms of female pleasure, we should not underestimate the satisfaction to be found in paying attention to women's stories, from their point of view. Feminist media theorists tell us that women are routinely ignored, overlooked, trivialised and infantilised in primetime television (Tuchman 1978, 8), and as such, the very fact that women are both seen and heard in the domestic drama helps us to understand the popular appeal of the soap opera for the female viewer (Allen 2012). The ways in which the genre values 'women's words, thoughts, and ideas [...] is comforting to women in a culture where the silencing of women's voices seems natural' (Brown 1994, 54). Soap opera asks us to invest in the female point of view and it is this viewpoint that continues to be understood as 'one of the most consistent pleasures offered to women' by the genre in question (Geraghty 1999, 47). The fact that the soap opera narrative is driven by problem solving and intimate conversations goes further to not simply acknowledge but to actually value the often-derided domestic, familial and emotional role that women continue to play, within and beyond the personal sphere (Brown 1994, 54). Soap operas recognise the ways in which women develop and maintain personal relationships and foregrounds the manner in which they balance individual, and often competing, demands for attention from friends, family, colleagues and the wider community (Geraghty 1999, 43). The domestic setting, the focus on family relations and the importance of personal friendships are also all said to speak to the woman in the audience (Brown 1994, 48).

Although some feminist television theorists might critique or condemn soap opera for reaffirming the long-standing link between women, motherhood and the domestic sphere or for reinforcing the 'ideological construct which naturalises "women's place" in the home' (Brown 1990, 203), it is worth noting that, even in the post-feminist period, women continue to take on the burden of housework (Williams 2001, 234) and the responsibility for familial and emotional relationships in society (Hollows 2000, 92). Indeed, it is precisely because the soap opera strives to reassure the homemaker of 'the importance of her situation' (Hartmann cited in Plant 2010, 42) and champion the 'culturally constructed skills of femininity' that the genre can be seen to speak for and about the women in the audience (Brunsdon cited in Abercrombie 1997, 51). The ways in which soap opera not only focuses on the domestic arena, but also applauds women's strength, power and control within this environment can be seen to offer pleasure and a sense of empowerment to the female. Indeed, if one considers that the most loyal viewers of soap opera are 'predominantly younger, working-class women, many of whom were at home all day looking after small children' then the pleasures on offer become clear (Geraghty 2005, 318). Theorists such as Mary Ellen Brown and Joanne Hollows suggests that those alternating storylines and open-ended plots that define the genre are also of significance to a female viewer who is living through multiple narratives, paying attention to alternating personal and professional storylines and finding herself amidst only ever partially completed domestic chores (Brown 1994, 58; Hollows 2000, 96).

Soap Opera and Motherhood

Early British radio soap operas such as *Mrs Dale's Diary* (1948–69) were presented as 'narratives of maternal sacrifice and redemption' (Plant 2010, 42), and when new television soaps were introduced, they were based around a range of mothering roles. While *Coronation Street* (1960–) presented Elsie Tanner (Patricia Phoenix) as the archetypal struggling working-class single mother, *Crossroads* (1964–88) gave us the epitome of middle-class working motherhood in the character of Meg Mortimer (Noele Gordon). However, although the matriarch has always been integral to the soap opera narrative, the figure of the housewife is becoming less prevalent and more troubled in the contemporary text (Brunsdon 2000, 81). *EastEnders* has shown us Angie Watts (Anita Dobson) as an alcoholic adoptive mother while *Brookside* (1982–2003) presented the viewer with a character who was struggling to combine motherhood with the wider personal and professional concerns of womanhood in the shape of Sheila Grant (Sue Johnston). Moreover, the popular – albeit imported – *Home and Away* (1988–) used and continues to use foster-mothering as a central narrative device in its weekly narratives. In short, it is not merely the representation of women but rather the representation of mothers that is essential to the genre. Peter Buckman tells us that 'the problems of motherhood' (Buckman 1984, 67) are crucial to soap opera, Christine Geraghty argues that the mother figure is the undisputed 'heroine' of the domestic text (Geraghty 1999, 81) and Dorothy Hobson notes that 'child-rearing' is one of the genre's principal storylines (Hobson 2003, 9). Soap opera does not merely represent motherhood, but rather, it represents the 'power of motherhood' within the family unit, and such maternal power is most evident in the ways in which the genre foregrounds 'the needs of children for their mothers' in the weekly narratives (ibid., 93). Tania Modleski's seminal work on the soap opera suggests that two of the most fundamental and oft-repeated narrative devices revolve around unwed mothers and the difficulties of balancing a career and motherhood (Modleski 2008, 31). Soap opera is routinely understood as a women's genre, but perhaps it is more fitting to refer to it as a mother's genre, due to the importance of motherhood, the significance of the maternal role and the acknowledgement of motherwork to the weekly narratives. With this in mind, it is surprising to find that although a range of theorists such as those outlined here have acknowledged the significance of mothers and motherhood to the genre in question, they have done little to examine, unmask or theorise those maternal roles, responsibilities or representations.

Although much feminist television criticism has been written on the subject of women and soap opera in terms of the power, pleasures and frustrations of the domestic sphere, little research to date focuses on the representation of the mother in the genre, which is surprising given the predominance of the maternal figure here. The focus on housework and personal relationships over motherhood and the maternal role is perhaps to be expected if one considers that the second-wave feminist movement itself directed 'much less attention to motherhood than to housework' (Fox 1998, 172). Ien Ang, Christine Geraghty, Mary Ellen Brown and Laura Stempel Mumford have all produced fascinating and enlightening work on women and television soap opera, and yet not one of these book-length studies has included motherhood as a specific chapter heading or as a key word in their index listings (Brown 1994; Mumford 1995a; Ang 1996 and Geraghty 1999). Moreover, Charlotte Brunsdon's work on the defense of soap opera overlooks motherhood as a central site of examination in a wider debate concerning women and soap opera (Brunsdon 1997), and Tamar Liebes and Sonia Livingstone's work on what they term 'mothers and lovers' pays scant attention to the representation of motherhood in an article dedicated to a broader exploration of the modern, multitasking woman (Liebes and Livingstone 1992).

Since the emergence and development of feminist television criticism in the late 1980s and 1990s, little has been written on the representations of feminism, femininity or the woman's role in soap opera. This early work has defined academic scholarship on the genre, and to date, scant attention has been paid to the depiction of mothers in the long-running domestic text. That said, even though the representation of motherhood has been largely overlooked in the genre, feminist television theorists have 'suggested that the multiple narrative structure of soap opera demands multiple identification on the part of the viewer, and thus constitutes the viewer as a type of ideal mother' figure (Brunsdon 1997, 17). Modleski informs us that the soap opera implies a feminine spectator 'who possesses greater wisdom than all her children, whose sympathy is large enough to encompass the conflicting claims of her family (she identifies with them all), and who has no demands or claims of her own (she identifies with no one character exclusively)' (Modleski 2008, 30–31). And yet, even as theorists continue to confirm or challenge the significance of the spectator in her role as the ideal mother, whether it be in terms of her endless tolerance and sympathy (ibid., 32), her passivity and isolation (Geraghty 1999, 45) or her inaccessibility to the working-class viewer (Seiter and Kreutzner 1991, 237) this interest has not encouraged the theorists in question to unmask, deconstruct or theorise the textual representations of the mother on the small screen.

EastEnders

EastEnders is the long-running British soap opera set in Albert Square, Walford, a fictional district of the East End of London. The drama is centered on a number of extended families including the Beales, Brannings, Butchers, Jacksons, Johnsons, Masoods, Mitchells and Slaters. The action and dialogue of the programme takes place in a range of public venues including the local public house, nightclub, café, launderette, beauticians, market stalls and garage. Although *EastEnders* was originally screened as two weekly half-hour episodes, it has more recently broadcast four episodes each week with a Sunday afternoon omnibus. Moreover, the Dish Network broadcasts *EastEnders* as a pay-per-view item in America, airing one month behind the British schedule. The programme is not only one of the highest rated soap operas, but one of the most popular programmes in Britain, averaging over 9 million regular viewers (MediaTel 2012). The show has won a seemingly exhaustive number of awards, with a BAFTA for the best continuing drama series, the British Soap Award for best soap opera, the Royal Television Society Programme Award for best soap opera and the Television and Radio Industries Club Award for television soap of the year, being just some of the accolades from the 2010 season.

Abortion, Miscarriage and Impending Motherhood

Pregnancies ending in abortion are routinely seen (or at least are heard being discussed whilst actually taking place off screen) on *EastEnders*. Over the show's long history, a number of female characters have refused motherhood and opted for this procedure, including – but not limited to – Dorothy Cotton (June Brown), Michelle Fowler (Susan Tully), Sharon Watts (Letitia Dean), Bianca Butcher (Patsy Palmer), Carol Jackson (Lindsey Coulson), Vicki Fowler (Scarlett Johnson), Zoe Slater (Michelle Ryan), Stacey Slater (Lacey Turner), Danielle Jones (Lauren Crace) and most recently Lucy Beale (Melissa Suffield). This is not to say that the frequency of the procedure is unrealistic. After all, according to figures from the Department of Health, 17.5 women per 1,000 have an abortion in England and Wales, with 189,574 procedures taking place in 2010 alone (Department of Health 2010). Likewise, 22 per cent of all pregnancies currently end in abortion in the United States (Guttmacher Institute 2011). The number of women having abortions is on the increase, and has been for the last four decades. Therefore, when popular female characters decide to have an abortion, be it as a young, mature, single or co-habiting future mother, the soap opera takes the time to understand the circumstances building up to the decision, and thus asks the female audience to at least understand, if not necessarily approve of, the choice made. It is clear that 'unintended pregnancy and abortion will always be facts of life because women want to make sure the time is right for them to take on the important role of becoming a parent' (BBC News 2010), and in the cases seen here, be it due to a cheating partner or an ill-advised first sexual encounter, these women believe that this is the wrong time. It is not uncommon for teenagers to become pregnant after their first and only experience of sexual intercourse in the soap opera; indeed, Carol's youngest daughter was in such a situation and in that instance the young woman did not know that she was pregnant until giving birth. She struggled to accept her new maternal role, put her baby up for adoption and eventually left Albert Square.

The abortion narrative might be considered both plausible and powerful in the soap opera – after all, voluntary abortion allows the woman to take charge of her own body and future destiny, removing male control and authority from an emotionally charged decision-making process. Laura Stempel Mumford makes this point when she says that the act of abortion within and beyond the soap opera 'represents an active exertion of control by the pregnant woman' (Mumford 1995b, 171). And although the woman in question might on occasion be assailed by regret over her decision at some time in the future, this does not change the appropriateness of the decision at the time in question. *EastEnders* does not go as far as to present abortion as a positive choice 'in the context of an intense social debate over women's reproductive rights', but what the programme does show is the reasons why women make this decision, and the ways in which they must then live with the consequences (ibid., 171). Alternatively, miscarriage allows the writers and producers to present the domestic drama associated with a pregnancy storyline without the recourse to abortion and without having to find a way to write a small child into future storylines for a popular female character. And if one considers that one in eight confirmed pregnancies end in miscarriage in Britain alone (NHS 2012), and that between 10 and 25 per cent of all clinically recognised pregnancies will end in miscarriage in America (American Pregnancy Association 2012), then seeing popular characters such as Kat Slater (Jessie Wallace) and Ronnie Branning (Samantha Womack) experience this emotional and physical trauma offers camaraderie and potential comfort to the female in the audience who might have suffered or be suffering a similar experience (*EastEnders* 22/12/2009).

Although miscarriage and abortion are routine and recurring stories in the soap opera, so too are later pregnancy and childbirth. Caroline Whitbeck makes the point that while most media audiences have witnessed several films about men in battle, few have seen a single media text that focuses on the experience of women carrying and bearing children. In this way, the theorist tells us that the soap opera has 'provided the only exception to the rule of the disregard of pregnancy and childbirth' in recent years (Whitbeck 1983, 191). Indeed, pregnancy, whether it be wanted or unwanted, expected or otherwise, is 'one of the major themes across all the soap operas' (Hobson 2003, 113). Indeed, there are currently two pregnancy storylines developing in *EastEnders*, that of twenty-something Janine Butcher (Charlie Brooks) and teenage Lola Pearce (Danielle Harold), with neither woman currently welcoming their future maternal role (*EastEnders* 24/12/2011).

The pregnancy itself, the revelation of paternity and the ensuing repercussions all create dramatic domestic context in this most gendered of television productions. Moreover, those couples who are unable to conceive or who turn to alternative reproduction technologies also create a focus for the domestic drama. Although the soap opera tends to stress that having a baby is 'the single most important thing in a woman's life', the course of the soap opera pregnancy, like that of friendship, marriage and indeed motherhood does not always run smoothly (Rogers 1992, 82). *Soap Opera Digest* (a weekly magazine founded in 1975 that looks at American soap operas, featuring on- and off-screen news about the genre, interviews with performers and plot summaries) makes this point when it tells us that a committed and loving couple who conceive will find that their pregnancy ends in miscarriage, whereas if 'the woman doesn't love her husband but wants to stay married to him, she'll get pregnant by another man, *accidentally* [...] and *claim* it's her husband's baby (cited in Buckman 1984, 74; italics in original). And although this narrative trope is in relation to the daytime American serial, the same is true for the primetime British soap opera, where the course of pregnancy and motherhood rarely meets the seemingly impossible standards of the 'good' mother set by contemporary culture.

Soap operas rarely include a plot twist that questions issues of maternity (with *EastEnders* offering a controversial example of such a story when one mother substitutes her deceased baby for another newborn in the maternity ward, *EastEnders* 01/01/2011); rather, the paternity mystery is a recurring narrative trope in the genre, whereby mothers deceive the community about the father of their child (Modleski 2008, 31). Like the abortion and miscarriage plots before it, the paternity mystery might be seen to reflect the wider social and sexual context. After all, between 10 and 15 per cent of the population as a whole are not genetically related to the men they grew up calling father (Baker and Papp cited in Feasey 2008, 17).

Although narratives that focus on paternity are easier to plot and offer more dramatic license than the maternity mystery, the sheer volume of paternity mysteries suggest that this is a popular narrative thread for the female viewer. Mary Ellen Brown makes this point when she says 'that the paternity plot contributes significantly to women's pleasure in watching the soaps' (Brown 1994, 58). Therefore, even though one might suggest that the paternity mystery figures so prominently in the soap opera because the genre reflects the wider patriarchal culture that 'privilege the father's role and identity over the mother's', it is worth noting the ways in which the narrative offers women within and beyond the soap opera a sense of empowerment (Mumford 1995a, 100). After all, the power to name or misname the father can influence romantic entanglements by uniting a previously hostile couple; that same power can also be seen to create economic advancement by situating a child within a particular family unit. Indeed, 'the power to define another person's family position is often the only power women are permitted to exercise with impunity, and the only exertion of power that generates even short-term satisfaction' (Mumford 1995b, 172). The power to name or misname the father gives soap opera viewers 'an opportunity to imagine a world in which women [...] are in control of the central fact of family life' (ibid., 175).

Stacey Slater gave birth to a baby girl from a one-night stand with Ryan Malloy (Neil McDermott). And although the new mother initially confessed to Bradley Branning (Charlie Clements) that the father of the baby was Archie Mitchell (Larry Lamb), she has since announced to friends, family and the wider community that it was in fact her now-deceased husband Bradley who was the true father of the baby. And although audiences know this not to be the case, her extended family and wider community were being deceived by the mother in question. Therefore, when we see Dorothy looking at the baby and commenting that she is 'the spitting image of Bradley, I think it's her eyes', the audience know that a paternity revelation and the ensuing repercussions are immanent (*EastEnders* 27/06/2010). More recently, Lola is refusing to name the father of her unborn child, informing one partner that 'you ain't the only guy I've been with you know' (*EastEnders* 22/11/2012). And yet, those familiar with the genre will be aware that even though the revelation of the true father will be the cause for dramatic tension and romantic repercussions, the longer-term effects of the paternity mystery will in time realign families rather than undermine that unit (Mumford 1995a, 98).

Stacey was pregnant at 19 and Lola is currently pregnant aged 15, and although paternity mysteries are not restricted to adolescent mothers, it is worth noting that *EastEnders* has, since the outset of the show, presented pregnancy narratives that do not conform to the 'good' mother myth, most tellingly in the figure of the homeless, alcoholic, bipolar and teenage mother. Such representations are routinely excluded from media narratives of mothering, and when they are covered in programmes such as *I'm Pregnant and …* either *Bipolar, Addicted, Homeless* or *In Prison* (2009–) it is merely in an effort to provide shocking, salacious and inappropriate images of childbirth and in turn reaffirm the 'good' mother myth. However, when audiences watch Stacey give birth, the scenes are distressing rather than shocking, disturbing rather than salacious. The young woman is strapped down in the ambulance against her wishes, her birth plan and requests for pain relief ignored; she faints after experiencing a panic-fuelled delivery only to then be chided for bottle-feeding her child. When we hear Stacey exclaim that 'I've just been ripped apart, I've had hands in me like I'm a lucky dip' (*EastEnders* 27/06/2010) the sentiment remains powerful for those mothers in the audience who tend to silence themselves about the painful and sometimes humiliating reality of childbirth (Arnold 2003, 6).

The number of conceptions to women aged under 18 was 38,259 in England and Wales (Office for National Statistics 2011) and 750,000 in America in 2009; indeed, recent statistics from the Center for Disease Control say that one-third of American girls get pregnant at least once before the age of 20 (The National Campaign, 2012). And even though reproduction 'on the part of this "excluded" group is discounted and regarded as of low value, or of no value at all, by those with high social influence' (Gatrell 2008, 45), there is a sense that *EastEnders* gives these women agency, autonomy and authority. Characters such as Michelle Fowler, Sonia Jackson (Natalie Cassidy), Demi Miller (Shana Swash) and Stacey all give birth as teenagers and each one has been seen to struggle with and on occasion remove themselves from their newfound maternal role and mothering responsibilities. This is not to say that audiences are asked to scrutinise and judge them as 'bad' mothers, but rather that the programme foregrounds the financial, social and educational changes that these young women, and indeed all women, have to make to their lives as new mothers.

Birth and Biological Mothers

EastEnders, like other British primetime soap operas, presents a diverse range of biological and other-mothers, crossing all manner of age, ethnicity, class and religious backgrounds, and I would suggest that the programme tends to use motherhood as a way of creating homogeneity among otherwise disparate female characters. Dorothy Hobson makes this point when she suggests that the 'concept of motherhood is seen as a quality which gives women status and unites them, whatever faults they may have or whatever they may do' (Hobson 2003, 92–3). Indeed, the show routinely concentrates on what pleasures and frustrations these mothers have in common, rather than exploring the difficulties and differences between them. Tamar Liebes and Sonia Livingstone make this point when they tell us that motherhood is presented and appreciated as a 'connecting force' for women in the genre (Liebes and Livingstone 1992, 108).

Tanya Jessop (Jo Joyner) is the birth mother of two teenage daughters and a baby son, and although she has split up with her husband, she is committed to providing emotional and financial stability to her children. However, rather than uphold the 'good' mother myth, the woman in question provides support for her children without compromising on her own social pleasures or professional aspirations. While the 'good' mother 'denies the mother any claims on herself, and requires her to find her satisfaction in helping her children to come to terms with and resolve their multiple difficulties' (Fiske 2003, 190), Tanya is committed to her friends and takes pride in her role as owner of the local beauty salon. Tanya has created a working model of motherhood that is empowering for her children and herself, a model of motherhood that is currently being referred to as 'feminist mothering' due to the fact that she has created 'a life outside of motherhood' (O'Reilly 2008, 6). Indeed, her maternal practices might be said to be in keeping with feminist parenting manuals as they 'challenge the excessive child-centeredness of contemporary parenting practices' (ibid., 1) and encourage women 'to grow as individuals, not just as Moms' (Tiemann cited in O'Reilly 2008, 1).

Likewise, Bianca Butcher is currently spending more time trying to find babysitters – so that she can continue her social life – than she is worrying about what nutritionally valuable meals she can feed her three young children and teenage stepdaughter. Indeed, when she was recently accused of having an extra-marital affair, it transpired that she was secretly texting her own husband, and the couple were heard having to admit that they were conducting 'a bit of *Dallas* role-play' (*EastEnders* 13/08/2010). Bianca defended her role-playing antics and secret rendezvous with her husband on the grounds that 'we never spend any time together, what with four kids and a mother-in-law' (*EastEnders* 13/08/2010). And likewise, when the woman in question finds appropriate childcare for her children, she looks jubilant at the thought of leaving the domestic scene (*EastEnders* 09/08/2010). This is a woman who looks to her own mother, friends and the wider community to care for her growing brood, not in order to shirk responsibility for her familial obligations, but rather to fulfil her social and sexual self. Bianca may not fit the culturally dominant image of the child-centred 'good' mother, but her refusal to funnel all of her energies into motherwork and her refusal 'to be defined exclusively in terms of motherhood' (Kinser 2010, 121) means that whilst she may be judged as a culturally inappropriate mother, she is in fact asserting herself as a competent parent, or what has elsewhere been referred to as a 'courageous' (Rich, 1977), 'radical' (Cooper, 1987), 'rebellious' (Douglas and Michaels 2005), 'hip' (Gore 2001) or 'feminist' (O'Reilly 2008, 4) mother. And although existing television scholars might suggest that characters such as Bianca are 'fallible, unsympathetic, or too preoccupied with problems in their own lives to support' their children (Liebes and Livingstone 1992, 101), one might suggest that these mothers are merely attempting to 'achieve and sustain a selfhood outside of and beyond motherhood' (O'Reilly 2008, 2). Characters such as Tanya and Bianca might struggle with the day-to-day realities of motherhood, but their social, sexual and professional aspirations are not entirely 'hindered by the responsibilities of childcare', as feminist television theorists have previously suggested (Liebes and Livingstone 1992, 104). Rather, these women are seen to live their social, sexual and working lives with authority, agency and autonomy, and as such they can all be seen to 'signify maternal practices that resist and refuse patriarchal motherhood to create a mode of mothering that is empowering to women' (O'Reilly 2008, 4–5).

Bianca's mother, Carol, is a fiercely protective mother of her three grown-up children and her grandchildren. Although the woman in question has struggled to balance her mothering work, her independence and her sexuality, she remains loyal to her immediate and extended family unit, and it is she rather than any present or previous partner who takes on the economic responsibilities as well as the emotional burdens of her family. Indeed, Carol is 'the central prop, sustaining the family through moments of crisis, [...] the emotional and practical head of the family combining moral insight with a dogged capacity to keep going whatever vicissitudes occur' (Geraghty 1999, 77). And although she has a somewhat volatile relationship with daughter Bianca, the two clearly love each other deeply. Carol and Bianca may argue, disagree and challenge one another on a daily basis, but there exists a 'consistent sense of underlying and active concern for each other' (ibid., 186). When we hear Carol telling her friend that 'Bianca and I have our issues – years went by when we didn't exchange a single word [...] but I love her – I really do' (*EastEnders* 12/08/2010), and later hear Bianca telling her mother that 'You're hard work, you're a miserable cow but I love you' (*EastEnders* 13/08/2010), the sense of antagonism that is expressed here does not diminish the intimacy of the relationship, but rather, speaks to the lived reality of the mother–daughter bond. Andrea O'Reilly makes the point that daughters have to distance and differentiate themselves from their mother if they are to assume an autonomous and mature adult identity, while mothers struggle to create a sense of self beyond their maternal role, and as such, this dual search for self goes some way to explain the conflict voiced here (O'Reilly 2004c, 243–4). The volatile relationship between these women is not unusual in the soap opera; rather, such relationships are routinely presented in the genre because they provide 'an irresistible combination of female solidarity and family intimacy' (Geraghty 1999, 49). Indeed, *EastEnders* continues to favour the mother–daughter dynamic, and storylines that focus on the biological or other-mother–daughter relationship far outweighs those that take the mother–son bond as their starting point.

The soap opera does not romanticise motherhood, nor does it ignore the fact that childrearing can be frustrating, challenging financially and a cause of genuine stress for woman. Those mothers outlined here have at some point neglected their children, had them taken into care and refused contact or faced economic hardship, and as such, they would struggle to fit the 'good' mother archetype that pervades the contemporary cultural climate. Soap operas present the reality of contemporary mothers struggling to live up to the 'good' mother myth that has dominated and continues to dominate the contemporary media landscape. The fact that soap opera has never, and can never – due to the formal demands of the genre – depict a 'good' mother in line with the romanticised maternal ideal should be acknowledged and applauded, and understood as one more reason why the genre appeals to the woman in the audience. The characteristics and expectations associated with the 'good' mother set women up to fail, and this pattern of failure is played out in minute detail in the soap opera. Therefore rather than critique the genre for its depictions of 'bad' mothers, we should instead be considering the ways in which these women are merely presenting a more candid, open and honest version of motherhood in the contemporary period.

Soap Opera and Other-Mothers

Pamela Downe informs us that contemporary society views biological motherhood as the normal, routine and ideal form of mothering, so much so, in fact, that other forms of mothering are rarely acknowledged and routinely overlooked within and beyond the television schedules (Downe 2004, 170). And yet, Grandparents Plus (a national charity which champions the role of grandparents and the wider family in children's lives) recently revealed that more than 300,000 children are being raised by grandparents, other family members and friends in England and Wales (Grandparents Plus 2012). Likewise, 2.7 million American families are currently maintained by grandparents who have one or more grandchildren resident with them, and it is worth noting that the majority of these carers are grandmothers (US Census Bureau 2009). Irrespective of whether these grandparents are co-parenting or custodial parenting, there is a clear sense that a large and growing number of children in Britain and America are being cared for by women who are not their biological mother. Foster mothers, stepparents, grandparents and non-custodial other-mothers receive little recognition in society; indeed, they are all but invisible in the 'popular and technical discourses of parenting and motherhood' (Downe 2004, 174). Moreover, although these women take on the economic, domestic and emotional burden of childcare they receive little financial support. Indeed, in Britain alone 'the childcare grandparents provide has been valued at £3.9 billion' at a time when three-quarters of kinship carers are said to be experiencing financial hardship (Grandparent Plus 2012).

Soap opera in general, and *EastEnders* in particular, is peppered with examples of other-mothers, be they stepmothers, female friends or grandparents, and as such, the genre might be seen to both recognise the reality of the contemporary family unit and respect the emotional and economic investments being made by those other than the biological mother within and beyond the small screen. This domestic genre presents a varied array of workable family arrangements. Indeed, we are reminded that the 'family in soap opera is not just Mum, Dad, kids and an occasional infestation of in-laws. People become related to one another at such a rate [...] that a term like "extended family" becomes laughably inadequate' (Buckman 1984, 76).

Patricia Evans (Pamela St. Clement), Peggy Mitchell (Barbara Windsor), Mo Harris (Laila Morse) and Dorothy Cotton all find themselves looking after their extended family, including grandchildren, nieces, nephews and in one instance her late husband's cousin's son. In some cases these women stand in as the primary caregiver when biological parents are absent, but in other cases they are simply offering one more voice in the communal rearing of children. Fiona Green informs us that such child-raising practices are currently in favour with feminist mothers as a challenge to the ideology of intensive mothering because these women take some of the weight of responsibility for the child's financial, emotional and moral wellbeing from the mother (Green 2004, 33). Moreover, the inclusion of and importance associated with the other-mother reaches beyond the extended family. After all, Dorothy may rarely see her own villainous son, but her maternal role has been acknowledged and confirmed due to the fact that she routinely takes in 'individuals who are not related by blood or marriage but who come under her care by an accident of geography' (Geraghty 1999, 82). Dorothy offers a number of Walford's younger generation both a roof over their heads and a moral compass in times of emotional and financial crisis. Patricia, Peggy and Dorothy are all biological mothers but are rarely seen nurturing their own children – rather, they 'act as a mother to the community' (Hollows 2000, 93). A family dinner at the Mitchells' brings this point home when Sally Martin (Anna Karen) tells Peggy 'this ain't your family at all – two bits of peroxide that you had nothing to do with three years ago, one old bird whose husband you stole until she stole him back, and one half cripple who is sleeping his way through the whole of the Mitchells, and your ex-husband's idiot cousin once removed […] I'm the only one at the table who is really related to you' (*EastEnders* 19/08/2010). The programme seems to suggest that it is these matriarchal figures 'who are the most successful in providing the nurturing strength on which a successful community is based' (Geraghty 1999, 125), After all, these women have 'the experience that would enable them to advise members of the community or comment on any matters that might come up within the soap' (Hobson 2003, 95). Or, to put it another way, these other-mothers 'have *earned* the authority they wield' over the extended family unit and the wider population (Buckman 1984, 52; italics in originals). Liebes and Livingstone make this point when they tell us that lone elderly women, such as those outlined here 'take turns in "mothering" whoever is in need' (Liebes and Livingstone 1992, 99).

However, this is not to suggest that these other-mothers are being presented as romanticized, idealistic mother surrogates; rather, they continue to remind us about the impossibility of 'good' motherhood and the implausibility of intensive mothering. When Peggy tells Patricia that she loves small babies, Patricia tells her friend that 'you are forgetting the pain and the mess and the sleepless nights – you can't be sentimental about babies; they're hard graft, actually – childbirth is hard graft' (*EastEnders* 27/06/2010). Moreover, when we hear Dorothy comment that 'my Nick was a difficult birth, I don't like to think about it', it acts as a powerful reminder of the true pain of labour (*EastEnders* 27/06/2010).

Soap opera has since its emergence been understood as a woman's genre, and perhaps more specifically as a genre for and about mothers. This is not to suggest that the genre upholds, applauds or circulates the 'good' mother myth. Rather, programmes such as *EastEnders* are dominated by those women whose maternal identities and motherwork practices negotiate the culturally appropriate and socially acceptable image of the ideal mother. Those women who refuse motherhood, those who refuse to reveal the paternity of their child, those who demand social independence and those who are not biological mothers can all be seen to challenge the ideological power of the 'good' mother myth by destabilising 'patriarchal representations of motherhood and family structures' (Reyes 2012).

Conclusion

This chapter has briefly outlined the history of the soap opera, the ways in which the genre appeals to women in the audience, feminist interest in the domestic drama and the importance of the mother in the genre. I have suggested that the soap opera presents a wide and varied range of mother roles, spanning different age, marital and economic boundaries, and made the point that these women are seen struggling to uphold the 'good' mother myth and failing to conform to the ideology of intensive mothering that this ideal demands. Mothers such as Tanya, Bianca and Carol demonstrate a powerful love for their children, but this maternal love does not overshadow their interest in friendships, working commitments, sexual pleasures and self-fulfillment outside of the home. And, at a time when 'beliefs in the importance of full-time mothercare for babies remain virtually unshaken' (Fox 1998, 172), the representations of these women helps to negotiate the unrealistic and unattainable ideal of motherhood that we are asked to aspire to.

Chapter 3

SITUATION COMEDY: THE (UN)FUNNY MUMMY WARS

Introduction

The situation comedy has witnessed a dramatic shift in representations of the family in recent decades. While programmes such as *Leave it to Beaver* (1957–63) and *The Donna Reed Show* (1958–66) made it clear that women were entirely satisfied with their role as full-time wife and mother, with the 'happy housewife' becoming a predictable trope of the genre, programmes such as *Maude* (1972–78), *Murphy Brown* (1988–98) and *Roseanne* (1988–97) depicted more controversial images of divorce, single parenting and the working mother. This chapter will explain that although the situation comedy has suggested, and indeed continues to suggest, that women are not complete or fulfilled unless they have children, contemporary shows such as *Outnumbered* (2007–) tend to challenge the 'happy housewife' stereotype by reflecting both the pleasures and comedic frustrations that come with modern-day mothering.

History of the Genre

The situation comedy is a repetitive genre that offers little in the way of shock, surprise or suspense. Rather, the genre draws on stock characters, limited locations and well-worn comedic plot devices. In this way, the pleasures on offer come from narrative circularity and the knowledge that things do not change in the genre (Neale and Krutnik 1995, 234–5). Although the situation comedy employs a classical 'narrative structure that involves the disruption of a stable situation and its resolution within each episode' (McQueen 1998, 57), this does not mean that characters cannot mature, marry or become parents in the sitcom; rather, friendships, family structures, locations and motivations must remain rooted throughout a shows history. The fact that *Joey* (2004–2006) struggled to find an audience after the eponymous hero left his friends and familial furniture speaks volumes about the pleasures at stake in the genre. And although the situation comedy has focused on both work and family arrangements as the basis of its setting and humour, the latter has proved to be the most popular since the emergence of the genre. The family comedy routinely deals with the drama of family comportment, sibling rivalry and the '*collision* of *values, identities* and *lifestyles*' that are evident within that unit (McQueen 1998, 58; italics in original). Situation comedies tend to focus on internal family roles, usually between parents and children, whether they are presented as blood family, melded family or metaphorical family (Hartley 2002, 66). In short, the institution of the family has served and continues to serve as the foundation of this comedy genre.

Situation Comedy and the Importance of Family

The situation-comedy format first appeared on American radio in the mid 1920s, and proved popular with listeners throughout the 1930s and 1940s. The format remained a firm favourite with audiences when it was adapted for the new medium of television in the late 1940s and early 1950s, with many popular shows and stars making the transition to the small screen. However, irrespective of the medium in question, the situation comedy has, since its inception, stressed the importance of the family unit, albeit in different guises over specific decades. While programmes such as *The Goldbergs* (1949–56), *Mama* (1949–57) and *Beulah* (1950–53) focused on the ways in which urban, ethnic and working-class families were coping with life in America (Morreale 2003, 2), later offerings such as *Leave it to Beaver*, *The Donna Reed Show* and *The Dick van Dyke Show* (1961–66) were more concerned with the representation of married life in the idealised middle-class suburbs, with *I Love Lucy* (1951–57) providing a clear transition between the two (Morreale 2003, 4). And although this conventional suburban comedy or what has since been termed the 'Hi Honey, I'm Home' show continued to be popular throughout the 1960s, programmes such as *My Three Sons* (1960–72) and *The Andy Griffith Show* (1960–68) modified the format by focusing upon the everyday situations of a widowed father struggling to raise his children (Feasey 2008, 21).

Although the single-parent sitcom continued throughout the 1970s, with divorced and widowed mothers in shows such as *Maude* and *Phyllis* (1975–77), this period was dominated by the single, childless urban woman, as typified by the character of Mary Richards in *The Mary Tyler Moore Show* (1970–77). And it is these single woman sitcoms that are said to showcase feminist heroines and speak of a liberal feminist agenda previously unseen in mainstream American programming (Rabinovitz 1995, 145). After all, it was these shows that dared to suggest that 'work was not just a prelude to marriage [or motherhood] or a substitute for it, but could form the center of a satisfying life for a woman in the way that it presumably did for men' (Dow 1996, 24).

The non-nuclear family unit that was evident throughout the 1970s continued to dominate the 1980s comedy, with American shows such as *Kate and Allie* (1984–89), *Who's the Boss?* (1984–92) and *Full House* (1987–95) focusing on two divorced mothers living together, a divorced mother and her widowed housekeeper and a widower and his extended family, respectively. The challenge that these programmes represented to the nuclear family unit was made explicit in shows such as *One Day at a Time* (1975–84) when we hear one character say 'Hey, we're a typical American family – a divorced mother of two, a twenty-year-old daughter who still lives at home, and a displaced teenager from Chicago!' (cited in Taylor 1989, 88). Indeed, if one considers, as Jane Feuer does, that 'the nuclear family is considered an ideologically conservative social unit that supports the status quo' then it might be suggested that 'sitcoms that undo the nuclear family are in a sense critical of it as a social institution' (Feuer 2002, 69). That said, even those non-nuclear family units such as those outlined here tend to be '*defined by the norm of the middle-class nuclear family*' (Morreale 2003, 210; italics in originals). Brett Mills makes this point when he tells us that these shows were not intended to critique the traditional suburban family, but rather to 'reflect that which broader society finds normal' (Mills 2005, 9). Moreover, the fact that these alternative families were screened alongside more traditional nuclear units in programmes such as *Family Ties* (1982–89) and *The Cosby Show* (1984–92) goes further to reinforce the cultural dominance of this idealised institution. And although the mother of the piece worked outside the home in these traditional nuclear texts, they continued to uphold rather than negotiate the romanticised middle-class suburban family as seen in earlier examples of the genre. In short, it was the mother who continued to be presented as the 'steady, loving person' who time and again met the emotional needs of her children (Spock cited in Kutulas 2005, 51).

One might be surprised to hear that even those irresponsible and unsentimental images of working-class families that dominated the 1980s and 1990s in programmes such as *Married... With Children* (1987–97), *Roseanne* and *The Simpsons* (1989–) were less interested in condemning family values than in challenging earlier incarnations of the contented middle-class unit. And even though more recent middle-class sitcoms such as *Friends* (1994–2004), *Coupling* (2000–2004) and *Will & Grace* (1998–2006) tended to focus on friendship groups rather than family units, they merely redefined friendship as the new pseudo-family rather than debunk the traditional family. The fact that these programmes ended with marriages, motherhood and babies for central protagonists goes further to blur the lines between the two. The situation comedy has presented such a myriad of family units since its emergence on commercial radio that the most daring and unique representation in recent years seems to be that of the traditional, nuclear, middle-class family, with shows such as *My Family* (2000–)

and *Outnumbered* being presented as 'plausibly novel' in their depiction of the patriarchal unit (Hartley 2002, 66). After several decades of divorced, widowed, working-class, quasi and queer representations, the middle-class nuclear family has returned to our screens, and it is the representations of motherhood in this seemingly traditional format that I will now explore in more detail.

Situation Comedy, the Family and Social Change

The situation comedy is often singled out as a genre capable of reflecting social, sexual and attitudinal developments within society. These developments are nowhere more evident than in the fluctuating representations of family life and the changing depictions of the maternal role seen in the genre. Indeed, television theorists have gone as far as to suggest that not only does the situation comedy reflect and respond to social change, but that the genre itself has 'offered oppositional ideas, depicted oppression and struggle, and reflected a critical consciousness that stops just short of political mobilization' (Hamamoto 1991, 2). The fact that the genre is based on a comedic narrative means that politically progressive and ideologically challenging ideas can be 'smuggled' in under a light-hearted veneer (Wells 1998, 181). Lynne Joyrich says it best when she says that the 'pleasure that they provide helps to mask the more sinister fantasies to which they give voice' (Joyrich 1996, 107). Serafina Bathrick suggests that it is the depiction of the mother that can 'mediate historical change through its representation of both family and the familial' (Bathrick 2003, 156), and as such, it is important to examine the changing representations of motherhood, motherwork and the maternal role in the situation comedy genre from the 1950s to the present day.

Pregnancy and Motherhood in the Situation Comedy: Lucy, Murphy and Roseanne

The 1950s sitcom centred on the comfortable and orderly traditional nuclear family located within a tidy suburban neighbourhood, and the small-scale problems that beset the middle-class male breadwinner, the homemaker mother and their precocious yet well-mannered children. These programmes presented a sweet, harmonious and innocent picture of family life or what is referred to as 'the electronic equivalent to the popular "Home Sweet Home" embroidery of the time' (Kanner 2002, 45). And although these sitcoms were popular throughout the 1960s, they *'remained rooted in 1950s conservatism and social values'* (Morreale 2003, 5; italics in original). Therefore, at a time when the women's movement was campaigning to release wives and mothers from the domestic sphere, the sitcom continued to naturalise a woman's place in the suburban home. Indeed, the period was defined by its televisual representations of good-natured and contented mothers who never complained and 'never expected anything from anyone' (Douglas 1995, 44). These mothers were wholly supportive of their children, they never belittled them and they routinely endured their misbehaviour with 'adoring bemusement' (Douglas and Michaels 2005, 217).

The dominant ideology of the period suggested that irrespective of rumours pertaining to the feminine mystique, women were only truly satisfied, fulfilled and complete as mothers. Indeed, family sitcoms such as *Leave it to Beaver*, *The Donna Reed Show* and *Father Knows Best* (1954–60) were infamous for their representations of 'smiling, benevolent, self-effacing, pearl-clad moms who loved to vacuum in high heels' (Douglas 1995, 36). Mothers such as June Cleaver (Barbara Billingsley), Donna Stone (Donna Reed), and Margaret Anderson (Jane Wyatt) presented a 'wholehearted commitment to family and their happy submersions into domestic life' and as such, these homemakers could be seen to not only uphold but also encourage women in the audience to conform to the 'good' mother myth (Kutulas 1998, 15).

These affable sitcoms were presenting a fantasy of economic security, social stability and family togetherness that was not necessarily in keeping with the wider social or sexual context. The economically stable nuclear family unit with a breadwinning father and a satisfied stay-at-home wife and mother has only ever represented 'a certain population, and only for a very restricted period that is now long past. *It was never, in fact, traditional*' (Kinser 2010, 26; italics in original). Amber Kinser makes this point when she tells us that:

> During the fifties, images of the 'traditional' nuclear family proliferated, even though such images misrepresented a majority of American families. The fifties were imagined then and are still imagined now as a time during which respectable families were self-sustaining on a single income [...] and were characterized by a full-time working father and a full-time stay-at-home mother. In fact a large majority of families were dependent on government assistance programs that funded and regulated federal housing loans and education payments [...] Not only was the suburban family in the 1950s more reliant on government 'handouts' than any group is now, but this decade also saw the highest rates of teen pregnancy in US history to date. The legendary family of the 1950s has no roots whatever in history or tradition; in fact, it stands out as an exception in US history rather than the rule from which we have supposedly and regrettably since moved away. (Ibid., 68)

However, even though this idealised suburban unit was a mere fantasy for many families during and since the 1950s, Thurer reminds us that 'even now we think of those mid-century family arrangements as good and right, and the way things were since time immemorial' (Thurer 2007, 337). In this same way, Judy Kutulas tells us that *Leave it to Beaver* 'remains the cultural ideal in American society; whether accepted, rejected, or reconfigured [because] it always looms over television's renderings of family' (Kutulas 2005, 59). Likewise, Sarah Matheson makes the point that these suburban sitcoms provide 'an enduring portrait of the American family that, even to this day, conjures a potent image of what the idealized domestic lifestyle looked like during this era' (Matheson 2007, 33). The idealised and homogenised image of the traditional middle-class nuclear family proliferated because the depiction of 'patriotism, consumption and family togetherness' that dominated these programmes proved popular with audiences, and thus advertisers of the period (Kinser 2010, 68).

These conservative sitcoms limited the role of women to that of the wife and mother, and the ideal maternal image was that of a woman 'who had no identity beyond the home and little real power within it' (Dow 1990, 264). Bernice Kanner makes this point when she tells us that these suburban mothers were 'loyal and loving homemakers [who] revered their husbands as more important than themselves [and whose] advice was rarely solicited' (Kanner 2002, 48). Moreover, the fact that they were routinely viewed performing a number of 'superfluous domestic tasks [such as] arranging flowers, polishing silver [and] filling candy dishes [went further] to underscore [their] relatively meaningless position in family life' (ibid., 48).

Indeed, these 1950s suburban sitcoms raised selfless motherhood 'to such exalted heights' that any woman in the audience would have questioned her own mothering capabilities and found them wanting on the back of this romanticised maternal depiction (Hamamoto 1991, 27). Even though this idealised postwar model of white, middle-class, consumer-driven, non-working, suburban motherhood would have been at odds with the reality of many women's lives, the romanticised image continued to pervade 'the consciousness of all women, in that they interacted with it, or internalised it and judged themselves by it, whilst also struggling against and re-negotiating such an image' (Andrews 1998, 55). Susan Douglas makes this point when she says that '[j]ust because the feminine mystique had become the official ideology by the late 1950s doesn't mean that all women bought into it. But it divided many of our mothers against themselves, pulled between idealized images and the more gritty reality of their own lives, pulled between defiance and self-abnegation' (Douglas 1995, 55).

The character of Lucy Ricardo (Lucille Ball) in *I Love Lucy* failed to find fulfillment in her domestic chores, and as such she could be said to negotiate the happy housewife myth that dominated the period. Indeed, her presentation of the discontented housewife might be said to speak to the frustrations of many women of the period who were themselves firmly situated within the confines of the domestic arena. After all, the 1950s 'was never the familial paradise it was cracked up to be, even in [...] middle-class suburbia, where outward domestic cheer often masked a good deal of quiet desperation, especially among women' (Thurer 2007, 337). Lucy merely 'endured the boredom and demanding routine of housewifery' rather than feel herself empowered by her role in the domestic space (Mellencamp cited in Mills 2005, 117). Lynn Spangler applauds the character for rebelling 'against her sex-typed role as housewife and the power structure [...] that limits her (Spangler 2003, 14) and champions the woman for conflicting 'with society's expectations of her' (ibid., 32). The fact that this character is desperate to leave the suburban home and find fame and fortune in the world of show businesses demonstrates an imagination, ambition and aspiration beyond the domestic arena. However, the fact that Lucy's antics frequently create frustration and friction in the marital home make it clear that there is an appropriate and inappropriate place for women, and the husband of the piece – played by Lucille Ball's real life partner Desi Arnaz – played to the dominant ideology of the day.

Although the character of Lucy might be seem to offer a feminist challenge to patriarchal authority, the dominant and preferred reading of the text must be that women should remain within the domestic space and care for the household. After all, her 'schemes to get into show business or earn her own money always end up with her happily returning home' (Spangler 2003, 14). The fact that Ricky strikes his wife on more than one occasion, with the nodding approval of friends and neighbours makes it clear that the show conformed to rather than challenged the patriarchal power structure of the period. And although seeing such patriarchal strictures played out on the small screen is of concern, the more worrying point of course was that 'the silencing of women in comedy [is] synonymous with that of women in the wider public sphere' (Goodman cited in Andrews 1998, 52). When the couple had a son in the second series (the birth of which was timed to coincide with the delivery of the couple's son in real life) it further naturalised Lucy's position as homemaker. Lucille Ball was the 'first openly pregnant woman to perform on television' and the comedy that resulted from her mood swings, food cravings and aspirations for the baby's future was new to television audiences (Landay 2005, 94). However, even though both the actress and character attempted to challenge 'accepted ideas about the impropriety of public representations of pregnancy', the show failed to offer a plausible challenge to the happy housewife myth (Landay 2005, 94). *I Love Lucy* managed to present Lucy's entire pregnancy without using the word 'pregnant' once, and those comedy moments that stemmed from her pregnancy were situated firmly within the domestic arena (Kisseloff cited in Mills 2005, 119). Indeed, rather than ridicule motherhood, the programme 'made it appear one of the most natural and normal things in the world' (Gould cited in Davies and Smith, 1998: 33).

Although pregnancy is today a common trope of the situation comedy, whether it is used to create a maternity story for an already pregnant actress or merely to add a new theme to an established television production, it was unknown and therefore potentially alienating to 1950s audiences (Kutulas 1998, 14). It was therefore crucially important that *I Love Lucy* present the pregnancy and ensuing motherhood story in a way that would appeal to the family viewer, in short, in a way that conformed to the ideal of the suburban middle-class family. *I Love Lucy* presented a traditional middle-class nuclear family unit, with Lucy in the role of the full-time housewife and mother, and as such, irrespective of what other comedy antics were evident in the show, the programme confirmed the dominant ideology of the period. Elaine Tyler May makes the point that the depiction of pregnancy in this popular sitcom merely 'reaffirmed the experience of motherhood as fulfilment' (May cited in Davies and Smith 1998, 39). What is interesting here of course is the fact that Lucille Ball herself was anything but a traditional wife and mother. Although Ball owned one of the largest television production companies in the United States and sought out medical intervention by opting for a Caesarean section, she nonetheless 'became the pre-eminent national icon of naturalized maternity' (Davies and Smith 1998, 44). The point here is that although Ball herself offered a potential challenge to the happy housewife myth, the way in which this working mother looked to find favour with the 1950s audience was by exploiting rather than exposing the 'good' mother myth. Thus, even though women were entering the workplace in ever-greater numbers throughout the 1950s and 1960s, the suburban sitcom continued to dominate that decade (Plant 2010, 39). These shows may not have reflected the reality of that period for audiences, but what they do demonstrate is the ways in which the happy housewife continued to dominate the ideology of the time.

Indeed, it was not until the 1970s that this idealised version of the suburban wife and mother was challenged. While the widowed Phyllis Lindstrom (Cloris Leachman) was seen struggling to combine motherhood and a professional working role in the programme of the same name, divorced Maude Findlay (Beatrice Arthur) opted for an abortion in the self-titled sitcom. And even though several network affiliates refused to show the episode in question, abortion continued 'to be mentioned as a right by pregnant characters' in the show (Kutulas 1998, 22). While characters such as Maude and Mary Richards focused on professional careers rather than creating traditional families, programmes such as *Rhoda* (1974–78) captured the ambivalence of the period for those young women who wanted both marriage and careers. Much of the humour and social commentary of these shows came from exploiting generational divisions between the childless career woman and her more traditional mother, with the suggestion that young women in the audience enjoyed the 'vicarious thrill' of challenging the traditional role of womanhood as motherhood (Kutulas 2005, 55).

While the American situation comedy appeared keen to present the single woman beyond the domestic space, the British comedy was also seen to negotiate the happy housewife myth. *Butterflies* (1978–83) was based on a suburban middle-class wife and mother who 'loves her family but hates being a housewife' (Mills 2005, 116). Rather than thrive in her domestic arena, Ria Parkinson (Wendy Craig) feels stifled by its routine, and rather than achieve satisfaction in her housewifely role, she feels bored by its repetitiveness, so much so in fact that she is seen contemplating an extra-marital affair as a way to escape the drudgery of motherwork, or what has elsewhere been termed 'The Problem that Has No Name' (Friedan 1963, 13). However, irrespective of national context or the marital status of the woman in question, these shows continued to present female anxiety as a personal narrative rather than a problem related to the wider patriarchal structure of society.

Although Lucy's visible pregnancy, Maude's abortion and Ria's consideration of adultery might have appeared shocking to audiences of the 1950s, 60s and 70s, no comedy has come close to triggering the sort of cultural debate over the role of motherhood caused by the 1991–92 season of *Murphy Brown*. *Murphy Brown* was the popular and long-running American situation comedy based on the personal and professional life of investigative journalist and news anchor, Murphy Brown (Candice Bergen), and her friends and co-workers on the fictional CBS television newsmagazine. The programme was applauded by feminist television critics for the ways in which the central female protagonist was able to achieve a notable professional role and a public voice in a competitive masculine environment, rather than conforming to any caring, nurturing or maternal images of femininity (Dow 1996, 137). Indeed, the controversy surrounding this show came not when the character of Murphy became pregnant from a one-night stand with her ex-husband, nor when the ex-husband admitted that he neither wanted to nor would attempt to adjust to life as a parent, but when Murphy decided to keep the baby and bring the child up as a single mother.

A media frenzy was ignited when then-vice president Dan Quayle drew attention to Murphy's decision to become a single mother in a speech to the Commonwealth Club of California during the George Bush campaign for re-election. Although the speech in question was about blue-collar African-American single mothers and what he believed to be their responsibility for the Los Angeles riots (because the rate of single motherhood approached 80 per cent in some ghettos), he included a brief aside, challenging the single parental status of the fictional Murphy Brown (Davies and Smith 1998, 57). Quayle commented that it 'doesn't help matters when primetime TV has Murphy Brown – a character who supposedly epitomizes today's intelligent, highly paid, professional woman – mocking the importance of fathers, by bearing a child alone and calling it just another "lifestyle choice"' (ibid., 57). This remark made headlines in the *New York Times*, *USA Today*, and *World News Tonight*, and the comment was addressed by the White House press spokesperson and key feminist activists. What this demonstrates of course is the importance of family values to contemporary American politics – or rather, the importance of those traditional, nuclear, middle-class family values that present the father as breadwinner and mother as full-time domestic to contemporary American politics. Dan Quayle made it clear that the happy housewife myth, as epitomised in the 1950s suburban sitcom, should remain the ideal to which we aspire, and Murphy Brown's decision to knowingly transgress this nuclear unit was seen as not just a problem for that particular family, but for society as a whole.

Although Dan Quayle seems to be suggesting that the single mother is at fault, there is no attention paid to the role of the father, the wider family or the state apparatus here. Moreover, although conservative critics attacked the character of Murphy for her liberated feminist stance on single parenting, what is interesting is the ways in which the programme seemed to rely not on an alternative or independent image of feminist parenting, but on a much more traditional depiction of the mother. The usually tough, brash and career-driven Murphy was softened by the birth of her child, even after the depiction of a gruelling delivery. The character seemed to be the victim of a cruel media backlash as she left the delivery room singing 'you make me feel like a natural woman' to her newborn child, with a dewy-eyed close-up of mother and baby harking back to those earlier representations of nurturing, naturalised mothers that fuelled the basis of Betty Friedan's (1963) work on the feminine mystique (S4:E26). Moreover, when Murphy struggled to combine new parenting with a masculinised work environment, there was no evidence that the character demanded flexi-time, job-sharing or on-site childcare in order to accommodate her newfound motherwork. And therefore, even though the character managed to work successfully while pregnant, she decided to focus less on her career after the birth of her baby. That said, this was only a temporary shift of priorities because soon after the birth of her son, the show went on to downplay Murphy's role as mother, focusing instead on her role in the workplace and the potential and promise of romance (Spangler 2003, 178).

Audiences might read Murphy's decision in line with a conservative agenda that stresses the incompatibility of motherwork with a public role, or as a feminist critique of the then-Conservative government to put in place those working patterns and childcare facilities that would enable women such as Murphy to have the choice of combining motherhood and paid labour. Either way, media interest in the representation of the single working mother points to the cultural significance of such depictions. Situation comedies of the period formed a consensus when they depicted strong female characters such as Rebecca Howe (Kirstie Alley), Christine Armstrong (Shelley Fabares), Jamie Buchman (Helen Hunt) and Monica Geller (Courteney Cox) vocalising a desire for motherhood because they were said to be 'ready' for the maternal role in *Cheers* (1982–93), *Coach* (1989–97), *Mad About You* (1992–99) and *Friends*, respectively. These programmes seem to be suggesting that women have a natural desire to mother, an innate need to take on the maternal role, and with this in mind, we might look to view Murphy Brown as less a critique of patriarchal working patterns, and more a further conservative take on this essentialist notion of gender. After all, even before Murphy got pregnant, she too was seen to acknowledge her ticking biological clock and speak of her desire for a baby (Spangler 2003, 174).

The one show that stood out during this period as a potential challenge to the dewy-eyed image of selfless middle-class motherhood was *Roseanne*. Although the programme was committed to the traditional nuclear unit, the family in question could be seen to critique this same unit. The character of Roseanne Conner (Roseanne Barr) was the emotional lynchpin of the family. However, she was also four things that women on the small screen 'are not supposed to be, working-class, loudmouthed, overweight, and a feminist' (Douglas 1995, 284). In fact, Roseanne might be said to epitomise the 'bad' mother due in part to her working practices and her socioeconomic status, and in part because she 'does not conform to traditional gender roles of behaviour' (Kinnick 2009, 3). While the mass media tended to 'idealize and glamorize motherhood as the one path to fulfillment for women, painting a rosy, Hallmark-card picture that ignores or minimizes the very real challenges that come along with parenthood' (ibid., 3), *Roseanne* was seen to re-write the 'boundaries of television motherhood' (Nelson 1989, 98).

Roseanne was a woman who, like the selfless and subservient mothers before her, loved her three children more than anything in the world, but who unlike them found motherhood and motherwork to be 'wearing, boring, and, at times, infuriating' (Douglas 1995, 284). This small screen mother did not seek out humorous, adulterous or endearing ways to escape the mundane routine of her day-to-day motherwork; rather, she complained in detail, at length, and with biting wit, about her role as cook, cleaner and family coordinator. And it is having to listen to this woman's feelings of anger, frustration and hostility that was said to break with comedy tradition and negotiate the image of the traditional wife and mother that continued to dominate the genre. Indeed, the programme negotiates the 'good' mother myth by making it clear that mothering young children is not necessarily satisfying or fulfilling, but rather, chaotic, conflict-ridden and a constant hassle (Andrews 1998, 62). Roseanne 'is definitely not the role model found in so many other television moms', and it is precisely her deconstruction of the myth of the idyllic family, and her anger, disappointment and rage, as well as her kindness, sacrifices and vulnerability that audiences are responding to here (Spangler 2003, 173). Therese Lichtenstein makes this point when she says that *Roseanne* rebukes 'the idea of even mutual love between a husband and a wife and their children [and] creates the kind of negative mirror image of what the positive American family was like' (Lichtenstein 1994, 201). Indeed, much of the humour of the show 'relies on a shared audience knowledge that media images of families and lived experiences are wide apart' (Andrews 1998, 63). In this way, the character gave credibility to 'a more ambivalent, frank, even jaundiced portrayal of motherhood' and thus offered women an alternative maternal role model (Douglas and Michaels 2005, 217).

Although working mothers appeared much more frequently in the 1980s and 1990s than in the previous decades of the situation comedy, these women tended to be professional women in respected careers, be it architects or reporters in *Family Ties* and *Growing Pains* (1985–92), respectively. These working mothers were not only professionally respected, but slender, attractive, relaxed, cheerful and playful (Kinnick 2009, 6). As such, they helped to fuel 'the myth of the super-mom: that doing it all, and doing it all with ease and style, was not only possible but was the new standard for modern moms' (ibid., 6). These women did not resort to fast food for family dinners, showed no need to pay for domestic help and never complained at the lack of government-sponsored social supports for working mothers (ibid., 6). In short, these women maintained the illusion of the 'good' mother while Roseanne continued to challenge the reality of this image. *Roseanne* depicts a struggling working-class family that relied on the mother's minimum wage to help pay the household bills, and as such, the show removes us from the comfortable and cosy consumerism of earlier decades, and from the public success of her middle-class counterparts. Roseanne routinely highlights not only her emotional significance to the family, but her economic importance to that unit, and it is her contribution to both spheres that is held up as an image of empowered working-class motherhood here. Rachel Horowitz makes this point when she says that 'Roseanne's feminism was for women who have to work because bills must get paid, who assert their role as head of the house despite the degrading work they often do during the day to pay for their kids' food and clothes' (Horowitz 2005, 9). Feminist television theorists championed the programme for challenging earlier depictions of idealised middle-class motherhood, and for making it clear that for some mothers, to work or not to work is less a lifestyle choice than an economic necessity, where concerns over 'opting out' (Belkin 2003) or worries about the 'mommy track' (Douglas 1995, 282) or the 'maternal wall' (Kinnick 2009, 17) are laughably irrelevant.

Although no programme has come close to *Roseanne* in terms of the ways in which it challenged both the 'happy housewife' myth found in earlier generations of the genre or the 'super-mom' aesthetic as seen in its contemporaries, it is 'certainly the case that there are now many more comedy depictions of women unhappy with the domestic social roles assigned to them and which show housewifery to be ridiculous' (Mills 2005, 116). Programmes such as *2point4 Children* (1991–99), *My Family* and *My Wife and Kids* (2001–2005) show mothers as strong-willed, working women beyond their domestic commitments. Whereas earlier sitcoms presented the mother as the selfless domestic with no real identity or as the 'super-mom' with no discord between her public and private responsibilities, these shows avoid the traditional housewife theme of earlier decades and show the struggles of those mothers who are trying to find a personal and professional identity.

And although one might suggest that the return of the traditional nuclear family over and above alternative family units might signal a nostalgic longing for an idealised suburban situation comedy-past, the fact that these families tend to be disorganised, disillusioned and in constant disagreement with one another makes it clear that this is not the case. Although middle-class television families of the 1950s and 1960s 'took harmony and order for granted, indeed took *the institution of the stable family* for granted' (Taylor 1989, 161; italics in original) these more recent shows can be seen to have to work at finding even a brief moment of tolerance, understanding or agreement. Indeed, one of the key repertoires of the genre is the way in which it teaches its audience 'how to live in families with tolerant mutual accommodation' (Hartley 2002, 66) when that family happens to be 'a less reliable, more complex unit than was previously the norm' (Mills 2005, 44). With this in mind, I want to examine *Outnumbered* for its depiction of the modern middle-class family, focusing on the ways in which the programme can be seen to both condemn and conform to earlier depictions of the 'happy housewife' myth.

Outnumbered

Outnumbered is a popular British domestic situation comedy, centred on the mundane trials and everyday tribulations of a middle-class nuclear family in South London. The show focuses on Pete (Hugh Dennis) and Sue Brockman (Claire Skinner) and their three children, 13-year-old Jake (Tyger Drew-Honey), 9-year-old Ben (Daniel Roche) and 7-year-old Karen (Ramona Marquez), with regular appearances by Sue's father, Frank (David Ryall), who is in the early stages of dementia and living with them at key intervals throughout the shows history. Pete is a history teacher at an inner-city secondary school while Sue is a part-time personal assistant at the outset of the show. The programme is committed to portraying the day-to-day reality of family life with challenging and curious children, focusing on such trivial and familiar stresses as the school run, finding lost car keys and trying to plan a family meal. *Outnumbered* presents a carefully observed portrait of family life; indeed, the creators of the show are so keen to produce a believable dialogue between the parents and children that the child actors are encouraged to improvise their dialogue in order to add authenticity to their performances. The show has been well-received by both popular and professional audiences, who cite the humdrum depiction of family life as the basis of its humour and thus popularity with audiences (Crompton 2012). The show regularly attracts between 2 and 6 million viewers (MediaTel 2012) – which is over a quarter of the audience share for its late-evening time slot – and has won numerous awards to date, including the Royal Television Society award for scripted comedy and British Comedy Awards for best situation comedy and best British comedy in 2009 alone. Moreover, the show has proved such a critical and commercial success that Fox has recently announced plans to make an American version, with Ken Marino playing the father of the piece.

Maternal Routine and Motherwork

Outnumbered presents the suburban family home in a state of chaos – the house is always in a mess with leftover food, crockery, homework, discarded toys and work files piled up over every available surface. The series begins with Sue finding a mouldy apple-core where the car keys should be, going to put the offending object into the kitchen bin only to discover that there is no bin liner, trying desperately to track down the ringing house phone that is not in its usual location before being heard screaming orders at the children to get ready for school so that they don't miss the bus, which, when missed, means that she has to take time out of work to then run each of them to school. Rather than spend time conversing with her husband, reading the day's news or finding time to clear away the breakfast dishes that she put out, all we see is a casually dressed and harried looking middle-aged mother repeating 'shoes, teeth and hair', with each order being ignored. She is so desperate to get the children to school so that she can herself get to work, that when she finds lice in her daughters hair she says it is clear just so she does not have to keep her home for the day and make alternative childcare arrangements (S1:E1).

Likewise, after school, Sue is left to feed not only her own children but also those of friends and neighbours who have either been invited or otherwise into her home. This is not presented as a peaceful family meal or even an emotionally nourishing example of quality time as a family; rather, it is merely another instance whereby the mother is being ignored, overlooked and unthanked for her efforts. The family meal does not demonstrate an easy or peaceful parenting experience, but rather the mundane frustrations and everyday challenges faced by the parents in question. Each child has their own special dietary and crockery requirements, and even when these are met, the food is either left uneaten on the plate or hidden under various soft furnishings, which must first be discovered before attempting to be cleared. We discover that daughter Karen has to eat out of her own special spotted bowl, and when Sue accidentally breaks the bowl, she makes a special journey to IKEA to replace the object with an exact replacement that same day, between juggling work and family, and even then her daughter still refuses to eat. Moreover, rather than use this time to talk about their day and share stories, the conversation at these meals consists of children talking about faeces (S1:E2). Although caring for children might at times be pleasurable, fulfilling and emotionally rewarding, the show, like *Roseanne* before it, makes it clear that 'the burden of caring for children can become routine drudgery or emotional torment when it is done constantly, repeatedly, because of one's obligations, and when it consumes nearly all of one's energies and time' (Held 1983, 11).

We hear that the family reluctantly go on day trips or holidays because they are more stressful then being at home with the children. And indeed, after watching Sue try to get her children ready for a family wedding, particularly after witnessing her daughter lock herself in the bathroom and refusing to take off her originally pristine bridesmaid gown, the audience understand her reluctance to travel. Indeed, seeing the behaviour of the children at the wedding creates humour and terror in equal measures as we watch the youngest bring a vicar to breaking point and put sardines in the chocolate fountain. Although the family are smartly dressed, the wedding merely demonstrates that day trips and family holidays are merely childcare in an alternative and less controllable location (S2:E1). When it is time for the children to go to bed, it is once again the mother who is seen to literally wrestle them into their bedrooms, only to find them up again, demanding food, drink and more stories an hour later (S1:E1). Sue is so busy trying to control her family, keep on top of the domestic chores and pacify her demanding boss that we rarely hear her complain, but when she does vocalise her unhappiness in the domestic arena she points to the gender imbalance in the home, asking 'why is it always mum who gets it in the neck [...] it's always me isn't it' (S2:E2).

That said, even though Sue is demoralised in the home and despondent at the lack of care or attention given to the domestic space by the rest of the family, she clearly defines herself as a mother and homemaker. When her husband does help with the domestic duties, she redoes them because he has not done them her way (S1:E4), and when her sister Angela Morrison (Samantha Bond) offers to help care for their elderly father, she initially refuses to accept the assistance (S1:E6). It is interesting to note that in these examples, Sue both wants to remove herself from and yet cannot help but continue to define herself in the domestic role. Although she is clearly frustrated with the day-to-day workings of family life, she struggles to let others take over these responsibilities, which reminds us of the ways in which earlier generations of the 'happy housewife' were granted power – albeit in limited form – based on their position in the family home. Sue is not a professional career woman, and as such, any respect or gratitude that she earns from her family is based on her position in the home; therefore even though motherwork frustrates rather than fulfils her, she continues to position herself in this role. A similar situation is seen in the long-running British comedy *My Family*, centred around another middle-class nuclear family. When Susan Harper (Zoë Wannamaker), the mother of the piece, realises that she doesn't have enough time to do both her paid work and household chores she decides to hire domestic help. After several interviews she appoints an incredibly competent and likeable cook and cleaner. However, rather than be thankful or grateful for the extra help, Susan starts to feel obsolete – so much so that she tries to sabotage the cleaner's efforts and family meals in order to reposition herself in the (albeit less successful) domestic role (S5:E8).

In *Outnumbered*, Sue is in a position of authority in the chaotic family home; it is her rules that are at least voiced, if not always adhered to. When Sue's sister brings presents for the children and tells them that they don't need to say thank you, Sue intervenes and makes it clear that her rules mean that the children will indeed abide by such social niceties (S1:E2). Moreover, Sue's position of authority in the home is often voiced by Karen when she tells her older brother that 'you're not allowed to leave the naughty step until mummy says so' (S1:E2). Indeed, mothers and daughters are somewhat interchangeable in the domestic arena, which itself speaks to the maternal role as a position of partial authority here. Alternatively of course, one might read this sequence and the programme in question as saying less about female power and more about the power of children in the contemporary family.

The children literally outnumber and overpower the adults in the family unit – so much so that the family dynamic seems to be less patriarchal or even matriarchal and more child-centred. This representation is fascinating because it cannot help but challenge extant literature from both within and beyond the field of motherhood studies. After all, much academic literature and popular advice manuals routinely focus on the close bond between a mother and child, with little acknowledgement of siblings and little advice being provided for second-time parents. Penny Munn's seminal work on mothering makes the point that existing psychological models of maternal care say little about mothering two or more siblings, due to the fact that any idyllic notion of intimacy, availability or appropriate mothering is challenged when mothers have more than one child because 'it is not possible to maintain the nurturant passivity and emotional availability suggested by popular accounts of mothering if more than one child is being mothered' (Munn 1994, 174). That said, when developmental psychology does present a model for second- and third-time mothering, it continues to uphold an unrealistic and unrealisable image of maternal care. It is suggested that a mother with more than one child should try and forge relationships between her children, exploring and explaining the needs of each child and introducing an acceptable moral code into the family. In this way, mothers are asked to 'monitor, keep track of and structure not only individual children, but also the relationship between' their children (ibid., 174). Even a cursory glance at *Outnumbered* makes it clear that mothers are struggling to maintain maternal authority over their children and finding it implausible to try and sustain relationships between them. Viewing Sue trying to keep the peace between Jake, Ben and Karen before school as they are shouting profanities and threatening to inflict grievous bodily harm on one another, makes a mockery of the mythical mother, able to mould, manipulate and monitor emotional bonds between her children (S2:E2).

Women, Work and the Mother 'Wars'

Watching Sue struggle with the double shift can be seen as one more way in which *Outnumbered* responds to developments in the family unit. Although Sue works part-time, she is phoned, emailed and texted by her boss each morning, afternoon and evening, always at inopportune domestic moments such as during the chaotic school run. When her daughter asks who keeps ringing, her father is heard explaining that 'Veronica is a lady your mummy works for, part-time, 16 days a week' (S1:E4). Sue is heard telling her boss in the first series that 'I work three days a week and Thursday isn't one of them' but to little or no avail (S1:E3). And later when she has reached breaking point with her boss in one heated phone call, she describes the conversation to her husband saying: 'I told her that she wasn't respecting the fact that I am part-time […] and I said that all the phone calls and emails at all the hours were interfering with my family time […] She said that wasn't her problem' (S1:E4). However, rather than discover that Sue has reset the boundaries of her working contract, we find out that she has in effect resigned from her post, and not forced the company or her boss to reassess their flexible work hours, job-sharing agreements or the insistence of 'face-time' in the office in line with family-friendly policies in the workplace. The programme presents Sue's struggle to combine paid work and domestic responsibilities as a personal problem based on her own lack of organisation or her children's penchant for chaos and calamity, and as such it fails to acknowledge that working mothers are struggling against corporate inflexibility and discrimination against mothers.

Sue leaving the workplace in this series does not provide further evidence of the 'opt-out' revolution or the reemergence of traditionalism whereby educated women are said to be leaving their professional careers to focus on motherhood (Belkin 2003). Rather, this is the reality of many women who are 'being *pushed* out of the workforce' (Kinser 2010, 125; italics in original) because they have 'tried, unsuccessfully, to arrange work hours, responsibilities, and opportunities that did not acutely penalize them for having family responsibilities' (ibid., 125). In order to 'receive full-time pay, benefits, and opportunities, workers are increasingly expected, especially in white-collar positions, to work more than forty hours per week, and they are unable to flex their hours according to needs of sick children, school days that end in the early afternoon, and summers that require several months of care or supervised activity that is rarely available, even if it is affordable, which for most families it is not' (ibid., 126). To talk about women 'opting out' rather than being pushed out by an inflexible work schedule 'ignores these critical issues and diverts attention away from the serious problem of women's unemployment and how public policy could mediate it' (ibid., 126). Many mothers who have been said to have 'opted out' would actually prefer to continue working, but a lack of support from their family, their employer or social policies leaves them unable to combine paid work and motherwork (ibid., 162). Alternatively, mothers are encouraged and coerced to position themselves on what is referred to as the 'mommy track', whereby women have increased flexibility in the work place 'in exchange for no promotions, no challenging assignments, less autonomy, and no raises' (Douglas 1995, 282). However, rather then present Sue's struggle to combine paid work and her domestic duties as evidence of a broader social concern, her inability to find a work and life balance is seen, as Murphy's was before her, as a personal rather than a political issue. We are asked to believe that Sue's problems in the workplace are not a reflection of systematic oppression, but rather, merely her experience of a particular employer who has been uncooperative and inflexible. In short, Sue's decision is individual rather than political. Brett Mills makes this point when he tells us that because the situation comedy deals with such standard fare as the politics of the home, the workplace and the family, this means that the genre rarely 'explores either macro social structures or the relationship between the individual and society as a whole' (Mills 2005, 45).

After losing her job the family are seen struggling financially, and Sue is soon looking for more work. Her husband questions her suitability for the workforce when he asks her 'what sort of company would offer a job to someone like yourself? [...] A mother with limited hours returning to the work environment, [...] you don't have any actual experience' (S2:E5). Not only is Pete disrespectful of her position outside of the family home, he also seems to be unappreciative of her role within it and the amount of energy and effort that goes into running a house with three children. During a restless night when both parents say that they are struggling to sleep, Pete tells his wife that he is desperate to rest because 'I've got that important meeting in the morning', and when Sue comments that 'I've got important things to do too' her husband makes it clear that his public role takes precedence, as he tells her that 'you haven't got any work to go to' irrespective of the challenges presented by the domestic environment (S2:E8). Sue is seen as both a working mother and a stay-at-home mother at different points in the show's history, and she is derided and dismissed in both roles. Although it is both disappointing and yet entirely in keeping with the contemporary cultural climate to see a woman's work within and beyond the home being so bluntly disregarded, what is even more damning is the way in which the show sets women in competition with one another. Sue struggles to make herself heard as she tells her boss that it is not appropriate to ring her outside of her part-time office hours, and we see her complain to her husband that her line manager 'hates anyone who's had children' because 'she looks on it as slacking' when the woman in question is anything but (S1:E2).

The divide between mother and non-mother is further established when Sue's bohemian, forty-something, single sister is heard talking about her chosen lifestyle in relation to the mothering role that her sister has dedicated herself to. When asked if she has children she replies that 'no, no – my lifestyle has never really left any room for it, I love my globetrotting too much. I couldn't do what Sue does, no, I couldn't do what Sue does – I really have to take my hat off to her, looking after Pete and the kids, day in day out. I mean always having to play second banana, as it were. No, I could never do that, no. I have huge admiration for my little sister, she's like this lovely supermum' (S2:E1). And although one could possibly read these words as a thoughtful commendation of the mothering role, the performance here is clearly asking us to see these words as denigrating and demeaning the decision to mother. In short, Angela, like Pete, does not appear to value the choice to mother or the efforts involved in motherwork.

That said, the fact that the programme dared to represent a woman who is without maternal thinking or mothering instincts might be seen as significant in itself. Angela does not have or seem to want children at the outset of the series, and as such, she might be seen to negotiate the unconscious weight of a culture that equates mature and responsible womanhood with motherhood.

Although there is a small and growing number of women who choose not to mother each year, over 90 per cent of women worldwide continue to bear and nurture children, and as such, one might suggest that women are socialised to believe that 'having children and caring for them is both natural and necessary' (Richardson 1993, 144). Feminists have long spoken about the need to 'value the decision *not* to be a mother at least as much as it values motherhood' and as such, we should perhaps value the representation of the non-mother here (Trebilcot 1983, 3; italics in original). However, although it might be useful to examine the depiction of the non-mother and consider the ways in which this figure is being used to comment on the representation of motherhood and womanhood on the small screen, this single non-mother is later aligned with the patriarchal family structure in a newfound stepmothering role. And yet although one might assume that Angela's status as a stepmother might bring the two sisters closer, replacing the earlier combative rhetoric with a shared maternal bonding, this is not the case – Angela uses her stepmothering role to further dismiss Sue's maternal practices.

Sue seems surprised that her sister has agreed to take on the role of stepmother because she 'used to think that kids got in the way of being a free spirit', to which Angela replies: 'God, no – what spirits could be freer than the spirit of kids? There is such wonderful energy in a big family' (S3:E5). And when Sue says that she understands the joys and pleasures of having a big family due to her day-to-day experience of raising three children, her sister manages to again dismiss Sue's motherwork when she says that 'yeah, you've got quite a big family Sue, but when you've got seven of you – believe me that's a big family' (S3:E5). Although the relationship between Sue and Angela might be understood as a commentary on sibling rivalry, it goes further to remind us of the mother 'wars' that are currently popular in the contemporary media landscape, be it between stay-at-home and working mothers or between birth and other-mothers. Recent research tells us that 'regardless of how a woman mothers, she can count on another mother disapproving of the choices she makes' (Goodman 2008, 38), and as such, these women further fuel the myths regarding appropriate and inappropriate mothering, 'while missing out on any opportunity to confront how society should treat women who, as a group, frequently set aside their own needs to fulfill the needs of loved ones' (ibid., 38). The point here is simply that mothers are encouraged to judge and rank other mothers, and as they do so, they are distracted from recognising that all mothers continue to be 'the ones held responsible for raising the children' (ibid., 38).

Outnumbered makes it clear that we should be sympathetic to – if not necessarily identifying with – Sue as the harried and hardworking mother figure, even when she is not necessarily depicted as the most efficient, organised or controlled figure of maternal authority. Sue is routinely seen trying to crowd-control her young children when they shout, swear and fight each other every morning before leaving for school. As contrast we see her next door neighbour Barbara (Lorraine Pilkington) calmly and politely sending all three of her own children to school without passing an angry word and without making a single threat. Indeed, like Barbara herself, these children are dressed as immaculately as they are well-behaved in their straw boater hats and pristine school uniforms (S2:E2). When Sue is heard shouting to her children to just 'get in the bloody car' because they have once again missed the school bus, Barbara tells Sue that 'they do get excitable don't they – mine are just the same'. Sue then mutters 'I think not' to herself as she watches with awe and admiration as the neighbours' children walk to school without incident. When Sue sees Barbara putting out her recycling bin she tells her that she is 'just saving the planet – the kids insist; you know what they're like' before asking what Sue and her family are doing that weekend. Sue replies 'oh you know, just vegging', to which Barbara responds 'oh, lucky you – Martin and I have to take the kids on this charity walk and then on the cycle ride. We've got to pick up a friend so they can be a proper string quartet, then we've got to finish making our puppet theatre and I've promised they can watch the *Sound of Music* tonight – we let them watch television on Sundays as a special treat' (S2:E2).

Rather than agree that just 'vegging' with the children is or could be fun, Sue feels the need to compete when faced with such extreme intensive parenting, or what has been termed 'professional motherhood' (Arnold 2003, 2). Barbara is presented as an example of the exhausting and exhaustive intensive mother in that she focuses relentlessly on her children's development and growth, supervises every detail of their day and bakes homemade cupcakes at every opportunity. In short, she is seen to respond to all the children's needs and desires, and to every stage of the children's emotional and intellectual development (ibid., 2). However, rather than acknowledge that such parenting is either unwanted, emotionally draining or financially restrictive, we see Sue question her own mothering, and as a result try in vain to ban all television and other computer devices in the hope of taking her family on an excursion to the local park. When her husband points out the futility of her request, she pleads with him and reminds him that 'next door do it all the time'. Her husband calmly reminds her 'that's their kids, who always say thank you and play musical instruments we've never heard of and don't eat insects – we can't compete with that' (S2:E3). When Sue is later heard complaining about having to load the dishwasher while her children ignore or overlook her and the chore in question, her husband tells her that 'Barbara's children next door have a washing-up rota, and they do their own sewing', at which point it is Sue who this time offers the reminder about the differences between the two sets of children, when she comments that 'I don't think comparisons are useful' (S2:E6). However, Sue's feelings and subsequent actions are not unusual because we are told that many 'working mothers who do not have the luxury of quitting compare themselves to this new superclass of stay-at-home moms [and] develop an inferiority complex' as a result of such comparisons (Kinnick 2009, 14).

Indeed, even though Sue realises that it is neither healthy nor helpful to compete with other mothers over the behaviour, educational accomplishments or social achievements of their children, she continues to question her own mothering techniques and spends time on internet forums talking to other mothers about the behaviour of their children. At one point we hear her tell her husband that 'this is a complicated age isn't it [...] I feel like I need re-training' (S2:E8). However, rather than trust her own maternal instincts, Sue routinely turns to Mumsnet for parenting advice and practical strategies, which then leaves her worryingly confused that she is both falling 'into the trap of over-parenting' whilst simultaneously 'under-parenting' (S1:E2). We see Sue question her own maternal capabilities and mothering instincts, but rather than judge her in line with the 'good' mother myth, we must acknowledge, as Diane Speier does, that mothers 'are human and flawed, and are learning on the job', and that because 'mothering is a trial and error experience, we need to respect that at best it will be "imperfect"' (Speier 2004, 149).

Sue is seen bribing her son to make him behave (S1:E5), calling her young daughter's bluff by helping her pack her bag when she says that she wants to leave home (S1:E6) and trying to avoid sitting next to her own children on a holiday flight (S2:E4). As such, one might assume that Barbara's parenting techniques and perfectly mannered children are being used to critique the chaos of the less structured household and dismiss Sue's role as mother here. However, when we later hear Barbara and her husband screaming at one another, see this woman changing the locks to their family home to prevent her husband gaining access and hear them talking about extra-marital affairs, it soon becomes clear that the ostensibly dysfunctional family is indeed the one that remains the cornerstone of society (S2:E8). In turn, this reminds us of the ways in which the situation comedy has throughout its long history continued to present alternative family units while simultaneously upholding long-established, traditional family values.

Conclusion

This chapter has briefly outlined the history of the situation comedy, paying particular attention to the representations of motherhood and the happy housewife that have dominated the genre since the 1950s, the alternative family units that saturated the genre throughout the 1970s and the more recent return to the traditional, albeit dysfunctional, nuclear family. The contemporary domestic comedy does not simply hark back to its earlier 'happy housewife' predecessors, but rather, makes it clear that motherhood and motherwork, especially when combined with paid work, create a raft of negative, challenging and perhaps unflattering emotions for the contemporary mother. Moreover, the fact that programmes such as *Outnumbered* make a point of playing to 'mother war' rhetoric does little to empower women, be they mothers, non-mothers, homemakers or working mothers. However, these shows are not presenting the unhappy mother and housewife in order to critique the institution of family or traditional family values. Indeed, even the most ostensibly anti-family texts are simply trying to critique those unrealistic and unrealisable ideals of middle-class suburban domesticity that have dominated the genre; so it is not the family unit that is of concern – instead, it is the feminine mystique of the contented homemaker that is being challenged here. In this way, the sitcom continues to foreground the importance of motherhood and motherwork to the family, but suggests that this role might be frustrating rather than fulfilling for the woman in question.

Chapter 4

TEEN DRAMA: ABSENT, INEPT AND INTOXICATED MOTHERS

Introduction

Teenagers and the teen experience have been a staple ingredient of television programming since the 1950s in a range of music shows, soap operas and situation comedies. However, it was not until the mid 1990s that the quality teen television drama series started to saturate small-screen schedules. Although parents were routinely absent or overlooked in 'must-see' teen dramas such as *Beverly Hills 90210* (1990–2000), *Party of Five* (1994–2000) and *Dawson's Creek* (1998–2003), parents and guardians have taken on a highly problematic role in contemporary examples of the genre. The teen drama shows parents as weak and irresponsible – be it socially, sexually or financially, and in many cases it is the mother who is the delinquent of the piece. Therefore, this chapter will look at the popular *90210* (2008–) and consider the ways in which motherhood and the maternal role are being represented in a genre routinely marketed to a young female audience. I am not assuming that middle-aged scholars will necessarily understand the adolescent media experience; indeed, Glyn Davis and Kay Dickinson make the point that very few media theorists tread into the murky waters of teen television for fear of misunderstanding the adolescent readings of such texts (Davis and Dickinson 2004, 5). That said, it remains important that we examine the depictions of motherhood that are being presented to this youth generation in order to at least attempt to understand the ways in which they are being asked to consider the maternal role.

The Teen Experience Within and Beyond the Small Screen

The teenager came to prominence in the Western world in the 1950s (ibid., 2). Although developmental psychologists such as Debra Haffner tend to categorise the life stage of adolescence into three overlapping periods, namely the early, middle and late stages (Haffner 1995, 15), it is worth noting that the teenage years are understood as a frustrating 'in-between' period that straddles and thus struggles with both new-found freedoms and strict limitations (Brown, Steele and Walsh-Childers 2002, 2). The life of the contemporary teen 'is a life of distinct limitations [...] and yet, concurrently, it is a phase when autonomy and a certain [...] notion of individuality is expected' (Davis and Dickinson 2004, 3). The teenage years are a prolonged and drawn-out period of physical, cognitive, social and psychological development, rather than a 'momentary rite of passage which initiates the child into instant adulthood' (ibid., 10). Moreover, these adolescent years are heavily monitored by dominant adult society due to the importance and gravitas of what is at stake in the movement between childhood and mature adulthood for the contemporary teen.

Television plays a crucial part in shaping teenage identity and forging adolescent entry into adult interactions. Indeed, teen television has been seen to play a pivotal role in not only representing but also managing the teen experience, by shaping adolescent roles, responsibilities and restrictions (Davis and Dickinson 2004, 10). Sharon Ross and Louise Ellen Stein make the point that teen television 'offers a crucial space for the negotiation of [those] political, social, and cultural issues' that are of importance to the average teen (Ross and Stein 2008a, 1). They go on to tell us that 'television featuring the lives and experiences of teens not only touch on [sic] coming of age [sic] issues, but also on questions of self, identity, gender, race, and community' and so speak to this same adolescent audience (ibid., 1). It is clear that teen television is an important source of information for adolescents, especially concerning those issues that are said to be of interest to the 'in-between' teen audience, such as sex, sexuality, friendship, family problems and anxieties concerning impending adulthood.

History of the Genre

British and American television schedules have routinely featured teenagers and issues that are of concern to a teen audience in a range of talent shows, variety programmes, soap operas and comedies (Feasey 2008, 45–8). As Rachel Moseley points out, there 'is a significant history of programming featuring and addressing teenagers and teenageness in the anglophone television landscape' (Moseley 2002, 41). However, although many of these shows were interested in presenting teenagers and addressing the teen experience, they tended to do so in a genre that was suited to the family audience. Sue Turnbull makes the point that although shows such as *The Many Loves of Dobie Gillis* (1959–63) were primarily concerned with the teen experience, they regularly featured parents and authority figures, and as such were 'certainly watched by all the family' (Turnbull 2008, 181). Indeed, it was not until the emergence of the quality teen drama in the mid 1990s that we witnessed the representation of a teen experience that was both made and marketed with the teen demographic in mind. And although teen television has been and continues to be planned, produced, distributed, marketed and in many cases even acted out by the adult population, there remains a sense that this is their programming (Davis and Dickinson 2004, 3).

The Fox network demonstrated the profitability of appealing to the teen demographic, with quality teen dramas such as *Beverly Hills 90210* and *Party of Five* proving popular with the youth market. As such, other quality teen productions followed, with shows such as *Buffy: The Vampire Slayer* (1997–2003), *Dawson's Creek*, *Charmed* (1998–2006), *Roswell High* (1999–2002), *The O.C.* (2003–2007) and *One Tree Hill* (2003–), with these shows leading to the success of more recent titles such as *Gossip Girl* (2007–), *90210* and *Glee* (2009–). One might notice that these titles tend to be female-orientated, and indeed, it is precisely these gendered youth texts that 'have shaped (and continue to shape) the predominant perception of Teen TV at this cultural moment' (Ross and Stein 2008b, 17).

There are debates surrounding the generic category of teen television, in terms of whether it is a set of shows that are grouped due to narrative characteristics, prominent pop music soundtracks, popular cultural reference points, thematic content, audience expectations, school environment, a teen community, audience engagement, publicity mechanisms, a melodramatic use of emotion or the embodied age of the characters on screen (Davis and Dickinson 2004, 1–12). Valerie Wee makes the point that these shows do share certain codes and conventions in that 'they feature a young and highly attractive ensemble cast and they all trace the experiences of youth and growing up with an appealing blend of intelligence, sensitivity, and knowing sarcasm' (Wee 2008, 48). Indeed, the youth being presented in these shows tend to be morally idealistic, introspective, responsible and self-aware. This is not to say that they do not have fun or suffer from 'numerous social, personal, emotional, and sexual crises' (ibid., 49), but rather that the teenagers being presented are in the main good, upstanding members of society. In short, the teenagers in question can be seen to respond to the overriding adult agenda of such productions. As I have suggested elsewhere these 'shows present teen life as a way of educating young people about their future role and responsibilities in both the home and the workplace, drawing on resourceful and respectful adolescents to act as role models for future generations of young people, and presenting the downward spiral of problematic and promiscuous teens to act as a warning to that demographic' (Feasey 2008, 47). With all these generic questions and classifications in mind however, I would simply suggest that the aforementioned titles might be considered teen programming firstly because, at the most fundamental level, they focus on issues that are of concern to the contemporary teen, and secondly, because such programming actually invites us to consider how the world looks from the adolescent point of view.

Ineffective and Absent Parents in Teen Television

Even a cursory glance at contemporary American teen television makes it clear that parents are either problematic forces in the life of a teenager or entirely absent in their lived reality. Sherri Sylvester makes the point that 'fictional adolescents without parents are a trend [and] parenthood is out of the picture' in teen television (Sylvester 1999). Likewise, Joyce Millman tells us that 'parents are mostly dead, absent or background static' in the genre in question (Millman 2000).

Dominique Pasquier echoes and elaborates on this point when she tells us that teen dramas tend to show an adolescent community growing up together, with little help, encouragement or support from outside their peer group. Pasquier goes on to comment that 'in series which cast parental roles, adult characters act childishly: teen series' parents have not solved their own problems. The message is very clear: to cope with the new self, friends might help, but not adults' (Pasquier 1996, 355).

Back in the 1960s, the eponymous *Gidget* (1965–66) was raised by her widowed father, and mothers were either dead or absent in such family-friendly programming as *Bachelor Father* (1957–62), *My Three Sons* (1960–72) and *The Courtship of Eddie's Father* (1969–72). More recently, a number of teenagers in the adolescent drama have experienced the death of a parent or parents, so much so in fact that it seems to have become a trope of the genre. While one of the central teenage characters in *Dawson's Creek* lost her mother to cancer, five siblings are left without parents due to a car crash in *Party of Five* and four adolescent girls are left without a mother in *Charmed*, when the witch is swept to her death in a tale of magic and sorcery. In both *Roswell High* and *Smallville* (2001–2011) young extraterrestrial teens have left their biological mothers on their home planets. And although in these latter examples the boys in question have been adopted by caring and responsible nuclear families, the mothers are seen to be impotent, ineffectual and uninvolved in their lives (Banks 2004, 25).

Moreover, while many teens have been orphaned on the small screen, so too have they been abandoned. In *Dawson's Creek*, one mother has abdicated her maternal responsibilities and sent her young daughter to live with her maternal grandmother; in *The O.C.* the central teen protagonist has been abandoned by his drunken mother and in *Heartbreak High* (1994–99) there is another example of a young teen who does not know her own mother. More recently, in *Glee* a pregnant cheerleader is no longer welcome in her family home by her father while her mother does nothing to alter his decision. Katharine Heinz-Knowles makes the point that 'the only relevant adults are often the teens' parents, and they are relevant primarily because of the interesting ways in which they are absent from their children's lives' (Heinz-Knowles cited in Aubrun and Grady 2000, 8). Indeed, on the rare occasion that we are introduced to a stable, supportive and well-meaning family unit, such as the Walsh family as they were presented at the outset of *Beverly Hills 90210*, the parents in question tend to conveniently move overseas, allowing the teen community to 'relish free time with little parental supervision' (McKinley 1997, 20).

Those mothers who remain in the family home tend to be presented as troubled alcoholics and drug addicts first and maternal caregivers second. *Beverly Hills 90210* introduced us to an alcoholic and drug-addicted former fashion model who routinely ignored, berated and abused her daughters. *Popular* (1999–2001) presented viewers with two alcoholic, abusive and emotionally unavailable mothers. In *The O.C.* the teenage Ryan was kicked out of his family home by his alcoholic mother before witnessing his then-adoptive mother following in her footsteps. Indeed, on the back of such representations of drunken behaviour *The O.C.* was said to be one of 'the worst shows for family viewing' in the United States in recent years (Van den Bulck, Simons and Baldwin, 2008, 934). Likewise, *Degrassi: The Next Generation* (2001–) depicted a young woman having to create a life with her alcoholic mother while her father is fighting in Iraq. *Veronica Mars* (2004–2007) presented a teen investigator selflessly sacrificing her college tuition to put her mother into an alcohol rehabilitation clinic, only to discover that the woman is clandestinely drinking and stealing from her own family. In this particular instance Veronica Mars (Kristen Bell) realises that 'her mother's presence is jeopardizing a secure and supportive home environment rather than creating it', and as such, it is the young daughter who asks this maternal figure to leave (Braithwaite 2008, 139). More recently, in *Beyond the Break* (2006–) we see a young girl running away from home to escape from her alcoholic mother, while *Hellcats* (2010) focused much of its drama on the turbulent relationship between a young pre-law student and her unreliable alcoholic mother.

Indeed, on the rare occasion when we do see an affectionate and considerate mother trying to forge a bond with her teenage daughter, these women tend to misunderstand, misinterpret and misjudge the adolescent generation. The classic example here is of course the relationship between Buffy Summers (Sarah Michelle Geller) and her mother in the teen vampire text, *Buffy: The Vampire Slayer*. Buffy's mother is at first ignorant of Buffy's supernatural status, misreading her daughter's erratic and seemingly irresponsible behaviour as teen rebellion, assuming that Buffy's mood swings and struggles with schoolwork are more about the Spring Fling than about the ensuing apocalypse. That said, the bond between mother and daughter is seen to grow, develop and strengthen as the secrecy of the slaying role is uncovered and otherwise-problematic behaviour thus explained.

One might suggest that this lack of mother figures in general and the destructive representations of those mothers who are in the family home belongs firmly within the tradition of teen television – as one way in which we can enjoy the trials and tribulations of the youth experience without the teen characters or adolescent audience being impeded by a controlling voice of authority or a civilising figure of maturity. However, this is less about a lack of parental figures or guardians of authority, and more to do with an absence of mothers. Several of the aforementioned shows make it clear that fathers and male guardians are to be respected because they and they alone 'provide structure, guidance and authority' for those teens under their care (Banks 2004, 19). What is surprising, however, is that this maternal absence appears not just in the American teen drama, but also in children's literature and mainstream Hollywood.

Gaye Tuchman used the phrase 'symbolic annihilation' to refer to the omission, trivialisation and condemnation of women in the media during the 1970s. The absence of female representations and the array of negative feminine stereotypes during this period were understood to be a way of maintaining patriarchy and social inequality (Tuchman 1978, 9). Yet even though Tuchman was writing about representations of women in the media at the height of the second-wave movement, the term appears fitting here in relation to both the underrepresentation of mothers, their lack of authorial presence in the family home and their social and sexual problematics within and beyond the contemporary teen drama. With this in mind we find that the greatest obstacle to 'investigating mothers in children's literature is finding the mothers' (Vandenberg-Daves 2004, 112). Barbara Chatton makes the point that a 'long tradition in children's books that plays to children's egocentricity consigns parents to little or no role in some stories' (Chatton 2001, 62). Indeed, 'there is also a common theme of parental death and a subsequent lost orphan experience that pervades the history of children's literature' (Vandenberg-Daves 2004, 112). However, although a lack of parents appears significant, a lack of mother figures is particularly striking. After all, a recent review of 'best-selling hardcover children's books revealed that Mother Rabbit in the Beatrix Potter books (who after all was not around when Peter got into the most trouble) was the only significant mother character in the top 50 books' (ibid., 112).

Likewise, Disney has routinely removed mother figures from their popular children's fairytales, so that *Snow White and the Seven Dwarfs* (1937), *Cinderella*

(1950) and more recently *The Little Mermaid* (1989), *Beauty and the Beast* (1991), *Aladdin* (1992) *Enchanted* (2007) and *Tinkerbell and the Great Fairy Rescue* (2010) show our young female characters without a maternal mother to turn to for care, compassion or consideration. The concern here is that a whole series of popular texts appear to be devaluing the role, responsibility and value of mothers and motherhood for a young female audience. After all, it is not simply that these young Disney princesses have no mother, but that the lack of a mother figure is deemed so unimportant as to be unworthy of comment. Marjorie Worthington makes the point that mothers 'have been so effectively erased from these [...] films that their absence is never remarked upon by the characters and, perhaps more importantly, their absence is therefore never noticed by the spectators' (Worthington 2009, 35). A lack of mothers means a lack of mother–daughter relations, which offers the suggestion that these maternal figures are either unimportant or unnecessary in the happy-ever-after of the young Disney princesses. Furthermore, the contemporary teen film has followed in these same motherless footsteps by showing mothers as absent and unavailable.

Angharad Valdivia tells us that single fathers play a prominent role in family films such as *Ghost Dad* (1990), *My Girl* (1991) *Sleepless in Seattle* (1993), *Getting Even with Dad* (1994), *Casper* (1995), *Fly Away Home* (1996) and *Clueless* (1995) (Valdivia 1998, 281). More recently, a protective father stands as the sole parent to his young daughter in *10 Things I Hate About You* (1999), while in *Sugar and Spice* (2001) a number of middle-class parents banish a pregnant teenager from their home, while another mother is in prison for robbery. *St. Trinian's* (2007) focuses on an adolescent living with her father, without mention of the whereabouts of her biological mother, and *Despicable Me* (2010) presents a super-villain turned doting father figure nurturing and being nurtured by three orphaned girls. And yet, if the lack of mothers appears as a problematic albeit predictable trope in the youth entertainment market place, nowhere is this theme more evident than in the original *Beverly Hills 90210* and in the later *90210* programme based on the earlier production.

90210

90210 is a classic American teen drama that focuses on the trials and tribulations of a group of teenagers who are trying to find their place in the world. The programme revolves around the students of the fictional West Beverly Hills High School as they experience new friendships, relationships, sexual experiences and family breakdowns. Although the show is set in a glamorous location and the young cast wear improbably beautiful clothes and drive breathtakingly expensive cars, the overriding themes of the teen experience remain. It is worth noting that the show is based in part on the earlier *Beverly Hills 90210* franchise that left the small screen nearly a decade previously, which also played to the troubled teen experience in an opulent setting.

Although the teenage characters who dominate the narrative shift over the show's short history, the central players are theatre student Annie Wilson (Shenae Grimes) and her adopted brother Dixon Wilson (Tristan Wilds), the young journalist Erin Silver (Jessica Stroup), teen mother Adrianna Tate-Duncan (Jessica Lowndes), socialite Naomi Clark (AnnaLynne McCord) and a number of interchangeable males who act as boyfriend backdrops and as the cause of female frictions in the narrative. Although this is a teen-driven drama, there are recurring adult characters in the shape of the homemaker-turned-personal-assistant Debbie Wilson (Lori Loughlin) and school teacher Ryan Matthews (Ryan Eggold). The series premiere proved popular on the CW network in America with over 4 million viewers (Gorman 2008), and debuted strongly on E4 in Britain with over 468,000 viewers when it premiered in 2009 (Barb 2012). In short, *90210* can be understood as a popular teen drama on both sides of the Atlantic, which plays to the genre codes, narrative conventions and characterisations of existing adolescent programming. With this in mind, it is interesting and indeed important to examine the ways in which motherhood is being presented or dismissed in this contemporary, popular text.

Domestic Privilege and Problematic Motherhood

There are a number of mothers who move in and out of the *90210* narrative through the show's first seasons, and in the main they are sexually, socially and financially irresponsible figures who 'become obstructions to be dismissed, derided, or overcome' (Miner 2009, 49). The overriding concern here, then, is that while much children's literature as well as the Disney franchise and the Hollywood teen movie are leaving motherhood and the maternal role out of the youth picture, teen television in general and *90210* in particular are situating problematic motherhood as a key trope in adolescent programming, focusing on the ways in which these women routinely and repeatedly disappoint, denigrate and disillusion their own children.

Dana Bowen (April Parker-Jones) is the biological mother of Dixon, who gave her young son up for adoption when she was a single, alcoholic mother, and more recently, when she comes back into her son's life, she is presented as an irresponsible mother and gambling addict. Tabitha is an alcoholic theatre actress who tends to swim naked and talk at length about her many and varied sexual conquests. Tracy Clark (Christina Moore) is a glamorous 'yummy mummy' who is more interested in her surface appearance than her daughters well-being, and when her husband moves his girlfriend into their beach house she leaves the family home and her daughter to go and 'find herself' in New York, leaving her teenage daughter to live alone. Laurel Cooper (Kelly Lynch) is a hippy who believes in free love and legalised drugs, who happens to sleep with her daughter's classmate and boyfriend, encouraging both the sexual freedom and intoxication of the adolescent in question.

Constance Tate-Duncan (Maeve Quinlan) is a secret drug-abuser-in-denial and an emotionally unavailable Hollywood mother who sees her daughter, Adrianna, as a theatrical client and as the breadwinner of their small family. The fact that Adrianna refers to her mother as 'Dina Lohan' (Lohan has been criticised by the popular press because her maternal and professional roles are intertwined, and as such, 'according to the narrative of bad celebrity motherhood' (Cobb 2008), she is not offering an appropriate maternal figure to her daughter), and that her friends ask after 'Mommie Dearest' (the name of the memoir and exposé written by Joan Crawford's adopted daughter, which reveals her mother's alcoholism, sexual promiscuities and child abuse) speaks to us about the ineffectual and inappropriate representation of motherhood being depicted here (S1:E7). Moreover, when Adrianna goes missing after a drug-fuelled binge, it is her friends rather than her mother who worry about her disappearance (S1:E7).

Jackie Taylor (Ann Gillespie) is a bipolar drug addict and abusive alcoholic who has no relationship with her eldest daughter and fails to notice that her younger daughter is sleeping in a women's refuge. Jackie's use and abuse of drugs and alcohol over the last decade means that she barely knows her daughters and thus is unable to recognise when they are in need of help or support. She wrongly blames her eldest daughter for the mental state of her youngest, and refuses to take any responsibility for these young women (S1:E18). Indeed, when she finds a new boyfriend she refers to herself as their aunt rather than their mother (S1:E18). Irrespective of whether she does this to hide her age, level of responsibility or any potential dating inflexibility, the end result is that she dismisses her maternal role in this and numerous other instances.

Heiress Jennifer Clark (Sara Foster) appeared in the series when her own mother disappeared, and although she arrived under the pretext of helping to care for her teenage sister Naomi, we soon discover that she has in fact returned to take advantage of her siblings' sizeable trust fund. When she discovers that she is pregnant she makes it clear that the baby will be presented as another of her fashionable accoutrements of femininity. When medical professionals explain that the final weeks of pregnancy are crucial because this is when the baby will put on weight, she looks horrified and retorts 'who wants a chubby baby?' (S3:E5). Moreover, when we hear that she is putting on a baby fashion show in the beach house, the father misunderstands her reasoning. He wants to believe that Jennifer is interested in meeting other mothers and talking about maternal experiences, although she merely sees it as another high-society event, because 'every mother in Beverly Hills with a Black card' will be there (S3:E8). When she does admit that she would be interested in talking to other mothers about 'diapers' one might expect a conversation debating the environmental and cost benefits of disposable and reusable nappies, but not here; Jennifer instead wants to ask them if there is 'any way around babies wearing them [because they] totally ruin the line of [her son's] clothes' (S3:E8). And at this point it is worth noting that her four-week-old son is wearing leather trousers. When another mother mentions that the little boy looks 'hot' (S3:E8) Jennifer takes this as a sartorial compliment rather than a concern about body temperature, and when she does eventually realise the issue at stake she merely replies that 'we all suffer for fashion' (S3:E8). This is a woman who goes on to take the wrong baby because it happened to be in a similar pram and voice the notion that breastfeeding is barbaric for mothers and should be avoided at all costs (S3:E8). On later realising that she is not prepared for and is rather unwilling to compromise her life for the new arrival, she leaves her baby with its father and a list of potential paid carers.

Although one might look to applaud Tracy's preference for self-interest over her maternal responsibilities, Constance's demand that her daughter contribute financially to the household or Jackie's desire for a single sexual subjectivity, there is of course little in the way of sympathy for these mothers due to the fact that the narrative asks us to identify with the teenage generation who are seen to be negatively affected by the life choices and narcotic dependencies of these maternal figures. That said, what the programme does demonstrate in a brutal way is the notion that maternal feelings and motherly instincts are not natural, fixed or innate for all women. Rather, there is a suggestion that maternal thinking is a learned skill that one can acquire with time, patience and practice, rather than an essentialist part of the female experience. In this way, Ruddick makes the point that 'maternal thinking is not the whole of a *mother's* thought any more than maternity is the whole of a mother's life' (Ruddick 2007a, 118; italics in original), but rather it is only one aspect of '"womanly" thinking' (Ruddick 2007b, 107).

Those absent and ineffectual mothers that are a common trope of the quality teen drama might be seen to pick up on early second-wave feminist writing which attempted to denaturalize motherhood and theorise the maternal without recourse to 'natural or biological explanations' (Miller 2005, 56). It was during the mid 1960s and early 1970s that feminist theorists started to suggest that 'there was nothing natural about women's responsibility for domestic life' (Hollows 2008, 57) and that 'women's "nurturing nature" was not a product of biology but culture' (ibid., 57). Indeed, feminism has tended to assert 'that motherhood and mothering are not *natural* for women, but that they are historically, culturally and socially constructed' (Bortolaia Silva 1996, 1; italics in original). With this in mind, feminism has sought to 'rescue mothering from idealizations and to reconsider it as a body of sophisticated skills and a form of disciplined and thoughtful work' (First 1994, 147).

In her work on motherhood myths and practices Abby Arnold makes the point that although some mothers do feel 'tied together' with their young babies and feel an intimate bond with their children, this connection does not exist for all women at all times. Moreover, this strength of emotional connectedness does little to assist routine day-to-day motherwork practices. Arnold goes on to state that we should not assume that mothering is natural, because to do so detracts from the efforts and energies that go in to motherwork. To suggest that the maternal role is somehow natural or innate merely takes for granted the skills, abilities and genuine labour that go in to contemporary childrearing. Indeed, we must remember that 'motherhood is not a natural act, it is a learned one [and] the more education, resources and economic security a woman has, the more effective a mother she will be' (Arnold 2003, 4). In this way, maternal connectedness does not a good mother make; rather, it is access to safety, security and social privilege that leads to agreeable mothering.

Sara Ruddick makes the point that mothers nurture and protect their children due to what she terms 'maternal practice' (Ruddick 1980). Miller picks up on this view when she tells us that the 'physical, emotional and intellectual dimensions of mothering' incorporate a set of skills that are purposefully learned and crafted through an engaged interaction with children (Miller 2005, 56). With this in mind, biological fathers, adoptive mothers and fathers, stepparents and other caretakers of children can all be seen to 'acquire maternal thinking' (Kinser 2010, 20) because mothering in this sense 'is not [...] the exclusive domain of biological mothers; it is a product of one's disciplined, focused, and persistent *effort*' (ibid., 20; italics in original). Research from within the field of psychology tells us that anyone can 'mother an infant who can do the following: provide frequent and sustained physical contact, soothe the child when distressed, be sensitive to the baby's signals, and respond promptly to a baby's crying' (Ehrensaft 1983, 48). However, even though an acknowledgement that maternal practices are learnt rather than natural is crucial in challenging essentialist notions of motherhood and maternal thought, this distinction does little to negotiate or update the ways in which female-dominated parenting, nursery and educational situations differently prepare men and women for the maternal role (ibid., 48).

Power, Patriarchy and the Single Shift

The ways in which these televisual mothers treat or mistreat their children is of concern in a genre committed to the young adult viewer, but perhaps more worryingly is the lack of reality being presented on the part of these maternal figures. I am not concerned here with the unrealistic dress codes, car purchases or beach houses of the women in question; indeed, it is clear that the themes of teen drama are central to these narratives, irrespective of the expense and expanse of the locations in question. Rather, I mean that at a time when the majority of mothers are having to balance work and family commitments (be it in full-time professional occupations that enable mothers to employ out-of-home childcare services, or lower paid service roles that demand the help of extended family and other mothers to help care for their children without financial reward, Gatrell 2008, 144–5), this programme fails to present the reality of this double shift. These women are, in the main, wives and homemakers who employ domestic help for mundane cooking, cleaning and domestic chores while they tend to their surface appearances, charity functions and home designs.

American teen drama in general and *90210* in particular depicts the privileged stay-at-home housewife as having a wealth of domestic help and personal assistants at her command. As such, one might suggest that the programme is in a position to depict the unattainable yet powerful image of the 'good' mother. However, the fact that several of these women discover that their husband is unfaithful speaks of the dark reality of the patriarchal nuclear unit and thus to the lack of social, sexual and economic power for the selfless 'good' mother, because women in this situation can choose to either ignore the affair in order to maintain their lifestyle or confront the adulterer and risk losing the family home and the lifestyle to which they have become accustomed. There are a number of mothers on the show who, given the choice between giving up their lifestyle and staying with an unfaithful husband, choose the latter. Although I do of course acknowledge that few characters on television drama, be it teen, medical, hospital or otherwise, have 'consistently fulfilling personal lives' (Dow 1996, 98), due to the fact that the drama of the piece tends to depend 'upon a continual disintegration of the family' (Feuer 1986, 105), the routine and repeated depiction of this scenario speaks not only of a need for dramatic action but also of the subjugation of women in the traditional nuclear environment.

Debbie initially stands by and watches another woman kiss her husband (S1:E8) and Colleen Sarkoissian (Sarah Danielle Madison) refuses to walk out of the family home even though her husband has been caught having another extra-marital affair, because as a full-time wife and mother she does not have the financial resources to do so (S4:E10). Indeed, we are presented with a number of scenes and sequences whereby a mother returns to the family unit irrespective of her humiliation, pain and anxiety at the hands of her husband, because of the unequal power dynamic that is structured around the male breadwinning role. After all, when 'a woman has children and becomes a full-time childrearer, she grows more dependent on her husband, her opportunities to meet men decrease, and her prospects for remarriage decline. The husband thus possesses the more promising alternatives outside the marriage, and his power increases' (Polatnick 1983, 31). In a rather more drawn-out story arc, Tracy is prepared to not only look the other way in response to her husband's regular affairs, but also to allow him to move his current girlfriend into their beach house (S1:E4). And even though she eventually makes the decision to leave her husband because she wants to be able to both respect herself and command her daughter's respect, she nonetheless struggles with this decision and later abandons her daughter.

Although one might read such narratives as evidence of the power inequality that exists at the heart of the traditional nuclear family unit, and therefore as a powerful commentary on contemporary family structures, the fact that these mothers tend to disappoint their children or disappear from their lives merely goes further to present motherhood as inept, ineffectual and failing. These women have the time, energy and income at their disposal to engage with 'professional' mothering and 'intensive' maternal practices (Arnold 2003, 2), and yet even these most privileged of mothers 'with the greatest resources at [their] private command' (Valeska 1983, 71) cannot come close to the 'good' mother archetype, and as such, they go further to remind us of the impossibility of this unrealistic and unrealisable ideal.

Imperfect but Available Motherhood

The most rounded and thus believable mother figure of the series is Debbie Wilson, biological mother to Annie and adoptive mother to Dixon. The fact that Debbie is awarded more screen time than those mothers previously mentioned, the fact that she is presented as more than a crude or cruel one-dimensional caricature of motherhood and the fact that she remains throughout the shows history means that she is being presented as the maternal figure of identification and thus, potential admiration. Like many mothers in this series and in the wider arena of teen drama, Debbie is presented as a slim, white, youthful and sexual mother, and as such, she can be seen to both uphold and subvert the culturally appropriate 'good' mother myth.

Debbie draws on a sisterly bond between herself and her daughter, and abdicates maternal authority for friendship. On the rare occasions when

Debbie feels that she needs to give her children some motherly advice, she actually asks them if they 'are up for some maternal wisdom' (S1:E14) or seeks their permission to 'be mom for a second' (S1:E5). Her husband gets upset when the children mistreat their mother and he demands that they apologise when they are rude or hurtful. However, rather than be grateful for such support, she is angered by what she sees as interference with her chosen maternal style. Debbie asks her husband 'why do you swoop in and save me when I'm dealing with the kids? I don't need to be saved'. In response her husband makes the point that they don't respect her because she tries too hard to be their friend and that 'sometimes they don't need a friend, they need a parent' (S2:E3).

Annie and Dixon do on occasion show a lack of respect for their mother when they leave the house after curfew, try and meet with friends even after they have been grounded or ignore her advice on love, sex, relationships and social etiquette. Annie genuinely hurts her mother when she mocks her employment prospects, asking her to 'show me the one ad for a housewife with no college degree, no experience and no skills' (S3:E5), and likewise, Dixon is seen distressing his mother when he angrily reminds his family that 'it's not like she's my real mom' (S2:E9). However, that said, this is a family that eats home-cooked meals together, has special chocolate cakes on their birthdays and has a family night that their friends are happy to be a part of. Even when Annie's glamorous friends mock her 'Pollyanna' mother it is done with heartfelt warmth and a sense of barely concealed envy (S1:E21). And other characters actually point out how special, supportive and – in their jargon – 'awesome' they find this maternal figure (S1:E6). Indeed, Dixon later admits that he has never questioned Debbie's role as his mother (S2:E12) and Annie goes as far as to present her mother as her hero in a college application assignment (S3:E8).

Although Debbie looks on the surface to be a soft and rather too sensitive stay-at-home mother, this woman is anything but vulnerable when her family is at stake. When she is recruited for a prestigious photography job she is happy to leave when there is an altercation between her boss and her son (S1:E6), and when she worries that her son is being lied to by an older girlfriend, she takes matters into her own hands and instructs the woman to leave (S2:E8). When her mother-in-law buys her children a car and lets them use and abuse the domestic help, it is Debbie who demands that they complete their chores and pay for the petrol and insurance for the new vehicle in order to instill a sense of responsibility (S1:E13). She tells Annie that she will not be selling her eggs to her current boss at any price because of the importance of the role of motherhood (S3:E5) and when she is in financial trouble she takes on a role as Jennifer's personal assistant and negotiates a better salary and health package than this woman was originally offering (S3:E5).

Debbie is a multi-faceted, rounded and believable figure of maternal love and failings, a woman who tries to do the right thing by both herself and her family. Even when she makes the wrong decision, it is clear that she always has the best of intentions. We never question her commitment to her children and their friends, and her new-found financial and emotional struggles as a single parent make her investment in her family appear all the more moving. She is a sexual woman who has an impromptu dalliance with her children's teacher in her living room (S3:E9) and she shows vulnerability when her divorce is announced and she discovers that her ex-husband is already in a new relationship (S3:E8). She demonstrates strength when her children are in need of her support (S2:E8), she opens up her home to other adolescents who are at odds with or have been abandoned by their own parents, and steps in to help with a number of school functions, theatre performances and fund-raising events.

In short, this is a believable and 'good enough' image of motherhood against a backdrop of otherwise monstrous stereotypes. The fact that this character was nominated for the Teen Choice Award for best parental unit in both 2009 and 2010 speaks volumes about the framing of the mother as both appropriate and acceptable in the series. That said, Debbie is not the archetypal 'good' mother because although she sees herself as a mother first, she acknowledges that she would like to focus more on her professional career (S1:E17). When kind-hearted television mothers tell their children that 'somewhere, there is that elusive balance between family and career, and right now that balance is a little off' (S1:E17) we tend to assume in most instances that the mother is lamenting her time spent in the professional sphere when she longs to be in the private domestic world, which is not the case here. Here we have an example of a woman who informs friends and acquaintances that 'I'm such a mom' (S2:E5) as she pulls family photographs out of her purse, but who admits that a return to the world of work would offer more than mere financial benefits. However, extant literature from within the field of motherhood studies tells us that there is a 'fine line that the contemporary mother has to tread between [...] independence on the one hand and claims of selfishness and censure on the other' (Woodward 2003, 29–30), and it is an awareness of that line that sets Debbie apart from her maternal contemporaries.

What is interesting in the series is the ways in which it problematises the lived reality of motherhood as a day-to-day practice while simultaneously revering the institution of motherhood. For example, although we hear untold accounts of the ways in which Jackie emotionally, verbally and physically abused her daughters, when she is seen dying from cancer her children forgive her for her past behaviours and re-establish a relationship with her (S2:E5). Although Constance does not die, she does have a similar moment of maternal salvation when she defends her daughter's decision to both have her baby and then give it up for adoption. When Adrianna's abilities to have or raise a child are being questioned, Constance steps in to defend her daughter and praise her work ethic and sense of adult responsibility (S1:E15). Dana returns from beyond the pale when she tells her son that 'I didn't contact you because I didn't want to disrupt your life, but it didn't stop me from thinking about you every single day; you're my baby, I want to be a part of your life' (S2:E16). Even Jennifer, who leaves her baby in the care of its father, is reminded about the importance and significance of her maternal role, however problematic; Ryan tells her that 'you're the most important person in Jack's life – you're his mother, which means that you're going to have more of an effect on his life than anybody else. You're the person who is going to make him the man he is going to be one day, and he's lucky to have you' (S3:E8). In this sense, teen television, like the wider television marketplace, simultaneously derides the unattainable myth of the 'good' mother whilst upholding this selfsame idealised image of maternal devotion.

Conclusion

This chapter has briefly outlined the history of the teen drama, paying particular attention to those representations of problematic motherhood that have appeared in the genre from the 1990s to the present day, considering the ways in which these inept and ineffectual images can be seen in the wider children's literature and teenage entertainment marketplace. *90210* offers a number of troubled and tortured presentations of motherhood, making it clear that maternal thoughts, feelings and practices may be less an essentialist and natural part of motherhood, and more a set of skills and disciplines that must be learnt by a range of maternal figures. However, although one might be delighted to see *90210* demonstrate the falsity of linking maternal thinking with biological motherhood, I cannot help but be surprised by those images of monstrous motherhood that are being presented on the small screen. After all, these mothers are seen to be sexual, social and financial problems to be overcome by the average teen rather than maternal figures of encouragement or support. It is a common trope of the teen experience in general and of the teen drama in particular that teenagers tend to turn to one another and instil a sense of community based on their peer group and generation, but that said, the extent to which mothers are either ignored or problematised is overwhelming here, especially given the dominant adult agenda that is otherwise evident in the genre.

The fact that those mothers who were seen in the first seasons of the show are being written out one by one might speak to the maturity of the teens on screen, but it also suggests a lack of respect for the parental role in general and for motherhood in particular. If young people continue to watch teen drama then they will be sent the worrying message that mothers are not needed, not wanted and of no importance to either the teen experience or a growing sense of adult maturity. And although much research exists to make the point that teen television addresses a broad youth demographic that could cover anyone from the 'tween' audience to the thirty-something, the concern over maternal representations still stands (Feasey 2006, 2–9).

Chapter 5

DRAMEDY: STRUGGLING, SEXUAL AND SISTERLY SINGLE MOTHERS

Introduction

The dramedy is a relatively new television genre that has received much critical and commercial success since its emergence in the late 1980s. Although the classification is relatively broad, recent examples of the genre tend to focus on a number of alternative family codes, conventions and complications. Indeed, programmes such as the *Gilmore Girls* (2000–2007), *Desperate Housewives* (2004–) and *Weeds* (2005–), base both their humor and dramatic tension on watching single mothers struggle within and beyond the home environment. Therefore, this chapter will examine the representation of those culturally acceptable and socially inappropriate single mothers, considering the way in which these women might re-imagine the parental role for the contemporary period.

History of the Genre

The recent genre classification of dramedy describes those hour-long television programmes that seek to fuse elements of comedy and drama, resulting in a drama with comic elements or a comedy with dramatic elements. While the television drama is said to focus on serious subject matters and complex characterisations, the small-screen comedy focuses on humorous repartee and self-reflexivity. The dramedy can 'blend the comic and the serious in different ways; some separate comic and dramatic storylines, while others combine drama and comedy together', while others do both (Lancioni 2006, 131). *Moonlighting* (1985–89) is said to have inaugurated the genre classification when the Directors Guild of America made an unprecedented decision to nominate the series for both best drama and comedy awards in the same year (Vande Berg 2010). *Moonlighting* and other early examples of the genre such as *Hooperman* (1987–89) *Northern Exposure* (1990–1995) and *Ally McBeal*

(1997–2002) generated both their comedic and dramatic narratives through the sexual tensions and budding romances of recurring cast members, and this remains a central element to contemporary dramedies such as *Gilmore Girls*, *Six Feet Under* (2001–2005), *Desperate Housewives*, *Weeds*, and *Parenthood* (2010–). However, although contemporary dramedies draw attention to the opportunities and anxieties surrounding sex and romance, they also exploit the contemporary family unit for both dramatic and comedic effect. Indeed, many of these shows seem committed to the presentation of alternative, non-nuclear and non-patriarchal family units, be it stepfamilies, single parents, surrogate parenting or homosexual partnerships. *Moonlighting* presented pregnancy and miscarriage, *Northern Exposure* depicted a phantom pregnancy, and the underlying narrative of *Ally McBeal* seems to grow out of the central protagonist's concern over her biological clock and the subsequent discovery of her 10-year-old daughter. *Six Feet Under* depicts accidental pregnancy, abortion, maternal suicide and a grieving family; *Weeds* focuses on a suburban widow resorting to desperate means to support her children; while *Parenthood* revolves around the trials and tribulations of one extended family, focusing on the pain of divorce and the financial, social and educational struggles surrounding single motherhood.

While the teen drama goes out of its way to remove motherhood from the small screen, the dramedy makes a point of exploring and indeed exploiting the maternal narrative. Representations of struggling mothers appear to dominate the contemporary dramedy, which leaves us questioning if the genre is perhaps not indebted to what Charlotte Brunsdon has termed 'heroine television', whereby women dominate the screen space, juggling work and family commitments, moving between relationships and trying to cope with the day-to-day routine of parenting (Brunsdon 1997, 34). Alternatively, the contemporary dramedy might be said to be borrowing heavily from what Andrea Press has referred to as 'post-family' television, whereby strong articulate women struggle with the day-to-day minutia of alternative home and family commitments, looking to other women rather than a patriarchal figure for social, financial and family support (Press cited in Dow 1996, 101).

Single, Sexual and Sisterly Motherhood in the Dramedy Genre

Although *Desperate Housewives* is more committed with the suburban domestic scene than the depiction of motherhood *per se*, the show nonetheless presents a number of fascinating representations of 'bad' motherhood and 'poor' maternal care, through a myriad of medicated, murderous, sisterly and 'stepford' mother figures. One might look to *Desperate Housewives* as an example of the struggles associated with both the working woman and the stay-at-home mother, considering the ways in which the show both challenges and conforms to unattainable images of the 'good' mother. Moreover, it is necessary to look at the depiction of single motherhood on the show in question due to the paucity of such images in the television landscape.

While motherhood appears to be a popular trope on contemporary television schedules, there are still very few representations of single mothers on the small screen. And if one considers that this particular family unit makes up a significant and growing demographic in the current cultural climate (Nock 2000, 255) then this oversight appears at best puzzling, and at worst problematic. Indeed, it is crucial that we see more single mothers on popular television due to the fact that such representations 'lessens the stigma [and] the sense of otherness that can come from being a child of a single parent' (Juffer 2006, 65). Alicia Skipper has suggested that the lack of single mothers on television stems from the fact that single parenthood defies the family-value rhetoric that drives the current right-wing political and religious agenda (Skipper 2008, 82). Alternatively, Amy Benfer has made the point that the lack of single mothers on screen might be due to the fact that this figure is seen to struggle socially, sexually or financially, without the necessary glamour, gloss or escapism that is central to much contemporary programming (Benfer 2000). Angharad Valdivia tells us that on the rare occasion when a single mother is presented in contemporary popular culture, she tends to conform to negative discourses, which suggest that she is failing her children and falling short of parenting ideals (Valdivia 1998, 272). With this in mind, it is important that we look at the representation of the single mother in the dramedy text, considering the ways in which these women adhere to negative stereotypes of the 'bad' mother, aspire to a more traditional family unit or offer a controversial, albeit current, take on the notion of a maternal role model.

Susan Mayer (Teri Hatcher) was the needy and damaged divorced single mother at the outset of the popular and long-running *Desperate Housewives*. According to Valdivia, Susan is a 'good' single mother due to the fact that she was essentially abandoned by her cheating husband, as opposed to being a single mother by choice, and as such, we are asked to sympathise with the woman in question (ibid., 283–6). This character is privileged in the sense that she is a children's book illustrator who can work from the comfort of her own beautiful and sizeable home, and yet she struggles with the financial reality of single parenthood because her ex-husband does not pay child maintenance for their daughter. Indeed, if one considers that only one in three lone parents receive child maintenance then Susan's financial situation, although desperate, is not unusual (Tagore 2010, 23). This forty-something character has a cheerleader's physique and perky demeanor, and although she attracts copious male attention, she struggles to find genuine commitment or loyalty from the men in her life. Indeed, Susan may well be an attractive and desirable image of single motherhood, but, following her painful divorce, she 'denies access to her sexuality' through celibacy (Bowers 2006, 95), and as such, the character is contained within appropriate motherhood discourses. However, the fact that Susan goes on to date and have sexual relationships offers the possibility of alternative and indeed potentially empowering images of motherhood.

After all, even though 'the standard of beauty is somewhat more muted for a mom than for a single woman' (Valdivia 1998, 282), the fact that a single mother is still asked to maintain a degree of physical attractiveness and sartorial taste means that there exists a potentially uneasy 'overlap between mom and single woman' (ibid., 282). Indeed, Susan might be said to present a significant break with earlier representations of appropriate and unacceptable motherhood because she is both a nurturing maternal presence and a desirable single female, or what Valdivia refers to as the 'parental Cosmo girl' (ibid., 289). However, although one might suggest that an attractive and optimistic figure such as Susan is 'not too shabby as a role model for sexy suburban moms everywhere' (Kenner 2006, 54), the fact that she is both incredibly glamorous and inconceivably clumsy goes some way towards taming the potential power of the sexual single mother. Indeed, it is commonly understood that those representations of motherhood that are the most sexual and alluring are also the same representations that are the most dysfunctional (Kenner 2006, 56). Abby Arnold makes this point somewhat bluntly when she tells us that 'conventional wisdom dictates that a mother who is truly sexy must be [...] a slut and [...] a bad mother' (Arnold 2003, 3). The fact that Susan 'can barely walk across the street without falling over' (Knowles 2005) may appear endearing to some, but it speaks to the infantilisation or more general incompetence of the sexual figure here. In short, this comedic device is merely a 'trait thrown in to tone down the sexuality of a television mom' (Kenner 2006, 54).

Likewise, even though Susan and her daughter share an open, honest, almost sisterly relationship, one might question the appropriateness of a mother who cannot pay her own bills, arrange custody conflicts or orchestrate romantic unions without the help of her teenage daughter, and although Susan has on occasion been seen to take a more responsible adult role in their relationship, the relationship is overwhelmingly based around a peer group rather than a more authoritative parental model. Alice Hart-Davis makes the point that such 'blurring of generations can be the social equivalent of a car crash' because although these mothers may suit their daughters youthful attire and want to be seen as young, fashionable and on trend, they are failing to 'respect [the] healthy boundaries' that parenting demands. Hart-Davis concludes by telling us that 'if your child likes you at the end of the parenting process, great. But that's best if it comes about by being a good role model for them to look up to, rather than being too pally' (Hart-Davis 2010). From this perspective, then, Susan may be a desirable and desiring single woman, but she cannot be a desiring, desirable and appropriate single mother.

Defining Single Motherhood in Society

The status of motherhood in general and of the single mother in particular has changed throughout different social, political and historical periods, and in relation to what are considered to be 'good' or 'bad' single mothers. While early forms of public assistance were put in place in the early 1900s to encourage widowed mothers to stay home and look after their children (Juffer 2007, 743), it is clear that American governmental support for low-income mothers has since been in decline (ibid., 729).

And it is not just government assistance towards the single mother that has seen a shift in previous generations; so too the role of the single woman as adoptive mother has been seen to alter over past decades. Historian Julie Berebitsky tells us that in the early part of the twentieth century, at a time before adoption became common practice, 'child rescue' reformers looked on 'mature single women as ideal adoptive parents, for they assumed that such women possessed a surfeit of unexpended mother love' (Berebitsky cited in Plant 2010, 95–6). However, by the 1920s, mature single women were being rejected as potential adoptive parents because of what was then understood as the negative force of those self-same pent-up maternal desires. It was suggested that 'woman could not be a good mother outside of a sexually satisfying marriage, for they regarded unmitigated mother love as a burdensome force, tinged with repressed sexual desire' (Plant 2010, 95). Therefore although a maternal figure that dedicated herself to her children and refused to remarry would have been applauded for such selfless mothering in the nineteenth century, this same woman would have been condemned as pathological mere decades later (ibid., 95).

And it is not just the government assistance or the appropriateness of the adoptive mother that has been seen to shift, but also the status of the single mother, or what was earlier referred to as the 'unmarried mother' in society. For example, up to and during the 1920s, all American unmarried mothers were said to be 'ruined' due to a biological defect: 'Illegitimacy occurred at the intersection of negative sociological and biological conditions and was an expression of an inhering, unchanging, and unchangeable '"physical" defect' (Solinger cited in Juffer 2007, 735). However, the number of unwed mothers was growing to such an extent that it soon became implausible to claim that these were all 'ruined' women, and as such, the problem of the unmarried mother was seen to shift from a biological concern to a concern with psychological neurosis. Thus, during the late 1940s and early 1950s those white women who found themselves pregnant outside of marriage were able to redeem themselves, but only if they were prepared to sign away custody of their child. Indeed, because 'the problem was psychological rather than biological, single mothers could be cured of their illness' (Juffer 2007, 735), and by 'admitting they were sick and agreeing to give up their babies [they] could be made marriageable again and assume their proper roles as mothers' (ibid., 735). However, only white women were able to find social and sexual salvation under this ruling because unwed black mothers 'continued to be portrayed as biologically unfit' maternal figures (ibid., 735). Indeed, statistics make it clear that black women were less likely to give their babies up for adoption compared with their white counterparts, which is said to have caused problems for social authorities because it 'conveyed that these women considered their motherhood legitimate and functional despite societal dissension' (Pietsch 2004, 73). Indeed, it was not until the mid 1970s that all unwed mothers were granted a level of individual respect and social acceptance, indicated by the shift in terminology from the 'unwed' to the 'single' mother – the term that retains its currency today (Juffer 2007, 736).

The single-parent household is becoming increasingly common in the contemporary era, particularly in Britain and America. In fact, the single-mother family is the fastest growing household demographic on both sides of the Atlantic (Nock 2000, 255). And although 'divorce and mortality were the traditional routes to single parenthood, births outside of marriage became the primary route to British single parenthood in 1986' (ibid., 255). There are currently 1.9 million lone parents in Britain caring for over 3 million children, meaning that a quarter of all children in Britain are living with a single parent (Tagore 2010, 23), and in over 90 per cent of cases, that parent is a single mother (Gingerbread 2011). And although the contemporary news agenda is saturated by stories concerning rising teen pregnancy rates, 'the average age of a lone parent is 36' (Tagore 2010, 23). Likewise, there are currently 12.9 million single parent families in America, with over 80 per cent of them being headed by a female. Indeed, since 2006 and 'for the first time in US history, a majority of all births to women under 30 were out of wedlock' (Roy 2009, 35).

The 'family of woman' has been said to have replaced the more traditional patriarchal unit (Stacey 1996, 51), and as such, there has appeared much research attempting to explain this growing trend. And although 'no consensus has been reached on the subject to date' (González 2006, 3) it has been argued that the rise of the single mother household is due in part to three interconnected developments: namely, welfare incentives, increased economic opportunities for women and a limited supply of marriageable men (ibid., 3). The continued research on lone parenting in general and on the single mother in particular stems from the fact that 'single motherhood seems to be associated with poverty and negative outcomes for children' (ibid., 1). However, although evidence does exist to suggest a link between single parenting, poverty and poor educational and career opportunities, the evidence also tells us that 'the unplanned child has no significant effect on the educational attainment of white mothers' (Bronars and Grogger 1994, 1148). Rather, 'the effects of unplanned births differ in many cases by race and across cohorts of unwed mothers' (ibid., 1155). After all, while 'nearly all unwed mothers experience substantial short-run decreases in labor-force participation after an unplanned birth', black women suffer from 'sizable and persistent negative effects' (ibid., 1155). However, even though extant research tells us that single white mothers do not suffer any long-term negative effects from their unwed maternal status, there is evidence to suggest that getting married and divorced is more physically and mentally problematic for single mothers, irrespective of race, when compared to their non-mothering counterparts (Williams, Sassler and Nicholson 2008, 1481–1511).

Marriage is said to offer a number of financial, social, psychological and physical benefits to both partners. Indeed a former British Conservative Party leader recently announced that 'we do a disservice to society if we ignore the evidence which shows that stable families tend to be associated with better outcomes for children' (Duncan Smith cited in Porter 2011), adding that 'there are few more powerful tools for promoting stability than the institution of marriage' (ibid.). Indeed, many marital and family welfare reforms have been put in place with the primary goal of encouraging 'the formation of two-parent families, especially among low-income single mothers' (Williams, Sassler and Nicholson 2008, 1482), and these 'programs are motivated in part by evidence that marriage improves the economic well-being of single mothers and their children [...] and that children raised in two-parent households fare better on several outcomes than those reared in single-parent families' (ibid., 1482).

However, those marital benefits – be they social, financial or physical – are less likely to extend to those women who were single mothers prior to the marital union. After all, single mothers who later marry are faced with a much higher risk of divorce than those who marry without children, and those negative financial and physiological effects of marital dissolution are said to be 'amplified among women who had a premarital birth' (ibid., 1484). Indeed, 'the poverty rates of disadvantaged single mothers who marry but later divorce actually exceed those of their never-married counterparts' (ibid., 1484). The fact that the economic burden of divorce undermines previous health advantages offered by marriage means that single mothers who marry and then divorce are actually worse off both mentally and physically than those single mothers who remain unmarried, and even worse off still than those women without children. After all, the 'strains of marital dissolution are likely amplified among single mothers who must cope with its consequences not only for their own lives but also for the lives of their children' (ibid., 1503). And if one considers that between 25 and 29 per cent of unwed mothers' marriages end within five years, such findings must be acknowledged and addressed (ibid., 1503). Moreover, it has been suggested that single mothers marry men with fewer socio-economic advantages and educational achievements than their childless counterparts, and as such 'marriage may not offer single mothers the same health-enhancing financial and economic resources that it provides to the average woman' (ibid., 1484–5).

Furthermore, some evidence has suggested that those women who marry after a premarital birth actually suffer from a lower quality relationship than those women who entered marriage without children. The suggestion here is that because single mothers who marry are 'more likely than are childless women to enter cohabiting relationships with men who already have children', then the emotional stresses and physical strains of uniting two previously separate families creates friction and frustration in the newly formed household (ibid., 1486). Ann Ferguson makes the point that stepchildren often struggle to accept or bond with their new social parent, which 'creates special problems for women, for as mothers and step-mothers [...] women are expected to be the ones to heal the conflicts within the family and to nurture everyone involved' (Ferguson 1983, 174). Therefore if one considers the challenges of creating a new family unit combined with the weaker economic position of those men who partner with single mothers, then it is perhaps unsurprising to find that these unions 'may have fewer positive consequences and perhaps some negative consequences for the health and well-being of single mothers' (Williams, Sassler and Nicholson, 2008, 1486). Furthermore, single mothers tend to move in with their new partners at a significantly faster rate than their childless contemporaries, and as such, the potentially hasty decision to create a new family might well be forged on either an inappropriate coupling or a lack of necessary communication (ibid., 1486). The findings here then suggest that those single mothers who marry tend to do so without the physiological or financial benefits previously associated with that union, because they tend to partner with an existing single father who is himself not privileged with educational or financial capital. These women go on to suffer in poor relationships, due in part to the emotional stress of trying to forge a new family unit and to the speed at which that unit came together. More worryingly perhaps is the negative consequences that both the hurried marriage and dissolution will have for the children involved, because 'entering and exiting any type of union is likely to have negative consequences for children' (ibid., 1503).

The 'Good' and 'Bad' Single Mother

Although extant research suggests that single motherhood is a potential cause for financial, social and sexual anxiety, it is important to note that there are differences between single parents. The forty-something 'woman who decides she wants a child and gets inseminated with donor sperm is obviously a single mom' (Juffer 2007, 750) but we are asked to question the single status of a 'divorced mom who shares physical custody with her ex-husband' or the twenty-something woman who lives with but is not married to the father of her baby (ibid., 750). Likewise, we are asked to distinguish between those 'women who have not ever been married to the fathers of their children, [...] single mothers who are divorced and are raising children without a live-in-spouse [and] women who have been widowed' (Skipper 2008, 81). Indeed, Arlie Hochschild has gone as far as to suggest that 'women are doing "single-mothering" both inside and outside the institution of marriage' because of the lack of male commitment to the domestic arena, which results in women either taking on the burdens of childcare or filing for divorce and taking their children out of the family home (Büskens 2004, 107).

Angharad Valdivia's research on motherhood in the media suggests that 'good' single mothers have not chosen their single-parenting status, but rather, have been tragically widowed or abandoned by the father of their children (Valdivia 1998, 283). These mostly middle-class mothers are exhaustively patient, unendingly caring and always compassionate, even in the face of the most trying of circumstances. These mothers maintain their beautiful appearances but never show interest in any relationship that would detract from or jeopardise the maternal bond with her children. And, perhaps unsurprisingly, such saintly goodness and external attractiveness is rewarded, as these mothers are routinely seen to find 'their way out of single motherhood and into wealthier status with perfectly adjusted children' (ibid., 284). Alternatively of course, the 'bad' single mother is without patience, tolerance or compassion, and although she is interested in pursuing a social life and sexual partners, this woman has no desire to find a stable father figure for her children. This 'bad' single mother is a 'morally, socially, and sexually aberrant [...] law-breaker' (Pietsch 2004, 66) who 'flaunts social conventions' (Phoenix 1994, 95). In short, the 'bad' unwed mother breaks 'multiple rules concerning femininity and sexuality, marriage and maternity' (Rolfe cited in Pietsch 2004, 68). The implication here is that 'good moms have happy children [and] bad moms have emotionally disturbed or delinquent children', and it is suggested that this message dominates the contemporary media agenda (Valdivia 1998, 288). With this in mind, future research must differentiate between a myriad of single mothers, but this is in order to create rigorous, accurate and thus credible findings rather than to offer any value judgements in favour of teenage never-married mothers, single mothers by choice or a range of other single groupings.

I have examined some of the ways in which single motherhood has been lived in different social periods, paying attention to the financial or physiological hardships that are said to be of concern to the unmarried mother. As such, it is crucial that we look at the representation of motherhood in general and single motherhood in particular in the popular and long-running *Gilmore Girls*. After all, this is a programme that was funded by the Family Friendly Programming Forum, a show that focuses on the relationship between a single mother and her teenage daughter, and, perhaps more importantly, a vehicle that depicts a contented single parent without financial or physiological hardship. There are only a small number of 'single mothers and even fewer representations of unwed mothers' (Skipper 2008, 82) on the small screen, and, given the rise of the single-mother family in the contemporary period, an examination of this maternal role is crucial here.

Gilmore Girls

Gilmore Girls is a popular dramedy text that focuses on the relationship between Lorelai Gilmore (Lauren Graham), a thirty-something single mother, and Lorelai 'Rory' Gilmore (Alexis Bledel), her teenage daughter, as they are seen living their daily lives in the fictional New England town of Stars Hollow, Connecticut. Their loving, caring, respectful and fun mother–daughter pairing is the central drive of the show, with little recourse to the usual social frustrations, miscommunications, quibbles and squabbles that are said to stem from more traditional mother–daughter relationships. Lorelai gave birth to Rory as a 16-year-old schoolgirl, and as such, the relatively small age difference between these two women creates a sisterly bond, which is exploited throughout much of the show's history.

The Family Friendly Programming Forum is a consortium that was set up by a number of mainstream advertising companies to fund programmes that offered multiple generation appeal, or, to put it more simply, an organisation that offers financial incentives to American networks to produce shows that parents can watch with, and enjoy alongside, their children. The organisation is said to support and promote 'the development of family friendly content', and the fact that it supports the single mother and teenage daughter dynamic makes it clear that 'the definition of family friendly is deliberately broad' to cater to the lived reality of the contemporary family (FFPF cited in Silbergleid 2009, 93). That said, some commentators have suggested that because the character of Lorelai goes on to marry the father of her child, Christopher Hayden

(David Sutcliffe), the programme 'conforms to the dark underbelly of the stipulations laid out' by the forum when it dictates that programmes are to be 'appropriate in theme, content and language' and portray 'a responsible resolution' of family issues (MacBain and Mahato 2008, 112). And although Lorelai does not remain happily married or even cohabiting with the man in question, it nevertheless points to the potential viability of the more traditional unit. That said, the long-running show is less committed to the nuclear family than it is motivated by the educational, social, romantic and financial trials and tribulations of the single mother–daughter relationship.

The WB's *Gilmore Girls* has been both a critical and commercial success, reaching an audience of between 3 and 5 million people per episode in America. The show is currently screened in rotation on E4 in Britain, and is proving particularly popular with female audiences across a number of age demographics on both sides of the Atlantic (Westman 2007, 25). The show has been nominated for the 'favorite family drama' category by the People's Choice Awards; Lauren Graham has been nominated for a number of best comedic and dramatic actress awards, including the Golden Globe, the Screen Actors Guild and the Television Critics Association awards. Moreover, as a nod to the teen demographic that is acknowledged in the show, Alexis Bledel has been nominated for the best dramatic actress award by the Teen Choice Awards, as well as winning their award for best comic performance, whilst Lauren Graham has twice won the award for the best depiction of a television mother. The series has also won a Family Television Award for best new series and was named 'best family television drama' by the Young Artist Awards. Indeed, *Gilmore Girls* is not only commercially successful and critically applauded, but also understood as a culturally relevant text, as evidenced by the fact that it was recently listed as one of *Time* magazine's 'Best Television Shows of All-*TIME*' (Poniewozik 2007).

A Myriad of Mothers on *Gilmore Girls*

Whilst negative stereotypes of the culturally inappropriate or 'bad' single mother abound in popular media culture, most commonly the working-class teen mother or the more mature and financially secure middle-class single-mother-by-choice, Lorelai offers an interesting and challenging case study of a self-sufficient teenage mother who is single by choice – who returns to school, sets up her own successful business and forges a close bond with her daughter, without sacrificing intimate friendships or sexual relationships. Depicting Lorelai as a hardworking and fiercely independent heroine, the show negotiates the predictable stereotypes surrounding both teenage pregnancy and the more mature single-mother-by-choice (McLoone cited in Coleman 2008, 176).

That said, even though the relationship between single teen mother Lorelai and her daughter Rory is presented as the driving force of the show, we never see Lorelai as a pregnant teenager, nor are we shown her struggling as a 16-year-old single mother. Rather, we are told through the very briefest of flashbacks and dialogue between the local characters that Lorelai not only became pregnant and kept the baby, but that she also refused to marry the father, ran away from home, dropped out of high school and went to work as a maid in a local hotel, aptly named the Independence Inn. The programme refuses to show us the years in which Lorelai struggled to bring up her daughter as a young teenage mother without family support or educational privilege. When we meet the characters, Lorelai is the manager of the Independence Inn, taking an evening course in business in the hope of opening her own establishment. She is single by choice, owns her own beautiful and sizeable home and is estranged from her parents. When we meet Rory she is seen to be an incredibly sweet, kind and educationally gifted teenager who is looking to a future as a foreign correspondent and a place in the Ivy League. Lorelai works hard at her job, but shows no interest in domestic chores, she and her daughter eat out at the local diner more often than they eat in and they share a love of fast foods and popular culture. In short 'the controversial politics of teen pregnancy as an issue are ingenuously sidestepped' (Coleman 2008, 176) because the characters are, from the outset, beautiful, confident, charismatic and intelligent, perhaps a long way from the negative image of the single mother and her daughter that is perpetuated in society and further still from the usual depiction of the lone parent in the current media landscape.

That said, more predictable and less rosy mother and daughter tensions are played out in the programme through the relationship between Lorelai and her own wealthy, privileged upper-class parents. Indeed, the relationship between Lorelai and her mother Emily Gilmore (Kelly Bishop) is at the heart of both the dramatic action and comic dialogue that is central to the show's success. Lorelai humiliated her proud parents when she became pregnant and ran away from home, and continued to hurt them by disowning them, their financial assistance and their upper class values. *Gilmore Girls* takes the relationship between Rory, Lorelai and Emily as a central focus, drawing attention to and offering potential judgements on the alternative mothering styles and mother–daughter relationships being presented in the programme. However, the once-physically and emotionally distant relationship between Lorelai and Emily becomes much closer, at least in terms of geographic proximity, when Lorelai goes to her parents for financial assistance to help with the costs of Rory's private schooling. Emily agrees to help Lorelai on the proviso that both Lorelai and Rory attend a Friday night dinner every week until the loan is paid, and these dinners fuel further mother–daughter frustrations between Lorelai and Emily, alongside a growing love and respect between granddaughter and grandmother as Rory enters and Lorelai re-enters the wealthy home that Lorelai left years earlier.

Gilmore Girls is a fascinating case study for several reasons: not only because it was the first programme funded by the Family Friendly Programming Forum, or because it puts a successful teenage single mother at the heart of the show, and not only because the child of that single parent is both socially and educationally gifted, but because the show dared to represent a number of mother–daughter pairings that each challenged the traditional nuclear unit. Indeed, a number of long-running and established characters can be seen to present the audience with a range of potential, if sometimes problematic, representations of motherhood, spanning class boundaries, generational differences, work ethics and cultures.

Mrs Kim (Emily Kuroda) is the Korean vegan matriarch and strict Seventh-day Adventist who rules her home, business and daughter with an authoritative voice. Mrs Kim does not allow her 16-year-old daughter to date, wear make-up, read non-Christian literature or listen to popular music. And yet although her daughter Lane Kim (Keiko Agena) spends much of the shows history hiding non-Christian paraphernalia under her bedroom floorboards and lying to her mother about her social activities, it is clear that Mrs Kim's stern tone stems from genuine love and concern for her daughter and Lane's deceit stems from not wanting to hurt or disappoint her mother. When Lane finally moves out of the family home, joins a band and starts dating, there is a period of time when the two are either unable or unwilling to communicate with one another. However, after a brief period without contact, the mother and daughter not only begin to talk, but embark on a more honest relationship, to the point where Mrs Kim not only helps her daughter to find bookings for her band, but actually supports her marriage to one of the band members, and does everything in her power to help her with the arrival of her twin boys at the end of the last series. The relationship between mother and daughter may not reflect the sisterly bonding or the open communication shared by Lorelai and Rory, but there is no mistaking the love and respect that these two women have for one another, which makes for a challenging but ultimately positive representation of motherhood in the series. Indeed, although these women share very different parenting styles, Mrs Kim and Lorelai share a motherly bond when they both talk of wanting to keep their teenage daughters safe and provide them with a wealth of opportunities (S1:E12).

Sookie St. James (Melissa McCarthy) is Lorelai's fun-loving and kind-hearted best friend and chef at the Independence Inn, and although she is single at the outset of the series, she becomes married and subsequently has two children, and was pregnant again at the end of the final series. And although Sookie is seen to cherish time with her children and adore her newfound maternal role, the character also demands time for herself, continues working without apology in a job that she finds fulfilling, spends quality time with friends and supports her local community. In short, Sookie is that rare depiction of a television mother who manages to combine a successful and demanding career with a growing family, without forgoing her own passions, interests and identity.

Sherry Tinsdale (Mädchen Amick) is the driven and hardworking career woman who becomes pregnant by Rory's father. This character is presented as a negative maternal force when she refuses to cut back on her working commitments while heavily pregnant, plans a Caesarean section around her working schedule and demands that Rory reorganise her work calendar while she waits impatiently for the birth of Georgia 'Gigi' Gilmore. Although her baby shower is filled with expensive gifts and well-dressed friends, it is clear that no one else in the party has children, or shows any interest in wanting them. Indeed, when Sherry has to have her Caesarean earlier than planned, these women make no effort to leave their work schedules to be there with her (S3:E6). The expectant mother being at a loss at her own baby shower is a common trope of contemporary popular programming, be it Rachel Green (Jennifer Anniston) in *Friends* (S8:E20) or Miranda Hobbs (Cynthia Nixon) in *Sex and the City* (S4:E17). However, Sherry seems to be singled out here, not simply for her lack of preparation for the birth, but for her misguided optimism about pregnancy, the birth and the ensuing role of working motherhood. Sherry makes little effort to convince us or herself that she actually wants this baby, and when she leaves her young daughter in the custody of her father and a range of paid nursing staff in order to take a permanent job in Paris, it merely reaffirms her earlier lack of maternal instinct (S5:E6). Although feminist mothering studies tells us that we should find a way to acknowledge and accept those women who are uninterested in or unable to mother, the ways in which Lorelai and Rory respond to Sherry's move makes it clear that the audience should view such actions as shocking, shameful and selfish. Moreover, the fact that the series ends with Sherry apologising for her actions and asking for her young daughter to join her in France makes it even clearer that her earlier work-centric model was unacceptable, and in this case barely forgivable. That said, even though Sherry's work-centric model of parenting may be at odds with the family-friendly image of maternal love and affection that drives the show, the fact that the programme dared to include this image of motherhood is powerful in itself, even if it was not presented as entirely positive. Other maternal figures are peppered throughout the shows history, be it Paris Geller's (Liza Weil) emotionally distant and newly divorced mother, Jess Mariano's (Milo Ventimiglia) socially and economically struggling mother, April Nardini's

(Vanessa Marano) artistic and bohemian single mother or Dean Forester's (Jared Padalecki) more traditional happy-homemaker figure.

However, although a number of different mothers and a range of alternative maternal styles are presented in the programme, Lorelai's open, honest and communicative relationship with her daughter is praised above all others, and her relaxed, sisterly and informal parenting style is, albeit sometimes begrudgingly, said to produce this respectful and loving relationship between these women. In short, Lorelai is constructed as the ideal mother because 'she listens, protects, teaches, and nourishes' her daughter and the wider community (Fleegal 2008, 146). This character acts as the mother surrogate to Lane, takes on the godmother role for Sooki's children and slips into the other-mothering role to young Gigi. She is always available for comfort and support for Paris and Dean when they ask for it, and she tries to offer maternal advice to the rebellious Jess. Moreover, she stands in as the mother surrogate during April's impromptu birthday party when the girl's own father is struggling to entertain a group of 'tweenage' girls. The programme makes it clear that although there are a number of mothering styles to adopt, only one will produce an honest, loving and respectful relationship between generations.

Lorelai, Rory and the Sisterly Bond

The bond between Lorelai and Rory is so strong and their relationship so open that they can talk about all manner of both superficial and serious concerns, ranging from clothes and accessories to sex and career opportunities, and we are asked to believe that this intimacy is due to their sisterly bond rather than the more traditional and authoritative mother and daughter relationship. When Lorelai wants to encourage Rory to talk to her about her recent relationship developments, we hear her tell her daughter that 'I was not thinking we had to talk like mum and kid, I thought we could talk like friends' (S5:E1). Likewise, when Lorelai gets into bed with Rory on her birthday morning she says 'you're a great, cool kid and the best friend a girl could ever have', to which Rory replies 'back at you', and when toasting her daughter that same evening she does it to 'my pal Rory' (S1:E6).

This mother and daughter pair eat together every evening, they double-date, attend town meetings and charity events together and even spend several weeks backpacking around Europe. Indeed, on Rory's first day at Yale, she rings her mother, requesting that she come and keep her company and stay the night in her new dorm room. Rory bemoans her own affections for her mother when she tells her that 'four hours at Yale, I'm already homesick; I'm 18 – you didn't socialise me properly, you made me a mama's girl. Why don't I hate you? Why don't I want to be away from you? […] I should hate you, not miss you. Do something to make me hate you' (S4:E2). But Rory genuinely misses her mother, their home and their shared life together, and Lorelai uses this opportunity not only to spend another night with her daughter, but to help her socialise in her new campus environment. Lorelai is heard telling us that 'Rory is my life – she's my pal, my everything' (S1:E5); indeed, 'her love for her daughter is almost palpable' (Millman 2000). However, this is not read as an unhealthy bond or an unnatural closeness, but rather, it speaks of the love between the pair as mother and daughter but also of their relationship as genuine friends. Indeed, a recent edition of *Newgen*, a magazine dedicated to inspiring and informing National Childbirth Trust supporters, presented what it sees as a positive case study of a single mother who commented that 'now [my daughter is] a teenager, it often feels as if we're flatmates, which is fun' (Tagore 2010, 24).

However, while the National Childbirth Trust might point to the success of this sisterly bond, others are currently condemning what is seen as an inappropriate relationship. Ann Erickson makes the point that Lorelai is emotionally stunted because she stopped developing as an adult when she gave birth to Rory, and that somehow she is growing up with her daughter rather than acting as an adult role model for her (Erickson 2008, 69). Moreover, Beth Kendrick voices her concerns because while Lorelai continues to play the part of the irresponsible teenager it leaves Rory having to take on the burden of adult roles and responsibilities at a time when she should 'feel secure enough to make mistakes and start establishing independence' (Kendrick 2006, 30). In short, commentators are asking how a teenage single mother can assert her independence when she herself is 'in some ways, still in need of financial and emotional parenting' (Benfer 2000).

However, to dismiss Lorelai as emotionally stunted or immature is to misunderstand the character in question. Indeed, Lorelai's 'charming and earthly house, her Jeep, her collection of t-shirts with funny and explicit phrases, her love of junk food – are all evidence of [her] personality, a personality she refuses to have stamped out by conforming to the standards of high society' (Fleegal 2008, 146). The character of Luke Danes (Scott Patterson) says it best in the show when he tells Lorelai that she is 'colourful and funny, [...] practically a cartoon character' (S6:E18). In this way, 'funny and colourful', 'charming' and 'earthy' are not euphemisms for 'irresponsible' or 'stunted', but cues to a fully rounded thirty-something independent woman and single mother. It has been said that the 'best gift a mother can give a daughter – and, as she becomes an adult, that a daughter can give her mother – is permission to be herself [because the] daughter can be who she wants to be because the mother is who she wants to be' (Tracy cited in Fleegal 2008, 150). In this case, Lorelai leaving her wealthy and claustrophobic parental home and forging a more liberating identity for herself has allowed Rory to then follow her own educational, geographical and emotional dreams. As such, we are not being asked to read Lorelai's youthful liberation as infantile, but as empowering for both mother and daughter alike. The fact that Lorelai can joke to her daughter that 'you have to do something bad while mummy is out of town' (S2:E16) speaks less of misguided mothering and more of the trust and respect that they have for one another.

Moreover, it is worth noting that although these women share clothes, intimate secrets and popular cultural reference points, Lorelai can and does mother in the more traditional sense of the word when she deems it necessary. For example, when Lorelai continues to put off informing her parents that she has become engaged, Rory tells her mother that she must do so immediately, and in this instance Lorelai tells her, albeit it in a jovial manner that 'I will tell them when I'm ready to tell them and you're just going to have to accept that because I'm the mother and you're the daughter, and in some cultures that means you have to do as I say' (S2:E2). And although on this particular occasion Rory chooses not to listen to her mother's words, when the issue is of more serious importance Rory does indeed accept her mother as a figure of authority. For example, when Rory decides that she does not want to attend the privileged Chilton Preparatory School because of an interest in a new boy, we hear Lorelai inform her that 'we always had a democracy in this house, but now I'm going to have to play the mom card' (S1:E1). In this same way, the usual mother–daughter democracy is overruled when Rory stays out, albeit innocently, with her then-boyfriend. In these rare instances 'Lorelai brings her back to the right path by showing Rory where she strayed instead of cutting her down even further' (Fleegal 2008, 149).

Lorelai, Rory, Sex and Conversation

Although Lorelai is seen dating throughout the show's history, both casually and in longer-term relationships, it is made clear that Rory would never be introduced to or asked to meet Lorelai's partners, and therefore form no attachments with them. Indeed, Lorelai has a 'distinctive ability to marry responsible motherhood [with] gratifying single womanhood' (MacBain and Mahato 2008, 97). It is only when Lorelei begins to date Rory's English teacher Max Medina (Scott Cohen) from her sophomore year at Chilton that this previously workable system is challenged. And on the first night that Max stays over at the Gilmore residence, it is Lorelai rather than Rory who finds the situation complicated and confusing, so much so that she asks to spend the night in bed with her daughter, fearing that 'it won't be the me-and-you, secret-special-clubhouse, no-boys-allowed thing anymore' (S2:E3).

A number of commentators have suggested that although Lorelai and Rory repeatedly extol the virtues of their open communications, there is evidence in the show to negate such claims. After all, even though mother and daughter are said to share their private thoughts and feelings, 'Lorelai does not share that she is dating Max or Digger, or that she is engaged to Luke and married to Christopher until well after the fact' (Erickson 2008, 79). And Rory does not tell her mother that she is dating her now-married ex-boyfriend. That said, one might argue that this speaks less about a lack of communication, and more about appropriate timing for what are potentially life-altering changes for the close-knit mother and daughter.

Moreover, when there has been a lack of communication, it is presented as a rare and upsetting time, with both characters coming to acknowledge that they have missed their usual dialogue and daily communications. After one period of non-communication, Lorelai tells Rory that 'we have to be able to talk' (S1:E20), and when Rory confronts her about her relationship with Max she apologises profusely, explaining that she was only trying to protect her daughter, promising that 'I won't keep anything from you again, my life will be an open book to you' (S1:E5). And when Lorelai discovers that Rory didn't tell her about a recent kiss, she asks her colleague 'why didn't she tell me, why didn't she tell me about the kiss? [...] We tell each other everything else, but this she keeps a secret [...] Not talking about guys and our personal lives – that's me and my mom, not me and Rory' (S1:E7). However, she and the audience are soon reminded of the strength of their relationship and thus Lorelai is once again reinstated as the 'good' mother. So even though, as some commentators have pointed out, mother and daughter disagree, argue or refuse contact on occasion – in some cases over several weeks and in different time zones (Erickson 2008, 65) – the fact that they are able to re-open communications means that their relationship can rebound from this lack of dialogue, which, again, ultimately repositions Lorelai as a positive maternal influence.

Critical commentators have suggested that Lorelai's inability to 'establish a solid relationship with a man' speaks of her sexual and social immaturity (ibid., 69). However, one might suggest that even though Lorelai dates casually, accepts and then cancels her engagement with Max, marries Christopher on the rebound from Luke, allows Christopher to leave and then realises her feelings for Luke, this is less a case of stunted emotions or an inability to commit than another example of the ways in which programmes such as this draw out the love story between characters who are known to the audience to be pre-destined soul mates. Either way, Lorelai offers a fascinating – and some have said 'seductive' – portrayal of contemporary single motherhood because her successful maternal role is 'dependent on her [...] ability to maintain the intimate relationship she has with her daughter in spite of the men in her life' (MacBain and Mahato 2008, 102–3). Indeed, 'Lorelai appeals to a viewership of married mothers, who envy Lorelai's youth, physical fitness, camaraderie with her daughter, ability to date and be free from marital constraints, and ability to parent and be free from co-parenting constraints or compromises' (Wall cited in Erickson 2008, 72–3). Cara Wall refers to Lorelai as the 'anti-Donna Reed – not the mother who's perfect in the way others want her to be, but the mother living the life all mothers secretly want to lead' (Wall 2005).

Recent economic data tells us that 'unplanned births may adversely affect a woman's prospects in both the marriage and labor markets' in part because they decrease her future marriage prospects (Bronars and Grogger 1994, 1141), and yet Lorelai is not without genuine proposals from single, childless and wealthy bachelors. Christopher has been proposing to Lorelai time and again since they were both teenagers, and as such one might put his most recent proposals down to nostalgia and a shared history, however when we see Max propose and Luke accept her proposal it can be seen to challenge the aforementioned economic analysis. In short, Lorelai does not seem adversely affected in the marriage market, because although she chooses not to marry the professional, personable and respectful Max, she does marry the charming, financially successful and doting Christopher.

Likewise, we are currently being told that 'single mothers [...] face the specter of long-term poverty with implications ranging from adolescent delinquency to depression and suicide among their children' (Valdivia 1998, 275), and yet, at a time when cultural commentators are signaling problems for those children from single-parent families, *Gilmore Girls* depicts a hardworking young woman breaking free from such negative life turns. And although 'it may be statistically unlikely that most unwed mothers will be as successful as Lorelai at this stage in [their] life', we are asked to acknowledge and applaud the fact that Lorelai supported both herself and her daughter by working as a maid at the Independence Inn while living in a single-room potting shed (Skipper 2008, 89). And although one might assume that such domestic duties and financial hardships were depressing, disappointing or mere drudgery, both Rory and Lorelai look back fondly on those years, talking glowingly about their close proximity and snug living quarters (ibid., 89).

It is worth noting that both mother and daughter are slim, white and beautiful; in short, they adhere to the beauty myth that abounds in contemporary media culture. However, Lorelai's beauty and sexual appeal is fascinating for it potentially challenges previous images of the celibate 'good' mother who puts her children's needs first and waits patiently for a 'desirable, decent, and therefore socially acceptable' husband (Valdivia 1998, 289). After all 'Lorelai does not allow her role as a mother to interfere with her identity as a woman and a sexual being; she is not completely willing to sacrifice that part of herself' (Skipper 2008, 91). However, whether one views Lorelai's sexuality as either 'bad' mothering or 'good' feminism, the character illustrates the potential social unease of combining desiring womanhood with single motherhood.

Lorelai, Rory and Domestic Indifference

Lorelai challenges the 'good' single mother stereotype, as she is self-sufficient, sexually aware and in a position to decline entirely respectable marriage proposals. Indeed, the 'basic premise that began *Gilmore Girls* unsettles the long legacy of clichéd representations of motherhood by having at its heart an affirming and positive presentation of a mother who is characterized by not only her sex drive and career, but also her single status' (MacBain and Mahato 2008, 99). Moreover, the character can be seen to negotiate the socially acceptable image of maternal domesticity, preferring instead to offer her daughter Pop-Tarts, take-away pizza and regular cheeseburgers at the local diner. Katherine Kinnick tells us that media images of appropriate motherhood conform to traditional gender roles and specifically that 'cooking and cleaning are embraced by good mothers, even those who work outside the home' (Kinnick 2009, 12). However, Lorelai is routinely constructed and circulated as the 'good' mother of the series even though she mocks housework, avoids laundry duties and uses her oven for extra shoe storage. On one occasion Lorelai leaves the house without underwear on laundry day, leaving Rory to wash both her own clothes, and her mothers, for fear of social humiliation (S1:E7). Lorelai also attends Rory's first day at school in denim hot pants and cowboy boots because she did not leave time to either do her own laundry or to pick up her clothes from the dry cleaners (S1:E2). At one particularly high or low domestic point, depending on your reading, we see the character refusing to make instant mashed potato because of the physical exertion of mixing it with water and the effort associated with washing up the bowl and spoon (S5:E9). Lorelai and Rory not only eat fast food at an alarming rate, they also stock up on sweets, crisps, peanut butter and marshmallows. Indeed much of the shows humour stems from the fact that these women continue to eat processed food with little negative effect on their skin, weight or other aspects of physical health. And although one should not and would not recommend the Gilmore diet to anyone outside of a fictional television series, the fact that these women spend mealtimes together and converse over their shared love of junk food can be seen as a positive take on mother daughter–bonding. In short, 'the dining habits of Rory and Lorelai challenge perceptions that women should be responsible for cooking and serving the meals' and highlight 'the significance of the experience of just sitting down together' (Skipper 2008, 92).

Lorelai, Rory, Other-Mothers and the Community Effort

Although Lorelai is presented as a hardworking, independent and resourceful single mother, the show does occasionally point to the ways in which the wider community of Stars Hollow has taken a turn in helping to raise Rory. The local dance teacher Miss Patty (Liz Torres) makes the point that the whole town takes pride in seeing Rory's successful graduation because each of them feels that they have contributed in some small way to her growing up, telling Christopher that 'we're all like Rory's parents around here' (S1:E15). Likewise, Lorelai comments that Luke was always a strong male presence, indeed a strong father figure, in her daughter's life (S7:E12). Therefore, although it has been argued that 'children of lone mothers do badly educationally and are more likely than children raised with two parents to become delinquent because they have less opportunity to observe appropriate models of male behaviour' this is not the case here (Phoenix and Woollett 1994b, 23). If one feels it necessary to question Lorelai's own status as a role model, then the fact that Rory is encouraged to look beyond her own mother for parental guidance and support speaks of a notion of other-mothering that is strongly encouraged by contemporary feminist mothers (Green 2004, 33). However, if we are to momentarily forget Lorelai's role in raising Rory, the programme goes to great lengths to remind us of Lorelai's role as a caring, considerate, loving and devoted maternal figure. When Christopher informs her that 'she's a great kid – she's all you, a chip off the old perfect block' (S1:E15), and later, 'God knows she doesn't need anyone besides you' (S1:E7), it speaks volumes about the role of Lorelai in shaping not just her daughter's looks, but her character, mannerisms and motivations.

Lorelai, Emily and the Mother–Daughter Dynamic

Although Lorelai is presented as the most appropriate maternal role model in the programme due to the consideration, care and compassion that she shows to her daughter, her peer group and her own friends, she demonstrates none of these nurturing characteristics towards her own parents; indeed, she often goes as far as presenting a rather cold, distant and even hostile front to her own mother. One commentator has gone as far as to ask if Lorelai's mothering skills are less a demonstration of her natural maternal instinct, and more a demonstration of 'a desire to continue her rebellion against her own mother by doing the opposite of what Emily did' (Fleegal 2008, 146). After all,

'Lorelai revels in her bad reputation; she pushes her mother's buttons like she's still 16, saying exactly the things she knows will set her off' (Millman 2000). Indeed, Lorelai goes to great lengths to stop her mother visiting her home, and when she does visit she goes to even greater lengths to stop her feeling welcome. When her mother announces a visit we see Lorelai hiding flowers and magazines, and when Rory finds her mother turning the heating down we hear her explain that she is trying to actively discourage her mother from staying in their otherwise warm, welcoming and comfortable home (S6:E17). Emily is fully aware that she is never invited and not much wanted in her daughter's house, and makes a point of telling her that 'it's not right, [...] you keep so much from me with these separate worlds of yours' (S5:E7).

Emily is a wealthy, upper-class, stay-at-home mother who dedicated her life to her husband, his business clients and their only child. The fact that Lorelai then ran away as a pregnant teenager caused Emily genuine upset, distress and anxiety. The fact that her daughter chose to remain at a distance throughout her adult life and Rory's formative years caused further disappointment and indeed humiliation to the proud woman in question. Emily views herself as a 'good' mother in line with the maternal codes and conventions of her class and generation, and she understands 'good' mothering to mean 'providing monetary items and opportunities that can be secured through money' for her daughter, and later, her granddaughter (Skipper 2008, 91), so when she tells Lorelai that 'I put you in a good school, I gave you the best of everything, I made sure you had the finest of opportunities' (S1:E9) she is presenting herself as a socially appropriate maternal figure. The fact that these maternal practices are at odds with her daughter's reminds us of cultural changes to the 'good' mother and the ways in which the ideal of appropriate motherhood is fabricated generation after generation depending on the social, sexual or political period. After all, rather than be grateful for such opportunities, Lorelai tells her mother that she felt stifled, stunted and claustrophobic in a world of debutante balls, society dinners and socially appropriate partnerships (S1:E9). Lorelai thus lives in what she refers to as a more 'colourful' house and indeed a more colourful world, filled with a level of laughter, friendship and fun which she considered lacking in her parents home (S1:E9).

When Emily suggests that Rory borrow Lorelai's golf clubs, she tells her that 'they are upstairs gathering dust, along with the rest of her potential' (S1:E3). Yet although this may seem cold, cruel and devoid of maternal care, the comment merely goes to remind us of the stark differences between the life that Emily wanted for her daughter and the life that her daughter currently leads. Therefore, it tells us less about Emily's hostility towards her daughter and more about her own maternal style. Emily does not approve of her daughter's colourful and bohemian lifestyle, her boyfriends, her clothes, her choice of home furnishings or her domestic routine, making her disapproval heard in each and every episode, and it is the ways in which Lorelai argues against and internalises these comments that creates the distance between the pair. Emily uses Lorelai's financial situation to demand Friday night dinners with her daughter and granddaughter, and although some might read this as another cold and calculated way to control access to her family, one might also acknowledge that it is a sadly desperate act from a mother who, although she doesn't understand her daughter, is desperate to try and rebuild a relationship with her and her teenage granddaughter. Emily is terrified when her mother-in-law, the original Lorelai Gilmore (Marion Ross), considers giving Rory her trust fund because it means that Rory will not need her. But again, one should not necessarily read this as a negative commentary on mother–daughter relationships, but as evidence of a mother, daughter and granddaughter struggling to relate and communicate effectively.

Indeed, Emily's deep love and genuine commitment to her daughter cannot go unnoticed in this series. On a small note, Emily makes pudding for Lorelai and Rory even though she does not care for it herself (S1:E6). Moreover, when Lorelai needed a loan for Rory's school and university fees, Emily obliged (S1:E1); when she needed a bank loan, she offered to act as guarantor (S2:11); when Christopher upsets Lorelai he is told to leave their home (S3:E2); and when Christopher's parents insult her daughter, they too are asked to leave (S1:E15). Moreover, when Lorelai is suffering with back pain, her mother insists on spending the night, bringing her food, stroking her hair, putting a blanket over her when she is tired and sleeping in the corner of the room just to watch over her daughter (S1:E19). And this last maternal act speaks of 'good' motherhood because Lorelai performs the same routine when her own daughter is injured in a later series (S2:E19).

Lorelai does not invite her mother to her college graduation ceremony because she understands that it will cause her pain, and when Rory pushes the point Lorelai tells her that

> I was supposed to graduate from high school, [...] marry a Yale man [...] Instead, I didn't finish high school, I didn't marry your father [...] I humiliated them – the two proudest people in the world and I humiliated them, I spoiled their plans, I took their fine upbringing and a world of comfort and opportunity and I threw it in their faces. I broke their hearts, they'll never forgive me [...] I don't want them to go, it will just hurt them and me. (S2:E21)

However, Rory does invite them, they do attend and both Lorelai and Emily are seen shedding a happy, proud tear (S2:E21). As if Emily's unwavering devotion to her daughter was not clear enough, we actually hear her ask Lorelai why they are not closer, and what they can do to become so, comparing their relationship to that of Lorelai and Rory. Lorelai tries to explain that the age difference between her and Rory and their relaxed home environment goes some way towards explaining their closeness, which leaves Emily hurt and frustrated because she feels that her decision to become a respectable wife and responsible mother means that 'I can't have a relationship with my daughter' (S2:E16). Lorelai goes on to explain that she and Rory are 'best friends first and mother and daughter second', whereas she feels that she and Emily are only ever, and can only ever be, mother and daughter in the more traditional and authoritative sense of that relationship. We can feel Emily's anguish when she tells Lorelai that 'I wasn't taught to be best friends with my daughter – I was taught to be a role model for my daughter, I did what I thought was right, I did what I thought I had to do to protect you, and because of this we have no relationship' (S2:E16). In short, Emily was the perfect role model of a 'good' wife and mother in accordance with her class and generation, which, we are asked to believe, has led to a lack of communication and a loss of a shared bond between mother and daughter. That said, this open exchange went a small, but significant, way to rebuild communications between the pair.

Emily genuinely wants to get to know Rory beyond the formality of Friday evening dinners, going as far as asking Lorelai to help her pick a special birthday present for her granddaughter, because although she loves her dearly she doesn't know her tastes and preferences (S1:E6). When Emily refers to Lorelai and Rory being in their own 'secret club' we can sense her pain at not being included or invited to join this Gilmore clique (S1:E6). And although a growing mutual affection develops throughout the series between Rory and Emily, the relationship between grandmother and granddaughter does on occasion mirror the relationship between Emily and Lorelai. After Emily throws Rory an extravagant birthday party, inviting people from her school that she does not know or like, but that are well connected, Rory makes her annoyance clear. However, although Emily should not have put on such a lavish display or should have thought to ask Rory for her advice on the guest list, there was genuine thought and consideration behind the celebration. Emily tells Lorelai that 'I spent a fortune on this party, I spent days planning it, making sure every little detail was perfect – the food, the linen, the music, and I did all this for Rory' (S1:E6), and although these things were not wanted, needed or requested in Emily's social circle, they speak of care, consideration and respect. In short, Emily may well be understood as a 'good' mother in the context of her own social class and generation, but Lorelai is presented as the more appropriate mother for the contemporary period, and each character in Stars Hollow pays testament to that fact. That said, even though Lorelai is depicted as the ideal mother figure, she remains a less-than-perfect daughter, which is perhaps why Emily's relationship with Rory becomes so important to Lorelai.

Rather than read Emily's actions here and throughout the narrative as a sign of her genuine affection for her granddaughter, Lorelai views it as Emily trying to relive and perhaps rework her failing relationship with herself, telling her mother that 'you finally get a shot of the daughter you've always wanted. Now you get your do-over – a new and improved Lorelai' (S6:E1). Indeed, many of the arguments between Emily and Rory are over how one or other of these women has treated the young Gilmore. Stacia Fleegal suggests that there exists a 'cyclic quality to the mothering' that takes place between these different generations of Gilmore women. Lorelai rejects Emily's parenting style and takes on a far more relaxed maternal role than her own mother, and this more relaxed approach allows Rory to find her own identity, which happens to be in keeping with the respectful, polite and bookish identity that Emily initially hoped for Lorelai (Fleegal 2008, 155). Emily clearly tries to indoctrinate Rory into her social world by encouraging her to marry into a respectable family, join the Daughters of the American Revolution (DAR) club, be seen at debutante balls and develop a more sophisticated palate; and yet I see this less as a woman trying to validate her own life or reimagine her own maternal and material role, and more as a grandmother trying to offer the young woman the best possible future, as it is understood within her social class. The differences between generations are most stark in those scenes between Emily and her own mother-in-law, the original Lorelai 'Trix' Gilmore (Marion Ross), because in these sequences we see the relationship between Emily and her own daughter in light relief. The original Lorelai appears as a genuinely cruel and cold matriarch, leaving Emily looking and feeling like a rebellious child in her own marital home. Indeed, we often see Emily relying on her daughter for emotional comfort during these sequences, which reveals a vulnerability about the character, which her class, wealth and pride tends to mask (S1:E18).

Conclusion

Lorelai is presented as a successful and seductive figure of single motherhood who 'never pushes vegetables on her child and is more interested in talking about the music of Sonic Youth or watching *Godfather* movie marathons than helping Rory with her science homework' (Haupt 2008, 121). As such, this popular maternal figure can be seen to challenge earlier versions of the unrealistic 'good' mother. Indeed, the series even takes it upon itself to openly mock the happy housewife as she is presented in *The Donna Reed Show* (1965–66). Lorelai watches the television re-run, whilst commenting that Donna was 'the quintessential 50s mum, with the perfect 50s family, never without a smile and high heels' and when another character suggests that Donna 'looks happy' Lorelai takes it upon herself to insist that the character looks 'medicated' (S1:E14). However, as audiences embrace this image of popular motherhood, it is worth considering the ways in which this youthful maternal role might simply be helping to recreate the 'good' mother myth, with teen pregnancy being 'rewritten as not merely choice but desirable outcome' in this instance (Silbergleid 2009, 105). The 'good' mother myth is shifting and changeable, depending on the social, sexual, financial and political period in question; yet irrespective of its social or sexual dimension, it remains an improbable and unattainable image of maternal care for each generation of mothers.

Chapter 6

REALITY PARENTING PROGRAMMING: FRAGILE, FAILING AND INEFFECTUAL MOTHERS

Introduction

Our television landscape is currently littered with documentaries, docu-dramas and reality programming that seek to expose a range of salacious and scandalous images of motherhood. Programmes such as *Half Ton Mum* (2007), *Octomom: Me and My 14 Kids* (2009) and *Too Old to be a Mum* (2010) present an ostensibly real look at some of the more shocking representations of motherhood that exist in the contemporary cultural climate. Moreover, even those programmes that seek to correct well-meaning but ultimately 'poor' parenting tend to focus on the image of the incapable, ill-equipped and incompetent mother. Contemporary parenting programmes find a myriad of ways in which to deride and dismiss motherhood and motherwork. The fact that the BBC refers in their television schedules to such programmes under the classification of 'parenting', while Channel 4 uses the term 'family and parenting' is in itself misleading because although it 'is mothers who continue to perform the bulk of child care, take responsibility for children's emotional development and are more likely to be called upon as principle executors of welfare and justice orders' the term 'parenting' suggests that childrearing is unmarked by gender (Jensen 2010, 177). From this perspective, this chapter will introduce a number of parenting documentaries before considering the representation of motherhood in the popular and long-running *Supernanny* (2004–), focusing on the ways in which women continue to be viewed as the primary care-giver and scrutinised in line with the ideology of intensive mothering.

History of the Genre

Television documentaries put real people on television and allow the audience to watch their stories unfold (Cummings et al., 2002, xi). And although there are debates concerning the role and relevance of staged sequences and re-enactments in the genre, there seems to be a consensus that documentary programming is a 'creative treatment of actuality' (Grierson cited in Kerrigan and McIntyre 2010, 111–30). If one considers that parenting documentaries depict direct and unmediated accounts of motherwork and the maternal role, then the genre can be said to offer some of the most realistic depictions of motherwork in the current cultural climate. Likewise, reality television can be seen to borrow from the documentary tradition in its use of ordinary people rather than actors, its focus on real experiences rather than scripted narratives, and its use of a neutral camera that records events rather than a more calculated shooting script. Indeed, even though the formal characteristics of such programming might vary in scope and emphasis, they tend to feature non-actors, present real lives, focus on personalisation and emotional engagement, draw on a 'window on the world' documentary-style of observation, include voice-over commentaries and exploit a soap-opera narrative structure (Casey et al., 2002, 196–7; Dovey 2002, 135). Jon Dovey makes the point that although there are clear differences in terms of subject matter and thus audience address in the reality genre, these programmes 'are unified by the attempt to package particular aspects of everyday life as entertainment' (Dovey 2002, 135).

The documentary series *An American Family* (1973) is understood as the first programme to present a candid rather than orchestrated depiction of family life. The programme was 'considered controversial due to its frank representation of [...] domestic life and for what it revealed about the less than ideal dynamics that underpinned the "typical" suburban family' (Matheson 2007, 33). Although such unscripted family exploits proved shocking, they also proved commercially successful and since that time 'reality television has [...] taken centre stage as the genre providing popular images of American family life' in the contemporary period (ibid., 33). Although those reality parenting television shows that reveal 'how families cope with children with behavioural problems have been around for decades [...] parenting programmes featuring an all-knowing expert are a relatively new' and indeed, growing phenomenon (Midgley 2007). This particular strand of expert-led makeover parenting programming has developed and flourished since the mid 2000s, with *Cutting Edge: Bad Behaviour* (2003) inaugurating such parenting productions. Indeed, the reality parenting shows, or what has elsewhere been referred to as 'parental advice' television (Midgley 2007), have their roots in self-improvement and makeover reality programming, whereby members of the public are transformed either in terms of their fitness levels (*The Biggest Loser UK*, 2005–), physical appearance (*Extreme Makeover UK*, 2004–), style and grooming (*How to Look Good Naked*, 2006–), surface appearance and marital harmony (*Trinny & Susannah Undress*, 2006–2007), relationship communications (*Tool Academy*, 2009–) and social etiquette (*Charm School*, 2007–2009). Irrespective of the transformation in question, these programmes follow a predictable format. The shows begin by introducing us to members of the public who are struggling with their weight, social skills or parenting abilities; these ordinary people are introduced to experts from the relevant field who give instruction and offer encouragement in relation to their chosen transformation; we then watch the participants fail, relapse and speak of their desperation before witnessing the successful makeover and an acknowledgement of the skills of the expert in question.

Although documentary and reality programming might foreground notions of authenticity, realism and transparency, such shows have been referred to as 'formatted documentary' due to the ways in which 'the action is substantially shaped through producers' suggestions and clever editing' (Gibson cited in Brancato 2007, 50). Indeed, one might suggest that the representation of mothers, motherhood and motherwork in parenting documentaries and reality parenting television goes some way to remind us of the careful use of editing and the clear sense of an agenda-setting function in the genres in question. In documentaries such as *Octomom*, *My Monkey Baby* (2009) and *8 Boys and Wanting a Girl* (2010), mothers are seen to move between ineffectual and pathological depictions, and likewise in reality parenting programmes such as *Supernanny*, *Nanny 911* (2004–) and *Extreme Parental Guidance* (2010–), these same women are seen to fail in what are assumed to be the most basic of parenting roles and responsibilities. Parenting television appears to offer some of the most conservative distinctions between the appropriate and ineffectual mother, and asks mothers, daughters and grandmothers in the audience to judge these women and find their maternal practices wanting. The genre routinely reveres the institution of motherhood while openly deriding real maternal practices, and as such these programmes can be said to reaffirm and revalidate the ideology of intensive mothering and the 'good' mother myth.

Zoe Williams tells us that 'BBC1's *Being Mum* season is the most laughably manipulative tug on maternal anxiety you've ever heard: who's way too old to be a mother (her! her over there! Look at her wrinkles!); who's done a really, really bad job (her! Her kids won't even talk!); the crowning anxiety, a whole programme about mothers whose children hate them [...] Just imagine the cynicism at the planning stage. I bet it stripped the paint off the walls' (Williams 2010). And although this 'tug on maternal anxiety' is nothing new, the focus of it has shifted over several generations from physical to psychological concerns. During the eighteenth and nineteenth centuries, philanthropic parenting advice focused on the prevention of infant mortality through better hygiene and nutrition, and although these 'interventions were marked by class prejudice' (Jensen 2010, 170) many of the 'humanitarian campaigns that emerged out of the work of the early parenting advice programmes did focus on social justice and the improvement of the living conditions of the poor' (ibid., 170–71). However, even though child and infant survival rates improved dramatically, the desire to watch, judge and rank motherwork remained. Rather than philanthropists offering advice concerning infant safety and physical care, childcare experts in the late nineteenth century became concerned with the *quality* of infant and childcare. The quality of childrearing was less to do with physical fitness or health regimes and more to do with emotionality, intelligence and personability, so that socially approved, and thus class-appropriate, parenting practices would 'guarantee not only a healthy, disease-free and nourished child, but a child who was in addition, variously and according to the context, mindful, respectful, resilient, autonomous and civically minded, with an inquiring mind and an enterprising spirit' (Hulbert cited in Jensen 2010, 171). Although we can understand the importance of childrearing interventions regarding health, safety and 'matters of diet, warmth, immediate environment, and physical development' (Smart 1996, 46), we should perhaps question the necessity of those parenting instructions that focus on the psychological nurturance of children, as they demand that mothers 'be continually attuned to the psychological, emotional or cognitive needs of her children' (O'Reilly 2004b, 7). Moreover, it is worth considering the lived reality of contemporary mothers who have little first-hand experience of mothering when compared to previous generations, due in part to the fact that women have fewer children and families live in more geographically dispersed areas. With this in mind, contemporary mothers 'do not possess the experiential knowledge to enable them to confidently make individual decisions' about mothering rules, routines and practices (Miller 2005, 140). And as such 'they increasingly look to expert bodies of knowledge and expert practices to guide them through this period of uncertainty' (ibid., 140).

Maternal Myths and the Monstrous Reality of Motherhood

Misbehaving Mums to Be (2011) focuses on a number of mothers whose pregnancy practices do not adhere to the 'good' mother myth, and we witness their emotional and physical shame and humiliation as they are shown the ways in which their smoking, eating and drinking habits are having a negative impact on their unborn child before a medical professional is asked to 'get these out-of-control mums in shape for the most important event of their lives' (S1:E1). *Fast Food Baby* (2011) is committed to showing the ways in which 'bad' mothers are failing to provide the correct nutritional food for their children, and witnessing their efforts to shift their inappropriate eating habits and practices; while *Half Ton Mum* documents the life and death of Renee Williams, the super morbidly obese mother who was 'unable to look after her two daughters' or even hug them due to her physical size.

The World's Oldest Mums (2009) focuses on a number of women who have chosen to use fertility technologies in order to have babies long after the menopause, *Help Me Love My Baby* (2007) focuses on the traumatic journey of a maternal mother who has only bonded with one of her twin girls, while *Cotton Wool Kids* (2008) allows us to condemn one particularly anxious mother for wanting to have a chip implanted in her daughter for the purposes of safety, security and surveillance. And although paternal fathers are seen in such shows, it is clear that it is the mothers who are most starkly under scrutiny here. *Four Sons versus Four Daughters* (2010) manages to not only question the gendered mothering that takes place in two family homes, but also to condemn what are set up as hypothetical maternal practices. When a mother of four boys cares for four girls and tells us that the obsession with ballet, shopping and appearances was 'tedious' compared to more active play with guns, water and go-karts, we are left feeling that we should somehow judge this woman in what is essentially a staged and artificial maternal environment.

8 Boys and Wanting a Girl examines the psychological condition of 'gender disappointment', in which a mother who has a number of sons is desperate to have a daughter, and it leaves us to question the appropriateness of those women who are unhappy with or unfulfilled by their existing children. One pregnant mother of four young boys tells us that 'I only ever wanted one child, one little girl'; she goes on to inform us that she has tried to sway the sex of her unborn child and that she has even considered adoption in order to have the daughter that she so desperately craves. We witness this woman weep with what might be considered a tactless frustration, anger and sorrow when she learns that her fifth child is another healthy boy, concluding that she will 'always be a little bit sad' about never having a baby girl in her family. Likewise, when we meet a mother of eight boys who 'has been trying to have a baby girl for over twenty years' we are asked to question her commitment to her existing children. We discover the true extent of 'gender disappointment' when a middle-aged and upper-middle-class mother of four healthy boys tells us that 'the feelings that I felt when after having my fourth [male] child [...] I would liken it to somebody who can't have a child [...] This is a deep-seated hurt and need that was never going to be fulfilled'. Rather than find a way to reconsider her relationship with her sons, this mother went to Spain where it is legal to choose the sex of a child. We discover that the mother in question went on to have twin girls after her second round of pre-implantation genetic diagnostics, and see how the news of twin girls left her feeling ecstatic. However, the mother's ecstasy leads to audience discomfort here.

Octomom: Me and My 14 Kids details the daily motherwork of Nadya Suleman, the woman who gave birth to the world's only surviving octuplets. The programme documents the shifting fame and fortunes of this unemployed single mother with 14 children under the age of nine, who has been dismissed as the 'most hated mother in the world'. Suleman already had six children who were conceived artificially through IVF when she became pregnant with the octuplets, and we discover that the doctor who implanted the embryos in this instance has been expelled from the American Society for Reproductive Medicine for ignoring the legal rulings regarding embryo insemination. However, the programme spends little time considering the broader legal, ethical or medical concerns regarding artificial insemination in order to deride and discount the mother figure here. When Suleman tells us that each *pair* of children 'gets ten minutes quality time with mom' the audience is being asked to condemn the woman for her selfishness in desiring such a large family. And even though the mother in question could not have known that she would have octuplets, the programme reminds us time and again that she already had six children before embarking on the later round of IVF. Suleman goes on to admit that she struggles to bond with all of her children, and had little maternal instinct after the birth of the octuplets. She tells us that

> the mothers that bond within the first day of their newborn being with them I admire, because it takes me a while to bond with kids, especially if there is so many. I found myself bonding more with three or four than with the others – it's so hard; I mean how can you possibly bond equally with that many?

Although there is the potential for a feminist discussion about natural maternal instincts and the sacrificial mother role, *Octomom: Me and my 14 Kids* encourages a far more patriarchal reading as it questions the appropriateness of an unemployed single mother who uses artificial insemination to produce her children and media contracts to provide for them.

Documentary representations of motherhood are at best conservative and at worst critical of real mothers and the lived maternal role. However, even when we are being asked to watch surrogate mothers the preferred reading remains problematic. In *Addicted to Surrogacy* (2009) we see a number of women who have carried babies for other families, and each one, without exception, is seen to be suffering physically and psychologically as a result. Indeed, these surrogates speak of 'a void' that being a surrogate temporarily fills and of the ways in which carrying a baby for another woman acts as 'a crutch' for a range of deeper emotional anxieties. These women are seen to bring happiness and fulfilment into the lives of other women, but the programme makes it clear that this joy is met by their own familial and financial disappointments.

For those women who are unable to have children, or who are not in contact with them, a recent documentary points to the ways in which these women might find familial harmony and maternal fulfilment. *My Monkey Baby* tells the story of a number of women who are raising a monkey as a member of their family. We are introduced to a childless young woman who is dating a man who refuses to have a family, and although the partner assures us that his girlfriend 'runs away' from children and thus is without maternal instinct, the woman in question admits to a desire for her own biological offspring. When we watch this woman hide her new monkey baby in her jacket, stroking her stomach as the primate sleeps, it leaves the audience with a sense of discomfort. Likewise, when we are introduced to a more mature childless woman who had a hysterectomy at the age of 32 we are asked to question the appropriateness of monkey baby motherhood. Although this woman tells us that she is happy looking after a menagerie of monkey babies, we are left with a feeling of unease when the woman in question talks of her fulfilment as a stepmother from an earlier marriage. We are told that 'becoming an instant mother was [...] wonderful – I got to be a mother, it was a very special time [...] My whole life, I wanted to be the nurturer, the fixer – I really loved being a mom, I really did'. This woman no longer has contact with these children, and has since devoted her time and energy to her many monkey babies. However, the most disturbing and disquieting example of monkey baby motherhood appears in the shape of an older maternal mother of six, who has looked to primates to fill the void that opened up when her own children left home and severed communication with their mother. When this woman tells us 'if you want a child for the rest of your life, if you want something to dote on for the rest of your life, then a monkey is for you'. When asked about her real children she tells us that 'If I could have kept them small I'd have kept them small forever, if I could have given them a little pill, you know I'd have kept them babies forever', and as such, we should perhaps not be surprised to learn of her desire for a monkey baby as a creature that would remain a dependent for its entire life span. When asked about her monkey baby we are told that 'I got my baby girl, [...] she was going to be my child, [...] a baby I was going to have forever [...] She wasn't going to graduate, she wasn't going to college, she wasn't going to get married, she wasn't going to leave me [...] She would be with me until I die'. These monkey mothers are at different times deluded, desperate and depressed, and yet rather than take a serious look at the emotions, anxieties and mental health of these women, the documentary merely invites us to scrutinise, judge and condemn them for their inappropriate maternal desires.

My Fake Baby (2008) introduces us to doll designers who make lifelike 'reborn' dolls with beating hearts, tiny veins, milk spots and other lifelike markings for a number of women who are unable to have children, who have seen their children leave home or otherwise feel that they have a desire to mother. But again, rather than look to the fragile mental health of the women in question, or the ways in which these dolls might be used as part of an infertility counselling programme where women can talk about their desire to mother whilst learning to develop strategies to cope with their childless state, the programme merely asks us to question the appropriateness of both the women who engineer these incredibly realistic creations and those women who mother them.

Mums Who Leave Their Kids (2006) is a documentary that ostensibly gives a voice to those women who have consciously and deliberately chosen to leave their children and the family home in favour of living a more independent and single lifestyle. We are introduced to Lesley Darcey, a mother who left her 6 and 7-year-old children to pursue a career in writing. Lesley explains that she was not happy in the family home, that she was not fulfilled by the demanding role of motherhood and that she was desperate to change what she felt was an exhausting, draining and suffocating reality. And although this mother admits that her young children were 'devastated' when she left, she makes it clear that she had 'a responsibility to' herself to pursue her passion for writing, and suggests that she is now a much better woman and mother for making that decision. Lesley sees her children regularly, on her own terms, rather than adhering to the notion that the mother should be the sole provider of childcare who puts her children's needs before her own, and as such, the programme is in a position to broaden the societal definitions of appropriate motherhood. Lesley might be understood as an outlier 'who refused to parrot the line that being a mother was an endlessly renewing, transcendent, ever-joyful experience that trumpeted everything else all the time' (Douglas and Michaels 2005, 220). However, rather than show any respect for Lesley's decision and demonstrate that there are alternative ways to mother and a number of ways in which to mother successfully, the programme makes no such claims to objectivity or impartiality. Rather, it makes it clear that mothers who leave their children are, without exception, selfish, shameful and open to condemnation. The voices of the mothers who leave their children are overlooked, their reasonings challenged and their life choices mocked.

Jane Moore, the tabloid journalist who fronts the programme, interviews mothers and professionals alike, presents a rather one-dimensional and unflattering view of the mothers who leave their children. Moore makes the point that although large numbers of fathers leave their young children, she sees those women who leave as 'more selfish' than their paternal counterparts.

And if audiences were in any doubt about Moore's views on the subject of mothers who leave their kids, she makes her own view clear when she tells us that 'they say their decision to leave was selfless, I still say it's selfish [...] No matter how tough my life was, the last thing I'd ever give up would be my children'. Moore goes further to present herself in opposition to these 'bad' mothers and in line with the 'good' mother as she reminds us again that 'I can't think of any extenuating circumstances that would make me walk out on my kids'. Extenuating circumstances indeed. Moore is a commercially successful journalist, novelist and television presenter with a beautiful, spacious, luxurious home in Richmond befitting a *Homes and Gardens* front cover, her husband is the former vice-president of communications at Sony Music Entertainment and owner of the PR agency, The Corporation Group. My point here is simply that Moore is financially secure, in a stable marriage, with a glamorous abode, and thus in a position to pay for domestic staff and childcare assistance, a position of privilege clearly not on offer to those women presented in the programme.

A number of academics and psychotherapists who were interviewed in the show tell us that postnatal depression may be one reason why many mothers are leaving their young children, making the point that mothers with young babies are vulnerable, in need of support and in many cases are suffering from low self-esteem. Indeed, there was much 'evidence to suggest that the women in the programme left their children due to mental health issues [and] extreme stress' (Jones 2006). Indeed 'given the cultural pressures on women to be mothers, and the attendant pressures of bringing up beautiful, talented and successful offspring, it's no shock that some women are less able to cope than others' (ibid.). However, rather than acknowledge the reality of this situation, Moore tells us that 'genuine post-natal depression can be a major factor for mothers leaving their children [...] But I also think many use it as an excuse to mask the real story – they dip their toe [*sic*] into full-time motherhood and found the water too hot'. Annie Pávlovic, Rosemary Aris and Audrey Mullender make the point that those women who leave their family home 'become, by definition, "unnatural" and, by implication, "immoral" women who somehow stand a "world apart" from "real" mothers' (Pávlovic et al., cited in O'Reilly and Porter 2005, 18). And yet, we must remember that as Andrea O'Reilly and Marie Porter tell us, these 'mothers are not judged against "real mothers", but against an ideal that is impossible for any mother to maintain' (O'Reilly and Porter 2005, 18).

The number of mothers who leave their children is 'increasing every year' and as such, one might presume that a documentary such as this would provide an opportunity for an impartial debate concerning those social, sexual, financial or other reasons why mothers do and do not leave their children, and the implications for the family unit (Arditti et al., cited in Büskens 2005, 265). However, Moore tells us that 'we've got the wombs, the hormones and the biological tie' and as such she is presenting an essentialist view of motherhood that does not allow for the possibility that some women are not satisfied with, fulfilled by or invested in the maternal role. Tanya Jones makes the point that a potentially fascinating and significant programme 'was marred by Jane's eagerness to parade herself as the perfect mother. We were subjected to her constant assurances that she would never leave her children, and that she couldn't understand why any woman would' (Jones 2006). In short, contemporary parenting documentaries tend to overlook the psychological disposition of those women who are either unable to have children, in relationships with men who are unwilling to have children, living away from the family home or who are in a situation where they are no longer in contact with their children, in favour of the more scandalous, salacious and shocking depictions of motherwork and the maternal role.

Class, Gender and Parenting Programming

It has been suggested that we are living in a culture saturated by representations of contented mothers and that those children who are depicted in the media are quiet, calming and 'trouble-free' individuals (Douglas 1995, 281). It is as if those 'good' mothers who adhere to the ideology of intensive mothering are being rewarded for their socially and sexually acceptable maternal practices by producing well-mannered, respectful, confident and productive children; children who are well liked by their peers and parents alike; children who will be productive citizens as they reach adolescence (Chase and Rogers 2001, 30). Sara Ruddick tells us that mothers hold themselves and others hold them up to be responsible for the social development of children. She makes the point that a mother 'must shape natural growth in such a way that her child becomes the sort of adult that she can appreciate and others can accept' (Ruddick 1980, 349). She goes on to say that even though mothers 'will vary enormously, individually and socially, in the traits and lives they will appreciate in their children [...] a mother typically takes as the criterion of her success the production of a young adult acceptable to her group' (ibid., 349).

For those mothers who do not conform to the 'good' mother myth, we are asked to bear witness to their shame and distress. Indeed, the makeover reality parenting genre delights in humiliating mothers. These women are scrutinised as they scream and swear at their children, smack them, ignore them and resort to sarcasm at their expense. The genre routinely depicts these women 'holding their heads in their hands – a visual sign of shame' after their children have been filmed in a number of dangerous, discourteous and disorderly situations (Ferguson 2010, 93). Galit Ferguson tells us that the voyeuristic camera spends far longer registering the upset, anxiety and humiliation of the mother compared to the father of the piece, with the suggestion that these women should be embarrassed by their parenting practices, reprimanded for their motherwork efforts and ridiculed for their attention-seeking and ultimately selfish excessive emotional outbursts (ibid., 98). The genre appears to encourage raw and painful displays of emotion, and it is soon clear that such displays are used less as a humbling and 'poignant moment of self-revelation' and more as a demeaning 'money shot' for the woman in the audience (Skeggs, Thumim and Wood 2008b, 139). What is surprising, then, is the fact that while this genre has 'received much criticism in terms of voyeurism, humiliation, and the oft-cited "dumbing down" debate […] little of this condemnation has addressed the crucial issues relating to the representation of women' (Fairclough 2004, 344).

While parenting documentaries tend to depict biological and other mothers as problematic and pathological, their reality television cousins routinely depict mothers struggling with the maternal role. Reality parenting programmes 'each purport to expose the backstage view of family life by allowing cameras access to average family interactions that are apparently spontaneous and unscripted', and in so doing, they shame and humiliate existing mothers before reinstating unattainable standards of maternal practice and motherwork (Brancato 2007, 50). Reality parenting programmes such as *Wife Swap* (2003–) are in a position to explore, examine and unmask gender roles in society due to the fact that they focus on the women's relationship with the domestic sphere. However, although there is the potential for informed commentary about the maternal role and mothering responsibilities, the programme tends to offer patriarchal conclusions concerning women's appropriate domestic duties and innate maternal instincts. Indeed, the very premise of the show seems to rely on measuring the success of women in the domestic sphere. Kirsty Fairclough makes the point that *Wife Swap* 'achieves nothing except to further emphasise the fact that women should be natural homemakers by virtue of their gender' (Fairclough 2004, 345). In this same way, Beverley Skeggs, Nancy Thumim and Helen Wood remind us that the 'home is not just a "natural" site of comfort, but one created through [the] sustained domestic and emotional labour of women' (Skeggs, Thumim and Wood 2008b, 140).

Mothers are assumed to have sole responsibility for childrearing, and any problems that they experience in the domestic sphere are positioned as individual failings rather than in the context of any wider social, sexual or political considerations. Ann Hall and Mardia Bishop state that the 'good' mother myth 'works to propagate a conservative agenda, pushing the responsibility for child care solely on the mother, making child rearing a personal issue instead of a social one' (Hall and Bishop 2009, xii). With this in mind, the programme can be seen to conform to the patriarchal 'good' mother myth that demands a mother be 'ever present in her children's lives when they are young, and when they get older she is home everyday to greet them as they return from school. If she works outside the home, she arranges her job around her children so she can be there for them as much as possible, certainly whenever they are sick or unhappy' (Chase and Rodgers 2001, 30). Indeed, it goes as far as to set up an opposition between stay-at-home mothers and working mothers, privileging the women's role as caregiver in the domestic sphere over her participation in the public realm. Any jobs, careers or other non-domestic labours are clearly and deliberately established as a troublesome 'interference' to their domestic lives (Fairclough 2004, 345).

Wife Swap seems to expect and demand an essentialist notion of motherhood and maternal care which dictates that 'women are *naturally* mothers, they are born with a built-in set of capacities, dispositions, and desires to nurture children' which are at odds with the working demands of the public sphere (Hall 1998, 59; italics in original). It is worth noting that in recent studies where adult females were asked to comment on a videotaped parent–child interaction, they were more negative about the interaction when the woman in the extract was described beforehand as a working rather than as a stay-at-home mother. In short, women 'who work outside the home are perceived as less nurturing and less competent in the role of mother compared to their counterparts who choose to stay home to raise their children' (Mottarella 2009, 224). The sequence shown was the same – the only change was the working description, but even the idea of a working mother created a negative reaction from respondents to the study. The suggestion here is that society continues to dictate the standards of 'good' mothering, dependent in the first instance on a woman's position within and beyond the domestic space. Even though evidence suggests that 'satisfaction with one's parental role is strongly linked to positive parental and child interactions' the 'good' mother myth continues to influence social readings of the working mother, so much so in fact that 'the happily employed mother [is] perceived in a negative light' (ibid., 224). The 'good' mother myth dictates that maternal care 'cannot be compressed into a manageable block of time' and as such 'no working mother's care can be fully adequate' (Tronto 2002, 44). And although no mother can ever be present for all of the 'essential care' moments that the ideology of intensive mothering demands, the fact that the stay-at-home mother is at least ostensibly available sets them apart from their working counterparts (ibid., 45).

Reality parenting television suggests that mothers are 'able to choose freely and cleanly how they will inhabit their space, speak to their families, the kinds of food they consume, and the sorts of practices and habits they perform'

(Jensen 2010, 189). What it ignores, overlooks and denies of course is 'the economic, material and geographical realities which shape and limit choices unevenly' and thus impact on maternal care and domestic duties (ibid., 189). In short, those women who are struggling financially, living in claustrophobic conditions and unable to find time to not only clothe and feed their children, but also to educate them inventively, entertain them and inspire them creatively are held up as 'poor' mothers.

Reality parenting television focuses on working-class families, so that incompetent, incapable and inarticulate motherwork, maternal care and domestic duties tend to be laid at the door of the economically, socially and educationally underprivileged. Tracey Jensen makes the point that culturally deficient working-class parents and in particular culturally inappropriate working-class mothers are over-represented in such programming (ibid., 189). Galit Ferguson goes on to tell us that these working-class mothers are, as in the codes and conventions of the makeover, asked to acknowledge, appreciate and adhere to a more restrained, rational and thus middle-class mode of parenting (Ferguson 2010, 95). Indeed, the 'healthy or "good enough", relationship between mother and child is represented as somehow lacking internality: any passion, tears, and affect between parent and child occurs before the techniques have been learned' (ibid., 95). While working-class mothers are deemed pathological and psychologically unhealthy, middle-class parenting practices, maternal dispositions and domestic proclivities are marked as appropriate, desirable and indeed normal (Jensen 2010, 189). Fiona Green makes this point when she says that 'mothers are the central characters, and through the structure, presentation, and narration of their stories, viewers are encouraged to evaluate and judge how they fulfil their roles. These programs constitute specific ways that mothers are to behave and be scrutinized' which exploits maternal, working, consuming and classed anxieties (Green 2007).

It has been suggested that the less-than-subtle class subtext that flows throughout reality parenting television stems less from the parental styles on display, and more from the post-production and voice-over narration. Zoe Williams makes the point that 'there's a sense in the edit [...] that the wealthier you are, the more agency you have, as a parent, the more your decisions ought to be respected as the result of considered thought' (Williams 2010). Williams goes on to suggest that a 'poor family is never idiosyncratic, it's always just doing it wrong. A rich family has to be doing things incredibly, grotesquely wrong, to garner the same judgment' (ibid.). In short, the genre positions middle-class stay-at-home motherhood as the preferred, correct and only acceptable version of maternal care, duty and attention. However, although one might look to reality parenting television in general, and the long-running and popular *Supernanny* in particular, as an example of patriarchal, misogynistic or class-based programming, some have suggested that these shows are entirely useful, necessary and significant in their depiction of appropriate and inappropriate parenting techniques. With this in mind, we will now look at the ways in which the experienced nanny Jo Frost presents motherhood, motherwork and the mother myth in *Supernanny* and *Extreme Parental Guidance*.

Supernanny

Jo Frost is a professional nanny with over 20 years experience in the field of infant and childcare in Britain and America. *Supernanny* sees Frost help a number of single, step and nuclear families with their unruly and disrespectful children by asking them to follow her clear, controlled and routinised parenting techniques. Her approach to parenting and childcare focuses on maintaining adult respect and authority while creating a safe and nurturing environment for the children. Her techniques are in no way controversial; indeed most 'of her recommendations are based on recognized authoritative positive parenting behaviours, that is, providing consistency, praise, routine and boundaries' (Ganeshasundaram and Henley 2009, 312).

Supernanny was an instant commercial success in the UK in 2004, and since that time, the programme has been viewed in over 40 countries worldwide and spawned numerous imitators. Frost has penned a number of popular childcare manuals such as *How to Get the Best from Your Children* (2005), *Ask Supernanny: What Every Parent Wants to Know* (2006), and *Jo Frost's Confident Baby Care* (2007). She has also set up a *Supernanny.com* website which 'serves as a portal for parenting advice and as a forum for discussing viewers' own families' (Tally 2008, 6). More recently, Frost has fronted *Extreme Parental Guidance*, which looks at issues that she sees affecting contemporary parents, such as getting children to eat healthily, sleep peacefully and play happily. And although these themes reflect those that were seen in *Supernanny*, her point is that they do not simply affect individual households. In order to understand the success, reach and popularity of this forty-something single, childless woman, it is worth noting that she has, since *Supernanny* first aired, become 'an Oprah-approved, world famous, multimillionaire childcare phenomenon' (Macaulay 2010). *Supernanny* is made up of discrete one-hour episodes, each presenting a heavily edited and univocal account of a struggling family unit, with unruly children, ineffectual parents and humiliated mothers. The programme reached over 13.5 million viewers on both sides of the Atlantic, with both the original British version and *Supernanny USA* being shown on Channel 4 and E4 (Tally 2008, 6). And although the programme attracts a diverse audience including parents, children and grandparents, it 'is clear from the bulk of responses on the various websites and listservs that discuss *Supernanny*, that the primary viewing audience is women with children' (ibid., 22).

Extant research on the show tells us that audiences tend to watch the programme for interest and educational reasons, and that these viewers were not only 'able to recollect unprompted many of the parenting techniques' being demonstrated in the show (Ganeshasundaram and Henley 2009, 316), but also point to a technique that would be helpful to their own family circumstances (Millar 2007, 45). *Supernanny* 'offers a way for viewers to watch a kind of docudrama unfold of their own dilemmas, with the inevitable resolution of families made intact, week after week' (Tally 2008, 19). The programme actively 'encourages viewers to measure themselves against the standards of the participants as well as idealized social norms' (Brancato 2007, 51). Indeed, it excels in both creating viewer identification with the troubled families and problem children on screen, while maintaining enough critical distance between them so as to not alienate audiences from their own parenting practices. After all, 'the behaviours of the children are so exaggerated that most viewers have the ability to distance themselves somewhat from the show, as they watch in fascination and horror as the family implodes in front of their very eyes' (Tally 2008, 1). *Supernanny* presents several examples of damaging and dangerous rather than merely socially inappropriate mothering, whereby children are missing (S2:E8), left and forgotten about in the family car (S3:E4), locked in bedrooms (S5:E4), seen running into main roads (S3:E2), sworn at (S2:E8), smacked (S2:E11), slapped (S5:E1) and force-fed (S2:E11).

Positive and Empowering Parental Programming

Much work on motherhood and the maternal role focuses on the transition to motherhood and examines the experiences of new mothers in that role (Phoenix and Woollett 1994a, 1–2). As such, little examination exists to account for the experiences of mothers with toddlers, adolescents and young adults. As such, the representation of motherhood on *Supernanny* addresses an important and, until recently, overlooked area of maternal care.

Supernanny not only exposes parenting problems, but offers parents in general, and mothers in particular, ways to create a more harmonious family unit, and as such, some commentators have been heard praising the show for its educational possibilities. *Supernanny* is said to serve as an educational device 'for parents, who may indeed be at a loss for how to deal with bad behaviour [and] in this view, Jo Frost becomes a kind of national spokesperson for audiences who need a kind of civic education in parenting' (Tally 2008, 26). Indeed, members of the Conservative party have recently praised Frost's routinised and organised methods in a parliamentary debate on anti-social behaviour (Macaulay 2010). The fact that each programme concludes with a short revisit to the originally struggling family, and that, without exception, these families are calmer, more courteous and the mothers more confident about their maternal practices demands that the audience acknowledge the success of the routinised parenting techniques being presented here. We are informed that 'over the course of one episode, Jo has changed lives and futures of families who were at the end of their rope. For viewers, she has taught them it is possible to improve family situations and behaviours by following her techniques and advice' (*Supernanny* 2010). Skeggs, Thumim and Wood remind us that reality parenting programmes such as *Supernanny* might well be 'highly edited and preplanned' in order to stage a particular version of reality, but the very 'repetition of the domestic and the everyday helps to obscure, or at least marginalize, some of these televisual devices' (Skeggs, Thumim and Wood 2008b, 139). Indeed, 80 per cent of those audiences surveyed agreed 'that the context as well as the improvements in the children's behaviour in the program [were] realistic' (Ganeshasundaram and Henley 2009, 314). In short, *Supernanny* is a commercial success; it has proved popular with politicians, policy-makers and parents alike.

The reality parenting genre is operating 'as an extension of women's emotional and domestic labour in which they have traditionally been constituted as moral guardians of the nation' (Skeggs, Thumim and Wood 2008b, 143), and these programmes might be said to pay women and mothers due respect for this role in the private sphere. However, the fact that 'these narratives provide helpful tips for parenting while systematically employing elements of regulation and surveillance to judge the abilities of parents, and in particular, mothers' must be of concern here (Green 2007). With this in mind I shall go on to examine the ways in which the programme confirms and conforms to the most patriarchal of mothering practices and in so doing upholds the unattainable and unrealisable myth of the 'good' mother.

Incompetent, Incapable and Ineffectual Mothers

Supernanny routinely emphasises the mother as the primary caregiver in the nuclear family unit, even when the mother in question works outside of the domestic space. Mothers are portrayed as the domestic manager, in charge of meal times, bath routines, bedtime stories, school runs, grocery shopping, household chores and general children's entertainment planning and activities. Even before these women are shamed for their parenting practices and rebuked for their bodily dispositions, they are in many instances challenged over the cleanliness, orderliness and the appropriateness of their homes (S1:E2). In short, mothers are portrayed as the primary parent, and as such, they are also depicted as the root cause of existing behavioural problems. Indeed, several of the infants, toddlers and older children who swear at, kick, punch and spit at their mothers tend to act very differently when their fathers are present in the home. Indeed, it is often clear that the 'men in the families are peripheral to these titanic struggles, as the mothers are ultimately left with the burden of raising the children' (Tally 2008, 21).

The programme suggests that it is the lenient, weak and fragile maternal figure that is the family problem that needs to be re-educated, not the ostensibly 'bad' children. Moreover, the fact that the parenting techniques are 'almost exclusively taught to mothers [...] whether stay-at-home or not' is particularly telling here (Green 2007). Throughout the show's long history, mothers tend to share justifications for their lack of formal, organised, coherent and constant discipline; namely, they are scared that such discipline will mean that their children will no longer love them (S2:E1) and they feel that going without discipline will lead to an easier family life in the present (S2:E1). Frost makes it clear within the ensuing narratives that both fears are unfounded, and indeed, both fears are the major cause of the children's bathtime, bedtime, eating, sharing and wider behavioural problems. When one mother admits that she is reluctant to discipline her son due in part to the intense grief that she still feels concerning the death of his younger brother, Frost registers the mother's grief but goes on to reprimand her for her lack of authority in the home. Telling this distraught mother to 'get it together' seems both inappropriate and insensitive in this regard (Jensen 2010, 187). Frost is heard telling one mother that 'it's you, it's you that hates leaving Matthew – it's you, not Matthew [...] Half of his mummy, mummy is you – you've created that' (S2:E7), while telling another mother that 'what you've got to do is realise that she has been mollycoddled by you and she has been allowed to get away with behaviour that is unacceptable for a three-year-old' (S5:E4). She tells another mother that 'your love has become destructive. It's shameful to watch' (S1:E1), and another that she has 'done it wrong, all wrong' (S5:E4). The programme even includes sequences where children point to the failings and fragility of their own mothers. One 7-year-old tells the camera that 'my mum's useless at looking after us, she needs some help' before pointing out that his stressed and fragile looking mother is 'going to cry in a minute' (S2:E3).

At the outset of the programme we are shown a number of filmed sequences where Frost observes the family dynamic, without comment or interference, and during these opening scenes we bear witness to two important facts. Firstly, we see how little power, control or authority these women have over their own children as they are routinely overlooked, ignored and even laughed at for their erratic and ineffectual attempts to parent; secondly, we hear Frost talk to these fraught, fragile and tearful mothers, telling them that 'they have a right to demand respect from their children' (Tally 2008, 24). However, although no one would question a mother's right to respect from her own family, the programme glosses over the fact that mothers are struggling with unmanageable workloads both within and beyond the domestic sphere. Rather than acknowledge that these women are failing due to a lack of spousal, family, friendship or other support networks, the programme suggests that women should be expected to take on what Angela McRobbie refers to as 'Herculean' responsibilities in both the private and public spheres (McRobbie 2009, 80). Indeed, the 'very premise of all of these programs is that modern home life is unmanageable, particularly for mothers' and yet rather than point to the structural reasons for these stressful conditions, viewers are asked to bask in the warmth of a temporary resolution offered by the portrayal of newly respectful, responsible and psychologically rounded children (Brancato 2007, 51). The strain of childcare and the burden of domestic management 'more often [than] not falls on the mother, who is left to parent with few outside supports and who nevertheless labours under the ideology of the "perfect mother"' (Tally 2008, 28). In this way, *Supernanny* suggests that 'good enough' mothering is not an acceptable level of maternal care, suggesting instead that mothers must not only dedicate their time to looking after the health, nutrition, sleep routines and homework of their children, but to find 'quality' time to play, inspire, educate and otherwise entertain them. *Supernanny* 'assists in regulating all women's mothering and results in pathologizing women who do not practice intensive mothering' (Green 2007). In this way, the programme adheres to a maternal myth whereby the mother 'lovingly anticipates and meets the child's every need. She is substantial and plentiful; she is not destroyed or overwhelmed by the demands of her child. Instead she finds fulfilment and satisfaction in caring for her offspring' (Winnicott cited in Bassin, Honey and Kaplan 1994, 2–3).

On the rare occasion where a mother dares to 'expresses her doubts' about the parenting practices on offer or question the appropriateness of such intensive behavioural methods, such challenges to disciplinary techniques are overlooked in favour of a challenge to the mothering skills being presented (S1:E1). When one mother suggests that intensive behavioural systems might work if she didn't have other demands on her time such as paid employment and household chores, her concerns 'are not directly addressed by either the parenting expert [...] or by the accompanying voiceover' (Jensen 2010, 179–80). The 'exhaustion incurred by the parental labour that the techniques require is not framed as a problem to be addressed, rather, it becomes another site of [maternal] failure' (ibid., 180). Therefore, the tiredness and fragility that the mother feels in this instance, and her subsequent lapses in the structured disciplinary techniques, are not presented as evidence of a mother struggling to balance domestic chores, paid labour and the demands of her children, rather they 'become evidence that [she] is not committed at an ontological level to becoming the "right kind" of parent' (ibid., 180). The 'casual underpinnings of [this woman's] exhaustion are silenced, and because they are not addressed or even acknowledged by the expert, she becomes positioned at the furtive moments of her to-camera doubts as something of a saboteur' (ibid., 180). This woman is oppressed by society in general and by *Supernanny* in particular because she does not adhere to the ideology of the 'good' mother, but what is missing here of course is any consideration of the context of her motherwork. *Supernanny* rigidly fixes the subject position of both wife and mother, and in so doing this limits the ways in which women are allowed to perform in these roles. Skeggs, Thumim and Wood remind us of the improbability of the socially accepted 'good' mother when they tell us that the programme focuses on the 'spectacle of performativity' coming undone (Skeggs, Thumim and Wood 2008b, 143). The show reveals the emotional and physical labour demanded by the 'good' mother and by revealing it as labour, the programme reminds audiences of the impossibility of achieving either the ideology of intensive mothering or the romanticised ideal of maternal care (ibid., 143).

When this mother suggests that Frost is able to see the family problems because she has the time, energy and opportunity to observe rather than run the family, she is dismissed for an inappropriate attitude towards and expectations regarding motherwork. This mother makes the point that 'when you're parents and you have your job and an eight-hour stint in the office [...] on top of that and then you have all the house on top of that as well, it's like you have three jobs and you don't ever take the time to sit down and look at where everything is and where it's all going' (S1:E1). This woman is not shirking her responsibilities to her family, merely struggling to maintain a mask of 'good' motherhood. Likewise, when another family is seen enjoying a McDonalds drive-through with their young sons (S2:E11), the visible 'pleasures they share of going to the drive-through, ordering and eating' are ignored in favour of situating the experience as evidence of maternal pathology and dysfunction (Jensen 2010, 180). Indeed, 'the "time famine" experienced by working parents in their food preparation [...] recedes into the background of [this and every other] episode' (ibid., 181). The programme simultaneously revels in the humiliation, shame and fragility of contemporary mothers, while making it clear that these women can be transformed into culturally appropriate maternal figures through middle-class motherwork and intensive maternal practices. Green makes the point when she tells us that 'viewers and participants learn that "good" mothers try hard and will eventually succeed in effectively disciplining themselves as they learn the techniques and, in turn, their children as they become a healthy and functioning family' (Green 2007).

Supernanny establishes mothers as primary caregivers, demands that they adhere to the ideology of intensive mothering and instead of acknowledging the social and structural conflicts experienced by modern working mothers, the programme merely presents childcare concerns as individual disciplinary, attitudinal, time management and other organisational failings to be corrected in the home. Tracey Jensen makes the point that 'structural inequalities are recast as individual failings that may be changed' in line with the makeover narrative (Jensen 2010, 174). Indeed, issues such as 'money, class, race, or any other sociological or political content [are never] used to explain the tribulations of the families depicted' (Brancato 2007, 54). The programme 'fails to offer any substantial exploration of issues surrounding child care [...]or the particular issues surrounding women's employment [...] which inevitably govern the options available to women and help determine the choices that they make' (Matheson 2007, 46). Rather, *Supernanny* seems to suggest that mothers can choose and control their working and parenting practices irrespective of other financial, social or sexual demands. Although one might suggest that the show be praised for acknowledging the lack of support networks for modern families 'in its heart-rending portraits of family life, it offers up not a call to better funding for working families, or other larger, social solutions, but rather individualistic disciplinary, behavioural techniques to re-establish parental authority in the house' (Tally 2008, 16). The point here then is that while the programme presents positive and supportive parenting techniques, it is 'only scratching the surface of a very deep societal problem, namely, the lack of supports available to women with children' (ibid., 13).

Each episode, without exception, sees Frost deriding, dismissing and berating mothers for being physically frail, mentally fragile and ineffectual in their parenting practices. The nanny in question tells us that one mother is 'a nervous wreck' (S3:E2), while another is 'completely out of her depth' (S3:E3). She tells another mother to 'stop copping out' of her maternal responsibilities (*Extreme Parental Guidance* S1:E3) and we see her disappointment when she tells a further caregiver that she is 'shocked to see how you have allowed [your child] to become this bad' (S1:E1). We hear Frost tell one mother that her treatment of her child is tantamount to 'neglect' (*Extreme Parental Guidance* S1:E3), another that her actions are a form of 'disgusting [...] abuse' (S2:E8) and another still that her maternal practices are 'unhealthy' (S3:E2). Frost shows disgust, disappointment and derision when these mothers become frustrated, angry or aggressive with their children. She is particularly vocal when she tells one struggling mother that 'you scare that boy, you scare him [...] and that [...] is not correct parenting [...] Your behaviour is threatening [...] I was livid with you, absolutely livid' (S2:E11). In another example, she tells a desperate mother that her behaviour 'is unacceptable no matter how bad things get' (S5:E1), and another that what she has witnessed in the household is 'appalling, absolutely appalling' (S3:E5), while another is 'disturbing to watch' (S5:E1). She tells yet another mother that 'we need to stop you from getting to the stage where you become the ugly person I just saw' (S3:E2).

Frost asks parents to witness what Green refers to as 'the pinnacle of their own parenting failure', at which point these primary caregivers refer to themselves as poor mothers, talk about their own inappropriate childrearing practices and berate themselves for their lack of consistent disciplinary techniques (Green 2007). While one mother is heard telling Frost that 'I just don't feel like a very good mum at the moment' (S2:E8), another tells her that she feels 'ashamed and guilty' at her own maternal practices (*Extreme Parental Guidance* S1:E1) while another confesses that she is 'failing [her son] big time' (*Extreme Parental Guidance* S1:E3). This theme of maternal shame, confession and failure continues as we hear one mother tell us that 'I feel completely frustrated [...] I'm at my wits end, I've got nowhere else to go – I feel like I've failed basically [...] I personally feel like I have failed my children, I feel like I'm not a good mother' (S2:E5), while another confesses that her children's behaviour makes her 'feel ashamed because people must think "what sort of mother is she?" [...] It makes me feel like I'm completely crap as a mother' (S3:E4). In her work on maternal thinking Sara Ruddick suggests that

> in the daily conflict of wills, at least with her children, a mother has the upper hand. Even the most powerless woman knows that she is physically stronger than her young children. This along with undeniable psychological power gives her the resources to control her children's behaviour and influence their perceptions. If a mother didn't have this control, her life would be unbearable. (Ruddick cited in O'Reilly 2004c, 250)

Unbearable indeed. Mothers routinely apologise for what they see as their maternal failings and acknowledge their inability to follow through with clear, consistent discipline in the household, aware that these failings are going to create chaos, disorder and disharmony in the domestic space. Elsa First makes the point that 'mothering, like most work traditionally assigned to women, has been simultaneously idealized and devalued by being considered merely natural and so taken for granted' (First 1994, 147). While parenting television is in a situation to 'rescue mothering from idealizations and to reconsider it as a body of sophisticated skills and a form of disciplined and thoughtful work', there is no such feminist agenda here (ibid., 147). One mother tells us that 'I feel like I'm some sort of mug to take it, but what else can I do? I'm still trying to do my best. [...] Nothing works, [...]nothing' (S3:E2); another confides to

Frost that 'I'm feeling hurt and sad that my nine-year-old daughter can treat me the way she is [...] I'm not like a mother to her,[...] she treats me so badly [...] I don't want her to shout at me and tell me she hates me' (S2: E5). Yet another primary caregiver speaks of her frustration at being unable to present a basic family meal for her children without tears and tantrums on both sides, telling us that 'it feels like they're all ganging up on me and I'm on my tod, trying to do this really basic thing, and it just makes me feel so stupid inside. It's such a simple thing, but me as a mother – I can't even do it, I can't even get a few smiley faces from A to B' (S2:E3). This woman goes on to tearfully recount that 'it upsets me – they should be able to behave for me, they're my children. If I can't feed them a bit of tea, that doesn't say very much about me as a mother' (S2:E3). This mother talks of the ways in which her youngest son drains her physically, mentally and emotionally, and goes on to blame herself for the fact that she had to have an emergency caesarean section rather than a home-birth as the explanation for the lack of maternal respect here (S2:E3).

Although several mothers admit to feeling miserable in their maternal role and talk of mechanically going 'through the routines' of motherwork (S2:E11), others express more extreme levels of frustration and failure when they tell us that 'it makes me feel like I'm completely crap as a mother [...] I keep thinking, "why did I ever had children?" [...] When it gets really bad I just want to get out, leave the whole lot of them' (S3:E4). A number of mothers confess to not only struggling with behavioural issues, but with the overwhelming role and responsibilities of motherhood and motherwork. One mother tells us that 'I don't want to be here anymore [...] I don't want to be here anymore, I just don't like it here anymore, it's not my idea of fun, it's not my idea of family life anymore [...] I've had enough, I had enough a long time ago' (S2:E8), while yet another confesses that 'the kids have got me very low, very extremely low. Sometimes I feel like walking out and leaving them in here on their own, when they get me to my lowest point' (S3:E2). Moreover, we are asked to question the maternal instincts of a mother who would 'choose to [...] work everyday [...] if I could' because it provides respite from her demanding and demeaning maternal role (S3:E3).

Reality parenting television in general and *Supernanny* in particular presents the ideology of intensive mothering as the correct version of maternal practice and care, and as such 'many mothers [...] strive to change and correct their mothering to more closely conform to the idealized mother and so avoid mother-blame. However, since no mother can achieve idealized motherhood, women bring to their lived experiences of mothering self-recrimination, anxiety, and guilt' (O'Reilly 2004d, 16). Extant literature tends to challenge the ways in which reality parenting programming holds up the ideology of intensive mothering as the only model of motherhood to aspire to and emulate.

That said, rather than critique or condemn the programme for exploiting fragile mothers or for humiliating depressed caregivers, the programme might be understood as a powerful, necessary and real voice for contemporary motherhood. Indeed, if one considers that contemporary mothers are said to bring inaccurate or ill-informed, disabling and delusional expectations to motherhood and the maternal role (Maushart 1999: xviii), one might suggest that the representation of motherhood in reality parenting television might be seen to bridge the gap between expectation and experience here. Furthermore, one could argue, as Skeggs, Thumim and Wood have done, that the depiction of motherhood in such texts might be seen to contribute to and refigure 'the value of women's emotional and domestic responsibilities within the neo-liberal economy' (Skeggs, Thumim and Wood 2008b, 135).

Conclusion

This chapter has outlined the ways in which motherhood and the maternal role have been and continue to be presented in television documentary and reality parenting programming, considering how shows such as *Wife Swap* and *Supernanny* adhere to the unattainable and unachievable ideology of intensive motherhood. These titles are seen to humiliate struggling mothers by adhering to the 'good' mother myth, and yet they are understood by participants and viewers alike to offer useful advice and practical support for contemporary parents. Nick Powell, executive producer of *Supernanny*, tells us that 'nannies provide the right combination of love and discipline that both kids and parents need' (Powell cited in Flynn 2005, 49) while Emily Flynn makes the point that nannies such as Frost are 'efficient, fun and much better with the kids than mom' (Flynn 2005, 48). Likewise, it is suggested that Supernanny sees all of the disciplinary problems in the home because she is a professional caregiver rather than a biological mother (S1:E1). Jo Frost is presented as a childcare expert, and as such, we are asked to respect her working experience over the lived maternal practice of existing mothers. In this way, reality parenting programming can be said to fit in with a 'wider professionalization of motherhood that infantilizes real mothers', which is in conflict with a feminist agenda that demands we respect mothers for their well-meaning if not all-encompassing motherwork (Cobb 2008).

Chapter 7

CELEBRITY REALITY TELEVISION: MAINTAINING THE 'YUMMY MUMMY' PROFILE

Introduction

Pregnant bodies are open to 'intense medical scrutiny and regulation [and yet] until recently the pregnant woman has been conspicuously absent from popular visual representation' (Tyler 2001, 69). Indeed, when a seven-month pregnant Demi Moore posed naked on the cover of *Vanity Fair* in 1991, the publication was placed on the top shelf of newsagents next to pornographic titles. Since that time however, numerous high profile pregnant women such as Cindy Crawford (*W* 1999), Britney Spears (*Harper's Bazaar* 2006) and Claudia Schiffer (*Vogue* 2010) have recreated the pose, and many more have gone on to present sexy and semi-clad pictures of their pregnant bodies, with the suggestion that such images are no longer shocking, scandalous or taboo, but rather, increasingly accessible and acceptable in the contemporary cultural climate (La Ferla 2002). Moreover, the celebrity pregnancy and famous 'yummy mummy' dominates the pages of both the gossip magazine and the more traditional women's titles, with much coverage focusing on the before-and-after weight and fashion makeovers of these famous mothers and mothers-to-be. Such media texts appear keen to not only judge and rank recognisable women for their ability to control, tame and constrain their growing bodies, but also to present them in a hierarchy of acceptable, unacceptable and unforgivable images of motherhood and maternalism.

Although it is not uncommon for stars such as Gisele Bündchen, Gwyneth Paltrow and Sarah Jessica Parker to talk about their changing bodies, personal lives and working commitments on the back of their new-found mothering role, it is less common for celebrities to open their homes to the public and allow them to view their parenting skills first hand. In this way it is important that we examine the representation of motherhood and motherwork in celebrity reality television in order to understand the ways in which such programmes articulate preferred, and otherwise, forms of motherhood in contemporary popular culture. With this in mind, this chapter will examine celebrity reality shows such as Kerry Katona's *The Next Chapter* (2010–), Katie Price's *Katie* (formerly known as *What Katie Did Next*) (2009–) and Alicia Douvall's *Glamour Models, Mum and Me* (2010), and consider the ways in which these mothers are at various times exposed, exhibitionistic and exploited because of what might ostensibly appear to be a lack of mature maternal responsibility.

Pregnancy and new motherhood might be understood as a great social, sexual and financial leveller amongst contemporary women, as concerns over conception, the anguish of pregnancy, weight gain, the pain of childbirth, sleep deprivation and postnatal depression might be understood as being beyond any classification of class privilege, wealth or social status. Indeed, in a recent afterword to a volume entitled *What They Know About…Parenting!: Celebrity Moms and Dads Give us Their Take on Having Kids* (2007), we are told that 'parenting is inspiring and meaningful and perplexing for *everyone*! […] No matter what level of fame people have achieved, they're not immune to being challenged by the awesome responsibility of being a parent' (Pearlman and Kramer 2007, 235; italics in original). However, the celebrity motherhood profile suggests that celebrity pregnancy and motherhood is less about finding a common ground between women as mothers and more about finding ways to distinguish between the serene, selfless and spontaneous celebrity mother and the lived reality of motherhood and motherwork outside of this gendered narrative.

Serene, Selfless and Spontaneous: The Celebrity Mother Profile

The celebratory celebrity-pregnancy story and the celebrity-motherhood profile became popular in the late 1970s and early 1980s in magazines such as *People* and *Us*. Since that time, the celebrity-mother profile has developed and flourished and continues to make up a routine, everyday and indeed expected part of today's celebrity gossip sector, with a wide range of irreverent and more respected titles from *heat* to *Hello!* detailing not only the love lives and romances of the rich and famous, but also scrutinising the pregnant bodies and maternity fashions of the female celebrity. The celebrity mother profile depicts a recognisable woman, routinely from the entertainment sphere, who is either pregnant or has recently given birth and is proudly showing off her new child or children for an exclusive interview and photo story. Indeed, it is only these glowing, proud new mothers rather than mothers with older children who are asked to grace the covers and offer parental insights in the glossy pages of such publications. Susan Douglas and Meredith Michaels make the point that the serene and contented celebrity mother has dominated and continues to dominate women's magazines, the celebrity gossip sector and indeed the wider media environment (Douglas and Michaels 2005, 115). Likewise, Angela McRobbie makes the point that 'the svelte figure of the high-income yummy mummy who can squeeze into size six jeans a couple of weeks after giving birth, with the help of a personal trainer, has become a favourite front-cover image in the celebrity weeklies' (McRobbie 2006). In short, the contemporary celebrity-motherhood story has become worthy of the mainstream news agenda (Goc 2007, 149–66).

Even before we read the serene stories and selfless interviews with pregnant stars and new celebrity mothers, it is worth considering the images that are being presented on the cover of these gendered texts. Women's magazines and the celebrity gossip sector tend to draw attention to and indeed celebrate the site of the pregnant body and the surface appearance and attractiveness of the new mother. However, irrespective of the reality of the celebrity pregnancy, delivery or the ensuing maternal role, what is represented is an orchestrated and deliberately considered image of motherhood. Women are asked to look at the pregnant bodies on display, and as such, are asked to note the lack of the usual markers of pregnancy. There are 'no stretch marks for these celebrities; their smooth stomachs accentuate bodies that look better than most women on a regular non-pregnant day' (Tropp 2006, 866). When a seven-month pregnant Britney Spears appeared naked on the cover of *Harpers Bazaar* we were told that not only did the singer look 'radiant' in her pregnant skin, but that she had 'not allowed her body to surrender unnecessarily to the demands of pregnancy' (O'Malley 2006). In this way, 'pregnancy is no longer about morning sickness, swollen ankles, mood swings, and bloating' (Pitt 2008), rather, 'women should look and feel absolutely fabulous right up to, and even during labour' (ibid.). Abby O'Reilly may sound facetious when she states that 'the newborn becomes nothing more than a side product of a problem that has to be overcome, a negligible nothing that has provided its mother with the opportunity to publicly display her self-restraint and high level of masterly control over her body' (O'Reilly 2007), however, the speed with which many celebrity mothers return to their pre-pregnancy shape, size and weight is nothing if not remarkable. Indeed, the 'photo of the new mum back in her size eight jeans has replaced the first portrait of the baby as the snap every picture editor wants' (Oldham 2003). And although one might suggest that an awareness of celebrity pregnancy, birth and new motherhood might be considered liberating for a generation of women who struggle with their own mothering role, the concern here is that the celebrity mother profile offers a limited and unattainable image of motherhood that romanticises that role, leading to maternal guilt and insecurity for the reader.

I refer here to a single celebrity-motherhood profile rather than a more plural notion of these maternal stories because these cover images and accompanying interviews appear interchangeable, allowing little in the way of deviation from the serene, selfless, sexy and self-fulfilled maternal pattern. Indeed, Douglas and Michaels have managed to reduce these glossy articles to a strict formula that demands that the woman in question be beautiful, in control of her destiny and in a loving relationship; she needs always to look radiantly happy when she is in the company of her children; she looks fabulous when pregnant because she follows a strict dietary and exercise regime; her children are her number one priority at all times and without exception, however high-achieving or high-profile her career; she must offer a modicum of frailty in order to allow the less privileged magazine readership to identify her as a maternal role model; she is spontaneous, fun and always ready to play with exuberance and enthusiasm with her children and she lavishes a wealth of material goods on her offspring (Douglas and Michaels 2005, 110–33). In short, this woman is presented as the archetypal 'good' mother, as she embodies, without ambiguity, the intensive mothering model that is seen to be the maternal ideal in the contemporary period.

These profiles make it clear that motherhood is paramount, irrespective of any existing entertainment profile. It is not enough for these mothers to talk about a devotion to their new child, nor to suggest that their career feels somehow insignificant in comparison to their newfound maternal role; rather, these mothers have to present the message 'that motherhood really is the best avocation in the world and women's place is, first and foremost, in the home' (ibid., 135), and that in order to fulfill the idealised maternal role, new mothers should put the children first and set themselves aside even if they continue to perform in the media marketplace (ibid., 135). The new mother profile adheres to a number of outdated, essentialist female stereotypes in that these women are in turn, and without exception, genetically predetermined to be nurturing, maternal and selfless. Douglas and Michaels go as far as referring to the profile as a 'powerful Trojan horse' due to the fact that what on the surface appears as a positive take on women who have managed to successfully combine loving motherhood with a satisfying career is actually just a front for supporting the myth of intensive mothering that women outside of the world of wealth and privilege cannot afford (ibid., 113). Indeed, the strength of maternal selflessness is so extreme in the celebrity-motherhood profile that these stories 'would have been right at home during the postwar redomestication program of the late 1940s and early 1950s, when mothers who wanted to work outside the home were deemed neurotic' (ibid., 135–6).

The women's magazine and celebrity gossip sector has paraded and continues to parade an exhaustive and exhausting list of famous new mothers who love their children unconditionally and without ambiguity and who are in control of their bodies, their homes, their careers, their relationships, their finances and last but not least, their new child. In short, the celebrity-mother profile offers 'a symbolic, fantasy response to the very real deficiencies mothers experienced in everyday life' (ibid., 116). Douglas and Michaels talk of 'Kathy Lee Gifford, Kelly Ripa, Gloria Estefan, Meg Ryan, Kelly Preston, Cindy Crawford, Vanna White, Angelina Jolie [and] Reese Witherspoon' (ibid., 114). However, we have more recently witnessed the celebrity mother profiles of Halle Berry, Cate Blanchet, Katie Holmes, Nicole Kidman, Jennifer Lopez and Gwyneth Paltrow, or in the British context, celebrities such as Mylene Klass, Tamzin Outhwaite, Melanie Sykes and Holly Willoughby.

Douglas and Michaels remind us that female film stars have, since the 1920s, been exploiting their new babies and young children in order to create a wholesome and ordinary public image and thus boost their box-office bankability (ibid., 117); the concern here however is that the contemporary celebrity-mother profile is less about ordinariness, normality or a sense of the mundane, and more about unachievable, unattainable and thus irresponsible depictions of the maternal role. The contemporary celebrity mother routinely ignores, overlooks or eliminates any references to her support network, be it the entourage of day and night nursery nurses and nannies to help look after the children; the personal trainer, dietician and chef to help work off any post-pregnancy baby weight; the stylists, hairdressers and make-up artists to ensure that the new mother looks glamorous and indeed perky during all public appearances and in deliberately 'candid' images of the new mother and baby; not to mention the drivers, personal assistants and managers to make sure that they are well rested, on time and always performing in line with the serene and selfless intensive mother profile. Indeed, so secure is the celebrity mother in her 'good' mother surroundings that many of these women find it possible and indeed plausible to step outside of their magazine profiles and give direction to other mothers from within the pages of book-length volumes on their motherhood practices (Klass 2008). With this in mind we are asked to consider the ways in which the 'celebrity mom image poses a paradox for women, as having it all is still an ideal to achieve while realistically most people know these celebrities have lots of help to achieve it all' (Tropp 2006, 863). The point here is that by 'erasing the kinds of support that celebrity and other wealthy mothers enjoy [...] and eliminating the challenges that even these most favored mothers face', these seemingly escapist and entertaining stories of new motherhood are asking real mothers to question their own standards of mothering and motherwork (Chappell 2005, 139). In short, these contented and comfortable stories of new motherhood are seen to play 'a subtle but important role in persuading so many of us to think about motherhood as an individual achievement and a test of individual will and self-discipline', which in turn sets us all up to stagger, falter and at times, fail (Douglas and Michaels 2005, 138).

Mothers and magazine readers know 'that famous yummy mummies are Hollywood fantasies; that in reality, celebrity mums actually have a team [...] that help [*sic*] to create and maintain their fantastic yummy mummy appearances' (Burroughs cited in Pitt 2008). Although the celebrity motherhood profile might cause its maternal reader to feel inadequate and ill-prepared for motherhood in contrast to such serene, selfless and glamorous standards, women continue to respond to and indeed invest in the maternal images and motherwork archetypes that are being presented in this gendered sector. Indeed, the copious and continued commercial interest in the celebrity-mother story must be seen as evidence of that fact. The appeal of a new mother who can combine a glamorous appearance, a spontaneous lifestyle, a deep maternal love and a successful career is obvious, if not actually obtainable. Abby O'Reilly makes this point when she tells us that the celebrity-mother profile 'does not provide the average new mother with a public figure with whom she can realistically identify. The average mother very often lacks the resources needed to pursue her ambitions at the same time as raising a family, whereas the celebrity yummy mummy has to make no such sacrifice' (O'Reilly 2007). Indeed, the point has to be made that even though a harmonious work and life balance is possible for the new celebrity mother, 'this should in no way place those who are denied the same opportunities in a position where we not only cast aspersions on her ability to raise her children, but also question her legitimacy as a modern-day woman' (ibid.).

Sarah Jessica Parker has been held up as the archetypal celebrity mother, based in part on her svelte appearance, her fashionista credentials, her long-term Hollywood marriage and the fact that she speaks the language of intensive mothering and thus adheres to and upholds the 'good' mother myth. Parker tells magazines such as *Glamour*, *Marie Claire* and *Grazia* of her overwhelming and all-consuming love for her son, and explains how she has had to shift her working patterns and priorities in order to spend quality time with her then-infant. Parker talks of being a 'hands-on mother' (Van Meter 2004, 85) who takes her son to work on set (ibid., 85) and makes herself available to her nannies if she happens to be working away from her child (Sullivan 2005, 704). She explains that although she used to sacrifice herself for her work, she now cannot wait to leave the set, hurry home and put her son to bed. She goes on to tell the female reader that she has found a new work–life balance since becoming a mother (Smith 2006, 137). Even though the actress tells us that 'I'm working 15 hours a day then running home to try and be a good parent' (Holgate 2003, 348), she continues to be presented as a 'good' mother in accordance with the intensive-mother myth rather than a partial and thus less able or available maternal figure.

Rather than present Parker as just another interchangeable example of the celebrity motherhood profile, the mother in question has actually been presented as *the* svelte and stylish figurehead of serene, selfless and spontaneous celebrity motherhood. In one interview with the pregnant star, *Elle* magazine referred to the 'baby bump' as 'her latest accessory' (Millea cited in Jermyn 2008, 166) and included what Debra Jermyn refers to as 'a montage of pictures of Parker pregnant in various styles of outfit', but which might also be understood as a pregnancy style-guide for the magazine readership (Jermyn 2008, 166). The magazine tells us that 'she wears it well', which clearly translates into applauding the actress for maintaining a glamorous, trim appearance and for bearing few physical signs of her pregnancy (Millea cited in Jermyn 2008, 166). Thus, even though Parker is keen to tell *Grazia* that 'since I had a baby, I'd far rather spend any spare time I have with my son than go shopping', the magazine continues to present Parker as the pinnacle of stylish celebrity motherhood in keeping with the celebrity-motherhood profile that dominates the sector (Gannon 2005, 15). It is as if, as has been suggested elsewhere, the physical appearance of slim, stylish and glamorous new motherhood 'is associated with being a good mother [which] creates particular aesthetic ideals for the lives of everyday women who now, apart from feeling the need to always appear to be in control, also have to look great while doing it' (Pitt 2008).

The celebrity-mother profile 'seems to suggest that appearance has become associated with a woman's maternal capabilities', with news and magazine media presenting Sarah Jessica Parker as the figurehead of this particular version of the unrealistic and unrealisable myth (ibid.). Parker presents us with an improbable and certainly unattainable image of working motherhood that is commercially and critically successful, stylish, svelte and available to and for her children. However, at the same time as Parker adheres to the image of the 'good' mother, she draws attention to the fantastical nature of the maternal role being presented here, putting a voice to the role of wealth, fame and privilege. Parker appears unique in the celebrity-mother profile due to 'her willingness to expose and condemn the impossible standards set by contemporary celebrity moms and the media's obsession with their post-partum weight loss' (Jermyn 2008, 171). Indeed, the actress is heard telling *Good Housekeeping* magazine that 'no real woman should look to any woman in this industry as an example. It's simply not applicable because of the enormous number of advantages we have' (Smith 2006, 138–9). The fact that Parker goes on to have twins via a surrogate is interesting here because, although Parker was happy to expose the fantasy of celebrity motherhood, the then-45-year-old Parker is less open or candid about the relevance of age in a discussion of fertility.

Although the celebrity-mother profile may not be a realistic role model for most new mothers, a number of aspirational mothers with time and financial resources at their disposal are said to be trying to imitate the physical appearances and mothering profiles of the celebrity mother. Stephanie O'Donohoe tells us that the 'yummy mummy' is a fashionable and assertive mother or expectant mother who retains her pre-conception sense of style and is able to resist other less flattering, albeit perhaps more realistic images of pregnancy and new motherhood (O'Donohoe 2006). The use of the term on an exhaustive array of kitchenware, clothing and other paraphernalia of femininity demonstrates both the popularity and currency of the term, with little hint of postmodern irony on display. There is evidence to suggest that the celebrity mother profile and the subsequent 'yummy mummy' phenomenon is creating pressure, stress and anxiety for contemporary women who can not live up to what they see as the maternal ideal (Devine 2008). Indeed, recent work makes it clear that the depiction of the 'yummy mummy' in the media 'contributes to a stigma of "failed femininity" for those mothers or potential mothers who can't live up to celebrity standards' (Hadfield, Rudoe and Sanderson-Mann 2007, 259). Janet Chan, the editor of *Parenting* magazine, tells us that her readers feel frustrated and inadequate in the face of such unrealistic and unattainable images of expectant and new motherhood (Chan cited in Ryan 2007). This is not to suggest that the readers are unaware of the celebrity machinery at play, the use of the celebrity mother profile in creating and cementing a favourable and thus bankable star image for a performer, or the agenda-setting function of the magazine in question; but rather, that 'women seem to know that the representations they see are idealized, at the same time they internalize the underlying messages' (Ryan 2007).

The popularity of makeover fashion programming in general and the plastic-surgery makeover show in particular provides evidence of the ways in which the celebrity-mother myth and the wider 'yummy mummy' profile are impacting on a generation of new mothers. There has long been a focus on age prevention and maintaining a youthful visage for women in society. Indeed, cosmetic advertising in the 1920s was trying to collapse the physical age distinctions between generations, as they asked women to 'Stay Young with Your daughter' (Addison 2009, 74). However, since that time, mothers have been asked to not only stay young with their daughters, but to rehabilitate 'themselves as sexualized subjects post-childbirth' (Gailey 2007, 111–12). Elizabeth Gailey makes the point that makeover television renders '*motherhood itself pathological*' because women are being asked to be sexually viable well into their late 30s and 40s (ibid., 112; italics in original). Gailey tells us that 'reclaiming the "blown-out" body parts sacrificed to childbirth is a routine aspect of responsible women's self-management and care' and reminds us of the ways in which the plastic-surgery profession views pregnancy as a pollutant on the female body (ibid., 112).

Unnecessary medical procedures are being 'sold to mothers on these shows as compensation for childbirth and "good" parenting' practices (ibid., 112), and such techniques are clearly effective. After all, in a recent survey of new mothers, nearly half of those women questioned said that 'their main concern after giving birth was to lose the weight they had gained during pregnancy', and more than 80 per cent of these women said that the celebrity mother profile was to blame for making post-pregnancy weight-loss look unrealistically easy and achievable (BBC News 2004). However, rather than question the wider cultural norms and mores that demand that expectant and new mothers retain a pre-pregnancy sense of style, serenity and surface beauty, many women 'self-blame and internalize a sense of private bodily failure, embarking on fitness routines, plastic surgery, and dieting practices to rectify anxieties about bodily lack' (Dworkin and Wachs 2004, 612). The celebrity-mother profile upholds the very highest standards of sartorial style, surface attractiveness, maternal bliss and selflessness, and although Parker has suggested that real women should not look to public mothers as maternal role models, there remains a sense that 'good' motherhood and appropriate maternal practices are linked with surface appearance, style and attractiveness, and the flourishing 'yummy mummy' profile and growing popularity of the 'mommy makeover' is testament to that fact.

Celebrity status, wealth and privilege can make a genuine difference to the lived reality of pregnancy and motherhood in terms of physical appearance and surface attractiveness, but one has to question whether such privilege has any bearing on the experience of the 'baby blues', postnatal depression or postnatal psychosis. Recent reports tell us that one in ten new mothers suffers from some form of clinical depression after the birth of a child (NHS 2011). Likewise, extant research tells us that 'half of all mothers with kids under five years old experience symptoms of intense emotional distress on a regular or continual basis' and that 'women are five times more likely to be diagnosed as mentally ill in the year after their first child's birth than at any other time in their lives' (Maushart 2007, 465). In short, research 'suggests that in our society motherhood can be and often is dangerous to our mental health' (ibid., 465). However, while half of all mothers are suffering with some form of depression, there is no statistical parity in the celebrity mother profile. Douglas and Michaels tell us, with only a hint of humour, that 'postpartum depression isn't an option for [...]celebrity moms [...] Unlike you, being subjected to sleep deprivation and raging hormones was a choice for these women, and they just said no' (Douglas and Michaels 2005, 122). Hilary Clark reminds us that self-control and personal discipline are key tropes of the celebrity mother profile and that, irrespective of the reality of the celebrity mothering experience, when these high profile new 'mothers expose themselves and their young children to the cameras [...] and their stories to readers [...] they give themselves over to the Celebrity Mom-making machinery' which is the 'myth-machine [that] powerfully shapes their own and ordinary women's perceptions of what good mothering involves' (Clark 2008, 458).

One might suggest that Brooke Shields' celebrity-mother profile and her extended volume entitled *Down Came the Rain: A Mother's Story of Depression and Recovery* (Shields 2005) stands out as the exception to the rule here. Shields uses the afterword of her book to tell women that postnatal depression is real and beyond their control and as such they should talk openly about their feelings and seek professional help. She makes the point that those suffering are not bad mothers, and that they should not feel guilty, ashamed or embarrassed by their emotions. As such, she goes some way to remind us that the serene, selfless and spontaneous celebrity-mother profile is an unrealisable and unattainable myth, with the suggestion that many of these women may talk of maternal bliss, work–life balance and the latest fashion apparels, but this may be another mask of acceptable motherhood. However, although one might refer to Shields as bold, brave or inspirational for penning her journey through postnatal depression and recovery, one might also argue that the mother in question was challenging the celebrity mother profile while simultaneously promoting the selfsame myth. After all, even though Shields admits to postnatal depression and talks openly about the literal and emotional wounds of her maternal journey, she also emphasises her 'wealth, privilege, and beauty in order to defend herself against the shame of confessing to mental illness' (Clark 2008, 459), so that the actress is re-appropriated as the trusted, loving and serene 'good' mother by the end of the volume, and thus, like Sarah Jessica Parker, presented in line with the manual of serene, selfless and spontaneous celebrity motherhood.

It is clear that the gendered magazine sector has presented and continues to present unattainable and unrealistic celebrity-mother profiles that adhere to the 'good' mother myth, and celebrity and entertainment programmes such as *Entertainment Tonight* (1981–) and *Access Hollywood* (1996–) draw on the same motherhood format as they feature stories of expectant and new celebrity mothers. Celebrity entertainment 'stories emphasize pregnant Hollywood moms "glowing" [...] and feeling sexier than ever. We see over-the-top baby showers, adorable baby gifts, and designer nursery décor. Once baby arrives, we see celebrity moms back in their size two couture within weeks' (Kinnick 2009, 4). Elsewhere we are presented with *Runway Moms* (2006–), a show committed to following the personal and professional lives of pregnant runway models. *Runway Moms* accompanies 'models on sexy photo shoots and learn[s] their prenatal secrets to staying fit and glamorous' (Discovery Health 2011), and as such, this programme, like the aforementioned entertainment texts, goes further to reinforce the celebrity-mother profile.

The celebrity-mother profile offers an unrealistic and unattainable version of the 'good' mother myth due in part to its presentation of impossible physical appearances and its focus on implausible working practices. Moreover, the fact that the profile routinely features mature first-time mothers is in itself misleading about the reality of fertility in this age group. The entertainment arena is 'riddled with questionable fertility miracles' for forty- and fifty-something mothers, with the suggestion that many of these women are either concealing their reliance on IVF treatment or hiding their use of surrogates (Groskop 2009). The celebrity mother profile routinely features mature mothers, be it Madonna (aged 41), Marcia Cross (44), Geena Davis (46), Holly Hunter (47) Beverly D'Angelo (49) or Cheryl Tiegs (52), and one might suggest that these women are merely reflecting a growing trend towards older motherhood, as an unprecedented number of women are choosing to delay having children into their late thirties and beyond (Khanapure and Bewley 2007, 20). However, although no one would want to deny these women their children, there is a sense that they are not telling the whole story. After all, although many women in their late thirties, forties and beyond can and do have normal pregnancies and give birth to healthy babies, the mature celebrity mother profile tends to 'lose sight of the risks to women's health' and misrepresent the emotional and physical consequences of older pregnancies (Wood 2008, 326).

Female fertility is reduced at 35 and reduced dramatically after 40, and as fertility decreases, miscarriages increase (Bonifazi 2003; Wood 2008, 326). For those women over 35 who carry their baby to term there 'is a higher incidence of haemorrhage [...] hypertension, pre-eclampic toxaemia and diabetes' (Khanapure and Bewley 2007, 21) and 'more problems with abnormal labour patterns and a definite higher risk of caesarean section' (ibid., 21). We find that 'older women have an increased incidence of preterm delivery and are more likely to deliver under 32 weeks' gestation with a consequent increased risk of prenatal mortality' (ibid., 21) More worrying still, we are informed that 'maternal mortality also increases several fold for older women compared with the younger pregnant patient' (ibid., 21). Older mothers, particularly aged 35 and upwards, have an increased risk of a Down's Syndrome baby, ectopic pregnancy, placental problems, high blood pressure, aneuploidy, stillbirth and low-birth-weight babies (Bonifazi 2003; Wood 2008, 326). Recent research has suggested that mature motherhood 'is also associated with a range of other, less well known, problems in children [such as] congenital malformations [...] schizophrenia [and] anorexia' (Berryman 1994, 108). And although such statistics have been well documented within the wider media landscape, they seem to have had little impact on the celebrity mother profile. Moreover, the use of IVF often goes unreported in these glossy texts, which goes further to mislead the female reader about the reality of late fertility, pregnancy and motherhood (Bonifazi 2003; Wood 2008, 326).

The reality is that even with reproductive assistance, the live-birth rate for older mothers is incredibly low. The 'live birth rate [*sic*] for women using assistive reproductive technology [...] with fresh, nondonor eggs or embryos is 15% at age 40, 5% at 43, and 2% after 43' (Bonifazi 2003). Indeed, a growing number of fertility clinics refuse to admit 45-year-old women for treatment (Gatrell 2008, 48). The concern here is that these statistical facts about fertility, pregnancy and new motherhood appear hidden from a generation of women who are delaying the maternal experience. After all, a 'recent survey of educated young professional women found that 90% thought that they could wait until age 45 to start having their own biological children, even though next to none over 44 are able to, despite advanced technology' (Bonifazi 2003). If female readers are looking to the celebrity magazine profile as a source of good, responsible and inspirational motherhood, and these stories about more-mature mothers overlook problems with conception and fertility, then no wonder readers are confused and ill-informed about the reality of the experience. Fertility problems do not appear to be part of the 'good' mother myth, suggesting that fertility is somehow linked to appropriate maternal practices. Anne Woollett tells us that women feel a sense of shame, embarrassment and humiliation when they struggle to or are unable to conceive, and as such, there is no place for such raw emotions or physical failings in the celebrity-mother profile (Woollett 1994, 47).

The Hierarchy of Contemporary Female Celebrity

The celebrity-mother profile dominates women's style and celebrity publications, and can be seen to have an impact on selected networks such as E! Entertainment Television. However, not all celebrity programming panders to this strict, serene and selfless maternal format. Celebrity reality television tends to present a number of mothers who struggle to maintain the mask of perfect motherhood, or rather, who are unwilling to adhere to the rules of the celebrity-motherhood profile. While the Hollywood actress, award-winning singer or supermodel are seen adhering to the celebrity motherhood profile in the magazine sector, there are other examples of recognisable women who are currently challenging these maternal myths by letting audiences view their day-to-day, mundane – and otherwise – motherwork. What is interesting here is where these different women are placed in the hierarchy of contemporary celebrity, with the suggestion that professionally respected celebrity mothers are able to uphold the motherhood profile, whereas those who demand media attention without the requisite skill, achievement or talent are less likely, or less able, to maintain this perfect maternal charade. Rather than critique or condemn those women who do not conform to the 'good' mother myth, it is worth noting that this less revered version of contemporary motherhood is popular with the young female demographic. A range of popular newspapers, magazines, supermarkets and fashion chains ask members of the public to vote for their celebrity mother of choice, and without exception these women tend to challenge the celebrity-mother profile, be it single mothers such as Suzanne Shaw, Ulrika Johnson and Kerry Katona or glamour models such as Katie Price or Melinda Messenger. These members of the public are clearly voting for a version of motherhood and the maternal role that does not conform to the serene and selfless 'good' mother myth.

Alicia Douvall, Katie Price and Kerry Katona seek publicity and promotion on the back of their sexualised, salacious and exhibitionistic performances in the public realm, and as such, each of these mothers has been criticised for fuelling media hype and thus demanding fame without any recourse to actual skill, talent or achievement. Although one might argue that 'it takes effort to be famous' (Marshall 2006, 647), cultural commentators appear keen to construct, cement and circulate the image of talentless celebrity. These women have each forged a career in the entertainment sphere, through a steady stream of reality shows, celebrity columns and autobiographies, with much commentary and accompanying imagery based around their sexual dalliances, romantic attachments, social engagements, sartorial choices, personal finances and health trials and tribulations. Like a number of other 'attributed' celebrities, their careers are 'an ongoing process of managing, repudiating, and creating the scandals that afford [them] media attention' (Bell 2008). Indeed, one cannot overestimate the importance of these reality television performances to their subsequent star image and celebrity status, with the charges of crudeness, exhibitionism and humiliation being thrown at both the shows and the stars in question – crudeness, exhibitionism and humiliation indeed. Alicia Douvall, Katie Price and Kerry Katona have each starred in celebrity reality programming, and it is to these reality texts that I now turn.

Mothering and Motherwork in Celebrity Reality Television

Celebrity reality television asks that recognisable people 'play' themselves on camera so that audiences can become acquainted with the 'real' person behind the media headlines and orchestrated photo-shoots. Indeed, while reality television creates a celebrity out of ordinary people, celebrity reality television creates an ordinary person out of the persona of an existing celebrity. In the case of Kerry Katona's *The Next Chapter*, Katie Price's *Katie* and Alicia Douvall's

Glamour Models, Mum and Me, we are being asked to view the maternal efforts on offer as true, authentic and as the reality of their mothering experiences.

These women have found fame playing themselves, and have continued to dominate the media schedules in this role, meaning that they appear to offer authenticity and sincerity to a willing audience. Their public images have been seen to be, from the outset, unscripted, unmediated and unapologetic, and these images have endured, irrespective of motherhood, marriage or media contracts. Douvall, Price and Katona play (and only play) themselves in the reality-media sphere, and their ability to find an interested audience is largely dependent on their ordinariness. The fact that they are able to secure a young, female, working-class fan base for their media enterprises at a time when they themselves are independently wealthy merely goes to demonstrate the power of their ordinary images. In short, these women are read, and continue to be read, amongst this grouping as both 'other' and yet 'one of us'; Douvall, Price and Katona personify a new breed of accessible, available and candid celebrity. The fact that these programmes do not shy away from showing these women as sexual and selfish means that they are not being produced in line with the celebrity-mother profile, and as such, we are asked to view these texts as a more believable – albeit still privileged – example of contemporary motherhood.

Alicia Douvall: One Teenage Daughter, Body Dysmorphia and Glamour Modelling

Alicia Douvall (born Sarah Howes) is a British glamour model, actress and reality-television star who first came to public attention due to a number of kiss-and-tell tabloid sex scandals, her penchant for plastic surgery and a propensity to dress provocatively in the media gaze. Although Douvall has been on several reality television shows, including *Celebrity Love Island* (2006) and more recently *Rehab* (2008), it is not until *Glamour Models, Mum and Me* that we start to acknowledge this woman as a mother, because this maternal role was not in keeping with the earlier image that the celebrity was keen to construct and circulate.

The programme begins as Douvall's teenage daughter tells us 'my name is Georgia Howes, I am 14 years old. When I grow up I want to be an architect, an actress and maybe a glamour model – I'm not sure yet'. Rather than be shocked by this revelation – hearing an educated and articulate young woman admit that she is still unsure as to whether to pursue an education and a professional career or to go into the world of topless modeling – this dilemma is said to be a rather common conundrum for the contemporary teenager. Indeed, in one significant survey, more than 60 per cent of teenage girls questioned said that they would rather be a glamour model than a nurse, doctor or teacher (Sky News, 2005). The shock-factor of the opening comes when Howes says that while 'I'm still trying to decide what to do with my life [...] my mum wants me to be a glamour model'.

Howes attends an exclusive boarding school and spends her weekends and holidays with her mother. She is presented as an incredibly compassionate, considerate, creative and hardworking young woman who has a desire to act, but not necessarily as a career objective. We see her studying diligently, getting upset at the prospect of missing school work and showing genuine enthusiasm for learning, be it science or Shakespeare. And although the appearance of such a model teenager is both inspiring and significant in its own right, it is the relationship between mother and daughter that is of interest here. Although at the start of the documentary Howes admits that she would consider working as a glamour model, by the end of the programme she has turned away from that option and is looking towards a place at university and a potential acting career after completing her education. What is fascinating, if albeit slightly uncomfortable to watch, is the ways in which her mother struggles to come to terms with her decision-making process. What is clear is that Douvall can relate to, befriend and act as a role model to a young daughter who is interested in style, fashion, celebrity and glamour, but she struggles to communicate with and find compassion for a daughter who is uninterested in the entertainment arena.

Douvall points to the differences between mother and daughter, and her inability to understand the younger woman, when she tells us that the teenager studying biology homework in the room next door is 'not the little girl I knew – my little girl likes bikinis and photo shoots, likes singing and acting and wants to be the next Britney Spears'. And when Howes demonstrates that she has grown out of this earlier fanciful stage and is making more mature and informed decisions about her future, Douvall tries to argue the case for topless glamour modelling, telling her daughter and the audience that 'it didn't do Jordan any harm, or me – it just cuts out the competition because if you're prepared to do topless [...] it's easier, you get more money, you get guaranteed work; you'll become famous within days'. And when her daughter suggests that she is uninterested in this line of work, Douvall presents a potentially post-feminist angle when she tells the camera that 'being a woman is powerful, and that's what I'm trying to teach my daughter, and that's the most important lesson you can teach a girl [...] You know that this [points to her body] is going to get you far'.

Douvall reminds her daughter that she only has two years left before she can have a breast enlargement, at which point her daughter says that she would not go under the knife after having seen so many procedures go wrong. Wrong indeed. We witness Howes drain the blood from her mother's breast after surgery, revealing the stitches and scarring left from a corrective operation. Douvall and her daughter went to Los Angeles to spend some time together during an Easter break, but the pair were unable to fly home due to a problem with Douvall's operation. We watch as they spend day after day in a small hotel room, mother taking strong pain medication after her surgery, and daughter desperately trying to keep on top of her schoolwork. When Howes admits her anxiety about missing crucial classes, Douvall offers to buy her daughter new clothes as compensation for her anxieties. And when Howes is frustrated by her lack of productivity outside of the school environment, we hear Douvall tell her daughter that 'you can do productive things – you can have your hair dyed, mummy will get your hair dyed blonde if you want. It is productive towards your modelling, towards your acting'. Douvall repeatedly misunderstands her daughter and desperately attempts to encourage her into the world that she herself understands and inhabits.

Douvall is clearly not presenting herself nor encouraging the documentary to present her as a selfless mother. Rather, this is a mother who is not committed to her child's education; indeed, she makes it clear that she does not know and is barely interested in the subjects that Howes is studying. Rather than take the time to engage with her homework, hobbies or general interests, she continues to talk about the surface appeal of celebrity and the lifestyle on offer through glamour modelling. What is at stake here is the relationship between mother and daughter, which Douvall makes clear on several occasions is akin to best friends and sisters rather than a more traditional mother-and-daughter pairing. We sit in on a therapy session with mother and daughter, and when Douvall makes the point that she has raised Howes as a sister rather than a daughter, the therapist reminds her rather firmly that her daughter is not her sister. When Douvall tries again to explain that the warmth and closeness of their relationship belies the more traditional unit, she is reminded that 'you're still the mom' before being instructed to 'meet [Howes] where she is, and not try to change her into who you want her to be'. This appears to be a turning point, because we then hear Douvall reflect on the reality of glamour modelling, reminding herself that 'it's really sad because I look back on all my friends who are glamour models - one of them is lap-dancing in a seedy club, [...] one of them is in prison, some of them are escorting and some are drinking'. On the back of this revelation she later tells her daughter that 'I think you'd be selling yourself short if you did topless modeling – you are much better than that, you don't need to dye your hair [...] you are perfect as you are'. Douvall offers an exhibitionistic and some might say selfish challenge to the celebrity-mother profile, and yet there is no mistaking the genuine connection and love that exists between this mother and daughter. Douvall is fully aware of the ways in which her sexual reputation will impact on her daughter, and goes as far as telling her that she has 'permission to deny who your mum is'. Rather than take her up on the offer, Howes states that 'I'm not going to be ashamed of who you are – you are funny and kind and caring, you do what's best for me. I wouldn't want to swap you', and at the programme's conclusion she goes on to tell us that her mother is 'trying not to pass her mistakes on to me and that's what makes her a perfect mum', and this comment speaks of genuine emotion rather than the 'cultural treacle' that constitutes the celebrity-mother profile (Douglas and Michaels 2005, 110).

That said, Douvall is an experienced media presence and as such, she understands the ways in which a programme such as this can help to construct, circulate and cement her celebrity persona, and so we have to question the ways in which she is using her child as a way to transform her own public persona for the sake of audience interest and thus economic investment. After all, even though the articulate, creative and eminently sensible Howes is an individual in her own right, her mother is able to 'bask' in her daughter's behaviour as if it were a reflection on her status as a successful mother. Jessica Collett makes this point when she reminds us that a 'mother's success is measured by her child's life and achievement' (Collett 2005, 329), so that in this instance, Howes's educational achievements, creativity and work ethic are the results of her mother's 'maternal instincts [and] worth as a human being' (Tardy 2000, 444). When Douvall asks us to look at the beauty, intellect and creativity of her teenage daughter, what she is really saying is 'look at me, Look what a great thing I've done', which is understood as a narcissistic and thus selfish rather than self-sacrificing and selfless maternal act (La Ferla 2002). In this way, one is left to question the ways in which Douvall is deliberately or otherwise choosing to use her daughter as part of her public profile, and the ways in which this image challenges or conforms to the 'good' mother myth that continues to dominate the contemporary cultural landscape.

Alicia Douvall allows her daughter Georgia Howes equal screen time and access to the camera, and this young woman is both seen and heard in her own right, which leaves us to question the ways in which younger children might be used in creating and cementing a public media profile. After all, younger children are, due to their status as 'incomplete and open persons [...] particularly suitable for use as impression management props' (Collett 2005, 328). And it is to this representation of media motherhood that I now turn.

Katie Price: Three Children, Two Fathers, Disability and Material Excess

Alicia Douvall has a consistent presence in the tabloid and reality sphere, but Katrina Amy Alexandria Alexis Infield, better known as Katie Price, aka

Jordan has, since the late 1990s, been a prolific and voracious media presence within the British celebrity, reality, tabloid and wider entertainment sphere.

Price first came to public recognition as a page-three glamour model in the British tabloid press, and after numerous plastic-surgery procedures she used her public recognition to expand her professional role into the wider entertainment arena. Since that time Price has continued to pose for men's titles such as *Playboy*, published four autobiographies, five novels and over 20 children's books. Price also released a platinum-selling album with then-husband Peter Andre, writes an advice column for *OK!* magazine, has her own lingerie range, jewellery line, hair-care brands and perfumes, not to mention her more recent equestrian range for adults and children. In short, Price is a commercially successful celebrity who has turned her fame into a commodity for trade. Price has appeared in a number of reality shows and series since the early 2000s, including: *Jordan: The Truth About Me* (2002), *Jordan: The Model Mum* (2003), *Jordan: You Don't Even Know Me* (2004), *When Jordan Met Peter* (2004), *Jordan & Peter: Laid Bare* (2005), *Katie & Peter: Unleashed* (2007) *Katie & Peter: The Next Chapter Down Under* (2008) and more recently *Katie*. Her most recent reality show, *Katie*, gives a seemingly open and candid account of Price as a new bride, as a successful business woman, as a woman who has natural maternal instincts, as a woman who is broody at the sight of a new-born baby, and as a woman struggling to move on from the grief of an earlier miscarriage.

In terms of her personal life, Price has had a number of high-profile relationships with men from the sporting and entertainment arenas, has been divorced twice and is, at the time of writing, said to be dating again. Price is the mother of three young children, 9-year-old Harvey, 6-year-old Junior and 4-year-old Princess Tiaamii. And although there appear to be days and even weeks when Price is not with her children, be it for work commitments, weddings, holidays or honeymoons, her reality shows tend to pay particular attention to Price's relationship with her children. Moreover, although her sexualised, self-confident and often selfish depiction of motherhood and motherwork is far removed from the 'good' mother myth, the lived reality of her maternal efforts appear popular with the young female audience in general, and young working-class mothers in particular. So much so in fact that Price has won a Celebrity Mother of the Year Award, appeared on the front cover of *OK!* magazine on mother's day and has her most recent television offering sponsored by Kiddicare.

Such personal accolades and financial endorsements might be linked to the fact that the voice-over for *Katie* is committed to presenting Price as the 'good' mother who is always thinking about her children and putting their needs before her own, irrespective of the demands of her career. At one point we are told that after a work engagement, Katie is 'back home enjoying being a mum again' (*Katie* S2:E1), which is later echoed as we hear that 'Katie gets back to what she does best: being a mum' (*Katie* S2:E7). Likewise, when she is snowed-in at her country estate it is considered as a blessing because 'it has allowed her to enjoy the thing in her life that she values above everything else: her kids' (*Katie* S2:E4). Indeed, it is her depth of maternal feeling which other mothers seem to invest in when they nominate Price for celebrity mother of the year awards and purchase the latest installment in her reality and tabloid experience. When these women voice their 'admiration' and 'respect' for Price they are responding to the ways in which the woman in question 'has become a symbol of how a person can constantly be in the public eye, whilst remaining a devoted and doting mum' (BBC 2007a).

Much is made in the programme and the wider media environment of the fact that Price's eldest son, Harvey, is clinically blind, autistic and diagnosed with septo-optic dysplasia, and of Price's unique relationship with the child. We see Price play with, kiss, cuddle and bestow great affection on her son; indeed, there appears a meaningful and committed relationship between the pair which demonstrates a level of patience, care and consideration not seen elsewhere in the Price persona. Indeed, we hear Price's brother talk about his sister's reliance on a local parent-and-toddler group for children with learning difficulties, telling us that 'it's like a self-help group really [...] Today she is a parent like any other parent [...] with a child with conditions of disability' (*Katie* S2: E2), and Price does appear at ease in this company. However, one is left to wonder about the appropriate depths of maternal feeling when Price tells us that 'I am quite a needy person, I need to be loved, all the time [...] Thank God I've got kids – they can love me and I can love them' (*Katie* S2:E5), and later when she tells us that she is relieved because while other partners and husbands have left, no one can ever take her son away from her (*Katie* S2:E2).

When we hear Price mention in passing at the turn of the new year that 'I want to get married – if I don't get married, I'll hopefully have another baby' (*Katie* S2:E2) the comment again brings to mind the woman's desperate desire for love, attention and affection, as well as the ways in which celebrity mothers tend to be judged differently than their less privileged counterparts. Price is a single mother with three children from two different fathers and she is talking here about adding another addition to her growing family, from an alternative paternal figure. Douglas and Michaels tell us that 'if you are a celebrity, you are entitled to have children whenever and however you want them, no matter how many you already have' or how many different fathers are involved in the process (Douglas and Michaels 2005, 137). There is no chastising here concerning the inappropriateness of the broken family unit, or 'impolite chiding [...] à la the welfare mother, about three kids by [...] different men' (ibid., 121). Rather, we are left with the suggestion that Price has the maternal instincts and material wealth to support whatever size of family she so desires and is capable of creating. Caroline Gatrell has suggested that 'women's reproductive labour is valued only in certain circumstances, and the notion of "value" is measured in relation to a woman's age, ethnicity, relative affluence and the number of children she already has' (Gatrell 2008, 49). However, in the celebrity-motherhood profile, the 'value' of motherhood is less in relation to a woman's age or number of existing children, and more in line with her affluence, her appearance and her ability to adhere to the 'good' mother myth.

Price's young children are often seen on screen, interacting with the film crew and acknowledging the presence of the camera, and Price makes no apology for allowing and indeed encouraging her children's media presence. Both she and the voice-over remind us that not only do her children attend professional photo-shoots to model Price's own children's clothesline, but that her 'kids can't wait to be on camera' (*Katie* S2:E7). Indeed, Price uses her daughter as the inspiration and future face for 'a junior make-up range' aimed at those little girls who like to play with fashion, hair and cosmetics (*Katie* S2:E5). Cultural commentators have questioned the ways in which reality figures such as Price use, manipulate or abuse their young children for the benefit of promotion, publicity, a reality career and thus financial gain (Dayna 2010). What is clearly at stake here is the celebrity-motherhood profile, and the potential destruction of the mask of motherhood. Price is a young, sexual and exhibitionistic woman who is deemed selfish rather than selfless, sexual rather than serene, self-indulgent rather than self-sacrificing, and as such she does not confirm to notions of 'good' motherhood. Although Price is presented as a devoted mother when she is with her children, with scenes of the family singing together on the sofa (*Katie* S2:E4), pony rides (*Katie* S2:E3) and trips to father Christmas (*Katie* S2:E2), she is not trying to suggest that she is either the sole caregiver for her children, or sufficiently fulfilled by this maternal role. Wealthy mothers such as Price, who can afford to hire a range of nurses, nannies and full-time child-minders to 'relieve them of the more burdensome aspects of childcare' (Polatnick 1983, 34), are able to 'enjoy the children's company when they want to, be active mothers when it suits them, but avoid the constant responsibility and the more unpleasant parts of the job' (ibid., 34). Indeed, any woman with access to such wealth is afforded 'considerable agency in the construction of their own maternal' identity (Woodward 2003, 29).

Indeed, in one of her earlier programmes she tells us that she is ready to go back to work just two weeks after giving birth, and laughs off the fact that she will be judged for her maternal practices by the tabloid press. Price tells us, 'Oh of course I'm going to get called a bad mum – I'm prepared to take it; the battle starts. I don't care if they call me a bad mum because they're not the ones living with me – they probably see me out, yeah of course. Every time I go out they're going to be: "Yeah, she's left her baby at home". So fucking what? I'm allowed out. Alright, it would be different if I was out every night of the week – I could understand it. I am allowed out, and I will go out, whether they call me a bad mum or not' (*Jordan: Model Mum* 2003). Although Price is presented as a devoted young mother, this is not her only role; she is a business woman, sexual object, desiring sexual subject and equestrian expert, and she makes no apologies or excuses for her personal or professional ambitions. However, the fact that she is 'not suitably, exclusively maternal' can and does on occasion leave her marked as an inappropriate and partial mother who has transgressed the feminine maternal ideal (Cobb 2008).

Katie Price may be simultaneously applauded for her serene maternal instincts while critiqued for selfish career ambitions and romantic interests. Indeed, Price was named as *OK!* magazine's Celebrity Mum of the Year in the very same week that a former nanny accused her of neglectful parenting (Northglow 2008). Price appears as a paradox of contemporary motherhood because while she is a single mother, her children appear surrounded by friends and supportive family figures; she bestows exhaustive material goods on her children while trying to teach them about manners and decorum; she leaves her children for work and pleasure while also taking them to business meetings and social events; she is clearly fulfilled by her career ambitions, but exudes maternal warmth and compassion when with her children; she is a sexualised figure who demands her own physical pleasure and yet she combines her sexual status with a more nurturing image of domesticity. In short, Price represents the lived reality of modern motherhood, not because all mothers are struggling to buy the right pony for their children or because we cannot decide on the style of the original crystal-encrusted mural for their newly refurbished bedroom, but because we too are multi-layered, multi-tasking mothers who struggle to wear the mask of perfect motherhood and maintain the 'good' mother myth.

Price may not be deemed a 'good' or appropriate mother in line with the celebrity-mother profile, but she demonstrates maternal care for her children, provides material comfort for her family and offers evidence of mundane yet meaningful motherwork, and as such we might consider her, like many women before her, an acceptable rather than appropriate mother, or rather what has been termed the 'good enough' rather than ideal maternal figure. However, while Price has negotiated the celebrity-mother profile, Kerry Katona's maternal efforts appear, in the first instance, to be beyond the pale.

Kerry Katona: Four Children, Two Fathers, Bankruptcy and Bipolar Disorder

Kerry Katona was a young, British glamour model who found fame with girl-band Atomic Kitten, before leaving the group to become a wife, mother and television presenter on shows such as *Loose Women* (1999–) and *Elimidate* (2002). Katona has, since her time in the public eye, published a regular column for *OK!* magazine, a number of autobiographies, a self-help book and three novels. Katona reached the height of her career success and public popularity after appearing in the programme *I'm a Celebrity…Get Me Out of Here* (2004) and being crowned 'Queen of the Jungle' in it. During this period Katona was married, divorced and had two daughters with singer Brian McFadden: 10-year-old Molly and 8-year-old Lily. Katona went on to marry, divorce and have another two children with taxi-driver Mark Croft: 4-year-old Heidi and 3-year-old Max. Since that time Katona has been consistently and aggressively condemned by the tabloid press and wider media marketplace for her parenting abilities, her financial mismanagement, her inebriated public performances, her disclosure of mental illness and her physical appearance and attractiveness.

Like Alicia Douvall and Katie Price before her, Katona has a recurring reality-television profile, appearing in a number of shows such as *My Fair Kerry* (2005), *Kerry Katona: Crazy in Love* (2008), *Kerry Katona: Whole Again* (2008), *Kerry Katona: What's the Problem?* (2009), *Kerry: Coming Clean* (2010) and most recently *Kerry Katona: The Next Chapter* (*TNC*) (2010–). These shows demonstrate an unnerving honesty, rawness and candor as we witness Katona's struggle with drugs, depression, bipolar disorder, physical transformation, marital breakdowns, bankruptcy proceedings, career turbulence and family disharmony. However, while traditional documentary and early reality programming demonstrates respect for its participants, this show 'betrays a deeply judgemental or supercilious attitude towards' Katona and her own maternal mother (Tyler and Bennett 2010, 386). Katona 'is portrayed, by turns, as infantile and demanding, brash, tasteless, outrageous and distraught, and the structure of the episodes emphasizes her instability' (ibid., 386).

Although Katona famously employed the services of publicist Max Clifford, with a number of television appearances, pubic apologies and media columns being used to brand and rebrand her media persona since achieving fame in the late 1990s, her authenticity and sincerity have never been in question. This does not mean that Katona's image has not changed in the time that she has been in the public eye, but rather, that any changes are seen as a natural and believable extension of the personality in question. In this way, struggles with her weight, mental health, custody battles, marriage, divorce and motherhood are all accepted and acceptable extensions of the public persona. Katona has maintained a media presence since the late 1990s, and since that time, the woman has garnered public affection and hostility, commercial success and professional humiliations. Emma Bell makes the point that Katona's 'vacillating status in the affections of the media can be charted through' her position within the Celebrity Mother of the Year awards. Katona won best mother of the year in 2002 and 2005, but went on to take the title for worst mother in 2008 and was later charged with being 'an "unfit mother" who should have her children taken away' (Bell 2008).

Katona is to all intents and purposes a working-class mother in terms of her upbringing, educational levels and her early career prospects, and as such, extant literature in the field of motherhood studies would deem her a 'bad' mother, with her single status reducing her to not only a 'bad' mother, but an emblem of wider social and sexual problems (Ferguson and King 2008, 174). Katona admits that she got pregnant with her fourth child because she did not want to have to commit to a contract that she signed for a fitness DVD (*TNC* S2:E2) and admits to drinking alcohol and smoking whilst pregnant (Katona cited in BBC News 2007b). We discover that Katona never missed her children when she had to travel and stay away from home for work because she 'looked forward to getting high on drugs' without their company or interference (*TNC* S2:E1). Katona was 'randomly drug tested by management' and currently sees a drunken, sexually explicit night out with other minor celebrities as a 'top night' (*TNC* S2:E7). Indeed, her then-management tells the audience that over a tragic and drug-hazed four-year period, Katona would sleep for 16 hours a day and spend no genuine time with her children (*TNC* S2:E1). Indeed, it is clear that she was not nor could be their primary caregiver in line with the 'good' mother myth. Katona is far removed from the maternal archetype or appropriate images of motherhood, and the fact that she appears happy to demonstrate her motherwork efforts on camera makes us question whether the former singer is either able to or interested in upholding the mask of perfect motherhood.

Katona makes it clear in her most recent reality series that her 'poor' mothering performances were due to an unstable marriage, mental-health problems, subsequent medications and an ensuing drug addiction. The woman stresses that she is committed to becoming a more appropriate mother for her children, and finds strength in her maternal role to leave her failing marriage and stop taking prescription and other drugs. She makes a point of reminding us time and time again in the programme of the importance of her children in her day-to-day life, and of the joy, fun and pleasures that they bring to her world. And although these can be understood as perfectly normal, healthy, albeit romanticized, maternal commentaries, it is important to note the professional implications of creating and maintaining a 'good' mother image for the woman in question. While Katona expresses her belief that 'letting the public get intimate with her as a mother could help her reclaim public affection' (Katona cited in Bell 2008), Bell reminds us that 'Katona's popularity depends on her ability to promote herself as a good, sane' and I would add sober mother figure here (Bell 2008). When Katona tells audiences that 'this is my life and its going on national television' she says that she 'wants people to like me' before adding 'for the kids', in order to present the only and correct presentation of selfless maternal thought as necessitated in the celebrity-mother profile (*TNC* S2:E3).

The voice-over seeks to situate Katona as a dedicated and devoted mother. The celebrity is often 'busy being a full-time mum' (*TNC* S2:E1), doing 'the school run' (*TNC* S2:E1), and we are told that although 'to the outside world image is everything to Katona, back at home it's all about being a good mum' (*TNC* S2:E1). The scenes in which we see Katona baking cupcakes (*TNC* S2:E2) sharing bathtimes (*TNC* S2:E1), singing with her girls (*TNC* S2:E8), making pirate breakfast treats for birthdays (*TNC* S2:E8) and supervising homework (*TNC* S2:E1) all adhere to the expected and appropriate image of a young mother fulfilling her maternal duties. Katona makes it clear that she understands the importance of quality time with her children when she says that 'this is crucial parts of their childhood, I've got to try and guide them', as if earlier instances of less appropriate maternal practices will be ignored, overlooked, forgotten or re-written (*TNC* S2:E2). Discovering that Katona's personal trainer arrives at the 'crack of dawn' before her children wake up goes another step towards positioning the performer in line with the celebrity-mother profile, in part because she has a grueling exercise regime that speaks of her commitment to surface appearances, and also because she does not let it interfere with her motherwork (*TNC* S2:E1).

Katona points to her earlier 'bad' mothering practices in order to redeem her current maternal efforts when she tells her audience that 'I'm enjoying being a mum more than I've ever enjoyed it […] I'm really embarrassed – I should have felt this a long time ago […] I got lost, massively got lost […] I got my priorities wrong (*TNC* S2:E2). Indeed, a number of famous young working-class 'ladettes' such as Gail Porter, Geri Halliwell and more recently Natalie Cassidy and Nicole Ritchie have attempted to rebrand their earlier excessive 'bad girl' images 'by claiming redemption through motherhood' (Bell 2008). In this way, their late-night drinking, sexual promiscuities and crude language are seen to be tamed and contained by an emerging yet innate maternal drive. Bell makes the point that Katona has 'conspicuously challenged [her] "bad girl" image by appealing to a virtuous, genuine, and material maternalism', and indeed Katona has made and continues to make a very public display of her love and affection for her photogenic children (ibid.). Moreover, 'for the ex-bad-girl, the transition to good womanhood seems largely to depend on her fitness as a mother, or better still, on the persona of the "yummy mummy"' that remains fashionable if not necessary obtainable in the contemporary period (ibid.). If we recall that the 'yummy mummy' is a privileged, style-conscious mother or expectant mother whose physical appearance and sartorial choices remain untouched and thus untarnished by pregnancy and motherhood, then it is relevant that Katona has lost several stone in weight, toned her body in advance of a fitness DVD, restyled her hair and appears dressed in designer apparel. In short, Katona has rehabilitated herself as a sexual subject; or rather, as a sexual object, post-childbirth, as is the want of the celebrity 'yummy mummy'.

Although one might challenge the appropriateness of a bipolar mother presenting her own life and the life of her growing children on national television, the use of her children in demanding celebrity photo-shoots, the crudeness of language expressed and the open hostility between herself and the father of her youngest children, there is an uncomfortable honesty being expressed here which is not seen elsewhere in mainstream programming or the wider media agenda. Katona makes it clear that she is a struggling single mother, and that the reality of being the primary caregiver becomes difficult when you try to be both the disciplinarian and a more nurturing force for your children (*TNC* S2:E6). She admits that she struggles with the lived reality of childcare because with four young children every day poses a new and unexpected social, emotional or financial challenge (*TNC* S2:E2). While we hear other stars and entertainment managers tell us that children adore doing photo-shoots to counteract any potential challenge to the selfless motherhood profile, Katona is heard telling her children, prior to the shots being taken, that 'this photo shoot we're doing today will buy your Christmas presents, so the better you are today [trails off]' (*TNC* S2:E2). In short, Katona's brash maternal style is not masked in maternal myth.

Katona's version of motherhood is compelling if not appropriate, honest if not ideal; but what is most meaningful here is the presentation of the motherhood cycle. We find out that Katona has lived in several foster homes and attended numerous different schools as a child. We learn that she witnessed her own mother's battle with mental illness, her suicide attempts and changing romantic engagements. We learn that mother and daughter used to go shoplifting together when they were suffering from financial hardship and that Katona used to purchase cocaine for her mother in order to 'cheer her up' (*TNC* S2:E2). Katona's own mother sold a drug story about her daughter, and is later heard telling the camera crew that 'honest to God I fucking hate her. I know it's on camera but I don't care – she's a selfish bitch' (*TNC* S2:E3). Mother and daughter share a troubled, turbulent yet committed relationship, not necessarily in keeping with the traditional mother–child dynamic, but important to both women nonetheless. What is genuinely meaningful here, and perhaps what appeals to the working-class female audience, is the way in which Katona is 'trying to break the fucking cycle here of my upbringing'

(*TNC* S2:E3). Katona did not have an 'appropriate' maternal role model, but she is trying to become one for her own children, and although it is incredibly easy to dismiss her motherwork efforts, one must also consider the ways in which the celebrity-motherhood profile, the 'yummy mummy' and the 'good' mother are all middle-class depictions of the maternal ideal. Katona appears as a reformed figure of maternal devotion, and although one might continue to separate her mothering from the 'good' mother myth, her mundane motherwork, the accoutrements of appropriate middle-class motherhood and her svelte figure allow Katona to move closer to the 'ideal of white, middle-class femininity as decorous, selfless, and deferential', which is in line with the celebrity-motherhood profile evident elsewhere in popular media culture (Cobb 2008).

Conclusion

There is a growing interest in the lived experience of recognisable mothers, be they idealised intensive mothers or less revered maternal figures. This chapter has outlined the ways in which celebrity mothers have been viewed on the small screen and in the wider media marketplace, suggesting that while the style and gossip sector has long been committed to a serene, selfless and thus unrealisable image of the 'good' mother, celebrity reality television has provided a space for more sexual and selfish depictions of contemporary motherhood. That said, such programmes use the voice-over narration to present these women in line with the ideology of intensive mothering and the socially acceptable 'good' mother even when such narration appears at odds with the maternal voices heard and the motherwork practices seen.

Chapter 8

FACTUAL TELEVISION: PREGNANCY, DELIVERY AND THE NEW MOTHER

Introduction

Niche reality television shows such as *Maternity Ward* (2000–2001) and *A Baby Story* (1998–) are committed to documenting pregnancies, childbirth and the early days of a new born life, and at a time when terrestrial television is being critiqued for taking pregnant presenters off our screens (Nathan and Mcconnell 2010), it is refreshing to find a cycle of programmes dedicated to presenting pregnant and childbearing women, and, at least ostensibly, the reality of that situation. This chapter will look at *One Born Every Minute UK* (2010–) and *One Born Every Minute USA* (2011–) and consider the ways in which the British and American version of the show either exploits new motherhood for ratings success or educates expectant parents in line with the lived experience of this role.

The Changing 'Nature' of Childbirth

Women have always given birth, and although this physical reality has remained unchanged since time immemorial, the social norms, mores and medical interventions associated with the experience have altered and shifted. During the eighteenth century it was common for midwives rather than physicians to attend to birthing mothers, and during this time it was not uncommon for a mother to lose a baby in delivery, or her own life amidst birthing complications (Plant 2010, 120). Pregnancy and childbirth were understood as 'intensely painful, debilitating, and potentially life-threatening' (ibid., 119) ordeals 'that should ideally be followed by a period of extended convalescence' (ibid., 126). Indeed, women of the period 'had no idea that childbirth should be easy and natural' (Cosslett 1994, 2). While 'maternal mortality remained a pressing problem, and many women continued to give birth without anesthesia' (Plant 2010, 129), it was difficult to challenge the notion that 'childbearing women braved great pain and danger' (ibid., 129). Indeed, pregnant women and mothers were respected for their potentially life-threatening self-sacrifices, and as such, were revered as 'pitiable yet courageous martyrs' (ibid., 119). Pregnancy, childbirth and motherhood were often physically excruciating, psychologically demanding and a risk to female health, and although some feminist commentators are critical of this period for presenting pregnant women 'as semi-invalid', these mothers were at least venerated and valued in their maternal role, albeit 'in an overwrought sentimental manner' (ibid., 145). It was around the mid-eighteenth century when a small number of socially privileged women who were concerned for their own safety during childbirth enlisted the medical assistance of, and reassurance from, male physicians that these early childbirth practices and the respect given to women who underwent them began to change (ibid., 120).

During the late 1930s and increasingly in the 1940s and 1950s 'a growing number of obstetricians, writers, and mothers' challenged the earlier view of childbirth as painful and debilitating, and embraced the experience 'as a wholly "normal" and "natural" event' (ibid., 119) that 'neither exacted a heavy physical toll nor necessitated a prolonged confinement' for the woman in question (ibid., 127). A number of childrearing experts from the postwar period were heard challenging the notion of maternal self-sacrifice of yesteryear in favour of presenting maternal fulfilment as the cornerstone of the pregnancy, birthing and mothering experience (ibid., 15). This change in maternal emphasis was due to the medicalisation of pregnancy and childbirth, which led to a dramatic reduction in maternal mortality rates.

Maternal mortality rates declined from '37.6 deaths per 10,000 births in 1940 to 8.3 deaths per 10,000 births in 1950' (ibid., 129), which coincided with a sharp rise in hospital births, from 55 per cent in 1940 to 88 per cent of total births in 1950 (ibid., 129–30). The sharp decline in both perinatal and maternal mortality rates is clearly linked to the move away from midwife care and home-births towards hospital-based deliveries and the medical regulation, supervision and professional management of pregnancy and childbirth (Miller 2005, 50). Postwar commentators suggested that 'the progressive "modern" way of giving birth was to divorce oneself from outdated servitude to biology by giving birth in hospital under total anaesthesia' (Davis-Floyd and Sargent cited in Miller 2005, 50). Thus, in less than a generation, pregnancy and childbirth had shifted from a painful and life-threatening ordeal to a safe and controlled experience to be embraced by mothers and the medical profession alike. By the mid 1970s 'virtually all babies in the United Kingdom and America were born in hospital', and by 2003 98 and 99 per cent of women in these respective countries gave birth in hospital (Miller 2005, 49, 50). This shift was so dramatic that 'the general sentiment, expressed in both medical journals and the popular press, was that modern medicine had finally conquered the age-old problem of childbed suffering and death' (Plant 2010, 130). Women of the period were said to have 'embraced the notion that childbirth – whether medicated or natural – could be viewed as predictable and even satisfying rather than dangerous and incapacitating' (ibid., 145). The 'development of confidence in our children's healthy survival is now so much the foundation on which the ideas and customs of the western world are built that we tend to take it for granted' (Dally 1982, 26). Contemporary labour and delivery 'has been made so safe that we tend to forget that it is potentially dangerous' (ibid., 39), and yet such maternal security seems to have come at a price, and that price is the ways in which society views and judges the birthing mother, and in many cases finds her wanting.

Postwar improvements in maternal health were seen to repudiate the notion of maternal suffering that was previously bound up with the ordeal of pregnancy, childbirth and mothering, and as such, women were no longer looked on with reverence or respect for their maternal role. Indeed, 'as the maternal death rate declined and anaesthesia became more widely available, the association between childbearing and self-sacrifice grew more tenuous, and claims to maternal authority premised on pain and suffering lost credibility' (Plant 2010, 144). Those women who experienced anything more than slight 'discomfort' during pregnancy and labour 'received little validation' and were challenged socially, scientifically and psychologically (ibid., 145). Alternatively, those women who blossomed during pregnancy and breezed through delivery were viewed and valued as the epitome of maternal femininity (ibid., 145). The postwar period denigrated rather than validated maternal suffering, and praised those women who made pregnancy and childbirth look effortless, and as such, it became 'difficult to acknowledge and accommodate the full range of birthing women's experiences' (ibid., 145).

Childbirth is officially understood as a 'medical event', and as such, medical institutions have gained a near 'monopoly' over pregnancy and hospitalised childbirth (Cosslett 1994, 4). Hospital births have been said to transform 'the unpredictable and uncontrollable natural process of birth into a relatively predictable and controllable technological phenomenon that reinforces American society's most fundamental beliefs about the superiority of technology over nature' (Davis-Floyd 1992, 2). The 'development of new technologies around reproduction and childbearing has further reinforced claims' to support the medicalisation of pregnancy and childbirth (Miller 2005, 52). Moreover, 'new reproductive technologies [...] are subtly altering women's lives by making conception, gestation, and birth something that predominately male authorities increasingly monitor, examine, and control' (Woliver 1995, 346). At the same time that pregnancy and childbirth have become medicalised, they have also become masculinized, and not only do male doctors dominate the delivery room, but they bring with them 'the increased use of instruments [...] and consequentially increased intervention' (Cosslett 1994, 32). With this in mind, the ideal birthing mother is 'one who believes in science, relies on technology, recognizes her inferiority [...] and so at some level accepts the principles of patriarchy' (Davis-Floyd 1992, 152–3). And although one might question a woman's acceptance of these principals, it is worth remembering that maternal appropriateness is equated with safety, security and well-being, and in this way, compliance with the medical model can appear not only appealing, but seductive (Miller 2005, 51).

Medical intervention may on occasion be unwarranted or unnecessary, but it is 'almost always intended to ensure the safety of both the mother and unborn child' (Arnold 2003, 6). Indeed, pregnant women in Britain and America 'go into labour with an almost 100 percent statistical certainty that both they and their child will survive. This is the first time this has been true in human history and is in large part due to medical intervention' (ibid., 6). However, even though recent technological interventions have been proven to decrease perinatal and maternal mortality rates, some feminists argue that hospital births and medical intervention is merely an extension of the 'patriarchy, male dominance and control over women's bodies' that is said to dominate the contemporary landscape (Miller 2005, 50). Tess Cosslett makes this point when she tells us that the 'hospital birth provides a symbol of women's oppression [...] It is a blatant physical enactment, a concentration and focusing, of forces that are better concealed in other social situations' (Cosslett 1994, 59–60). Adrienne Rich echoes this when she notes that the image of the drugged, sheeted and strapped-down birthing woman lying on her back with her legs in stirrups – as is routine in the medicalised version of childbirth – is a scene of ritualised humiliation that speaks for the wider patriarchal oppression and masculine coercion of women in society (Rich 1977, 170–1). Moreover, we are informed that the practice of caesarean section is 'presented as evidence of the technology and skill of the surgeon in question' while offering complete male control of the passive and thus coercive female body (O'Reilly and Porter 2005, 10). Theresa Morris and Katherine McInerney support this thesis when they tell us that 'birth by Caesarean section is the ultimate way to control the bodies of women during birth' (Morris and McInerney 2010, 135).

The medicalisation and hospitalisation of childbirth 'has been achieved at considerable emotional cost' (Dally 1982, 39) because many mothers 'experience the "factory belt" system and the clinical and scientific atmosphere that accompanies it as dehumanizing' (ibid., 39). Sheila Kitzinger tells us that 'what parents learn in childbirth classes does not prepare them adequately to deal with the highly medicalized environment and crisis atmosphere in the hospital' (Kitzinger cited in Wolf 2002: 73). Likewise, Rayna Rapp suggests that 'reproductive medicine offers both benefits and burdens' (Rapp 1994, 204) because contemporary 'technologies are aimed at reducing maternal and infant mortality and helping assure normal, healthy outcomes. At the same time, however, it controls conditions of pregnancy, birth, and parenting in ways that scientize our most fundamental experiences' (ibid., 205). The concern is that by adhering to what is deemed a safe, secure and controlled birthing experience, we are also being removed from, and thus alienated by, that selfsame process. Women are 'robbed of their individuality' when they become mothers in the hospital environment; each pregnant woman wears the same gown in the same bed, eating the same food, looking at the same plastic cot, and as such, they become 'generic' maternal figures without voice or identity (Cosslett 1994, 60). The fact that hospital births insist on separating the newborn from its mother immediately after it has been born in order to be 'washed, weighed, wrapped, given shots and eye drops' goes further to create anxiety and apprehension at the medicalisation of the birthing process (Miner 1996, 10).

Although antenatal monitoring and hospitalised childbirth has reduced perinatal and maternal mortality rates, the medicalisation of maternal care in the contemporary period is in question. The number of inductions for non-medical reasons has increased dramatically since the 1970s (Cosslett 1994, 50) and the numbers of caesarean sections is rising year on year with no evidence of improved outcomes for either the mother or baby (Beech 2004). Although less than 10 per cent of pregnant women need a caesarean section on medical grounds, be it for the health of mother or baby, the number of women choosing or receiving this procedure is far greater than that figure (ibid.). During the mid 1980s, the number of caesarean sections was over 30 per cent and growing in the United States, and approaching 18 per cent in Britain. Since that time, the number of women needing a caesarean section has remained at 10 per cent, but the number having the operation continues to grow (ibid.): 'In the UK, the rate is now 23 per cent, but many hospitals have rates approaching 30 per cent. If you book into the Portland private maternity hospital, almost 90 per cent of their patients emerge with a scarred uterus' (ibid.). In short, '140,000 women a year undergo caesarean sections [and] 75,000 women a year are having unnecessary major surgery' (ibid.).

A caesarean section constitutes major abdominal surgery, involving one incision through the abdominal wall and another around the uterus. As a surgical procedure, it carries a number of medical risks associated with anaesthesia and infection, and demands a lengthy period of convalescence. Suzanne Arms makes this point when she tells us that the risks associated with the operation 'are the same as those of any major surgery: unexpected adverse reaction to the anesthesia or other drugs used, uncontrollable hemorrhage [...]

or infection that does not respond to treatment [as well as] risk of an injury to other organs such as the bladder [*sic*]' (Arms cited in Wolf 2002, 149–50). Moreover, the 'long-term dangers of Cesarean are adhesions in the scar tissue that can cause chronic pain, bowl obstruction, infertility or miscarriage; and placenta acreta [...] in the next pregnancy' (ibid., 149–50) With such risks in mind, the decision to have the operation should not be taken lightly by mothers or the medical profession. And yet although one might question a mother's desire to have a caesarean section, we can perhaps understand their appeal to the medical profession. After all, private obstetricians practicing in America currently 'earn far more for performing Caesareans than for attending vaginal births, and hospitals bring in more income that way as well' (Wolf 2002, 151). Naomi Wolf tells us that if 'unnecessary Caesareans were avoided, American hospitals would lose *$1.1* billion in revenue a year. Cutting the Caesarean rate back to 5 per cent of all births – the rate in some European countries today, and just under that in the United States before the boom – would wipe out *$175* million a year in personal income for obstetricians alone, for whom the Caesarean section boom means shorter hours at increased pay' (ibid., 151–2; italics in original).

Although childbirth has become increasingly medicalised and thus masculinised in recent decades, a non-interventionist and more natural childbirth movement emerged in Britain during the 1930s, developed in America during the 1940s and is popular with a small but growing number of mothers in the present day. The 'natural' approach can be defined as those 'birthing technique[s] in which women chose to forgo anesthetics (or rely only [on] drugs that did not dramatically dull consciousness) in order to experience the thrill of childbirth' (Plant 2010, 136). Grantly Dick-Read is regarded as the founding father of the natural childcare movement, and his bestselling book *Childbirth Without Fear* (1944) told women that labour was a natural and normal function of the female body and that the fear and pain associated with childbirth 'could be eliminated by inducing the right state of mind in a birthing woman' (Dick-Read cited in Cosslett 1994, 9). Since that time, Sheila Kitzinger has foregrounded the female and feminine view of childbirth in her pioneering volume, *The Experience of Childbirth* (1962). The book speaks to pregnant women from the point of view of the experienced mother, teacher and confidante, and although the work does include medical expertise, Kitzinger is not writing as a qualified obstetrician. The point here is that while hospitalised childbirth is seen to reduce the pregnant woman to an objectified body in need of masculinised and medicalised interventions, the more natural approach seeks to 'reclaim natural childbirth for a female-centred approach, which can empower women against institutionalised medicine and its mostly male practitioners' (Cosslett 1994, 15). The natural childbirth movement seeks to challenge the masculinist view of childbirth that values the expertise of the health professional over and above a childbearing woman's knowledge of her own body. As such, this particular approach can be seen to speak to two different and seemingly oppositional groups of women: traditionally feminine women who want to recover an essential and innate maternal subjectivity, and feminists who want to challenge patriarchal power in the hospitalised birth (ibid., 35).

Although it is necessary to understand the developments in both the growing natural childbirth movement and the dominant hospitalisation of childbirth, what these narratives do not account for is the ways in which birthing women experience these medicalised, masculinised or other conditions. It is important to look at extant literature from within the field of feminist, motherhood and women's studies that addresses female voices as they relate to their pregnancy and labour experiences.

Women's Voices and the Childbirth Experience

In Ann Oakley's seminal work with new mothers, we are told that 'less than half the mothers said they enjoyed the experience of having a baby in hospital [and] more than a third felt that feelings about the management of the birth in some way overflowed into their relationship with the baby' (Oakley 1979, 296). If we are to understand that the birthing experience can have a positive or negative effect on a mother's relationship with her baby then it is crucially important that women understand and can make informed choices about the experience. After all, in some cases it is not so much the painful reality of childbirth or the medicalised environment that cause upset, discomfort or anxiety for women, but the lack of relevant and real birthing knowledge that creates the problem.

Prior to the actual birth of their baby, most women tend to see natural childbirth as the most positive delivery for both mother and baby because they assume that it allows the new mother to be able to bond and breastfeed with baby immediately and to be fully conscious of the life-changing experience as it happens. This is perhaps understandable when helpful manuals on childbirth only hint at the pain of delivery, referring to the 'increasing discomfort' (Eisenberg 1996, 293) of contractions during the active phase of labour and the 'exhausting and demanding' (ibid., 297) nature of the transition stage. Susan Maushart makes the point that although contemporary discourses on childbirth are anatomically explicit, they are less clear about the subject of pain in delivery. She makes the point that 'a woman could read all the definitive popular texts, conscientiously attend her prenatal classes and listen with minute attention to her obstetrician's every word, and still come away with the impression that having a baby won't hurt much, or at least not terribly much' (Maushart 1999, 91–2). With this in mind, those women who were keen to have a more natural childbirth experience tend to go on to request pain relief in some form, or require further medical assistance when faced with the painful reality of childbirth. The point here is simply that 'normal childbirth is excruciatingly, outrageously painful' and yet women are being asked to prepare birth plans under the impression that it is anything but (ibid., 92).

According to both mothers and the medical profession, the definition of a successful – or rather, 'good' – birth is one that is under control, be that control imposed externally by way of medical interventions or internally through controlled breathing (ibid., 79). All mothers visualise a 'good' birth and birth plans are written with this level of control in mind. However, although all pregnant women and future mothers visualise a 'good' birth, the reality is that most women will have – and none will expect – a 'bad' birth that is out of control and refusing to progress according to plan (ibid., 79). Abby Arnold makes this point when she tells us that some women do experience a controlled, controllable and bearable 'good' birth experience, whereby the waters break, the woman is taken to her chosen place of birth, labour pains are intense but manageable and, with the help of a loving partner, breathing exercises, back massages, ice chips and the picture of her new baby in her mind, she feels an overwhelming sense of power and empowerment as she gives birth, bonding on eye contact with her newborn. In this narrative, everyone cries at the power and joy of the birthing experience, the baby is placed onto the mother and immediately feeds (Arnold 2003, 5). However, while we are told that labour and delivery does follow this narrative on occasion, for the vast majority of women this experience is a fiction that goes some way towards tarnishing their own birth experiences. The painful reality of labour is overwhelming and unimaginable, and nothing in our lives prepares us for that pain. For many women, breathing exercises, back massages, ice chips or the image of their unborn child do little to numb the ordeal (ibid.).

Arnold is candid about her own birthing experience as it is seen against the rosy hued narratives of natural childbirth. She refers to 'the full force of active labor' as 'living in […] hell', and although she was encouraged to visualise her baby to get her through the pain until the anaesthesiologist arrived to deliver her epidural, she roared 'fuck the baby' because an 'unknown baby was no match for the contractions of labor' (ibid., 5). What is interesting here is that the nurse who helped deliver her baby later told her that her seemingly insensitive ferocious outburst 'was a mild statement compared to what she'd heard many other women say' (ibid., 5). And yet, it seems as if medical advice, childbirth manuals and the appropriate codes and conventions surrounding birthing narratives choose not to enlighten women about the ordeal of childbirth, instead focusing on the importance of what is essentially an impossible, improbable and unobtainable 'good' birth experience. Arnold goes on to remind us that the 'image of the labouring mother maintaining her power and control, where the pain remains manageable and support surrounds her like a warm bath, where medical intervention is solely devoted to enhancing the mother's birth experience, where the birth plan works and breast feeding is easy and mutually enjoyable, is held out to be the ideal, what all women should not only strive for but naturally, automatically want' (ibid., 6). Mothers are told that they should 'take responsibility for orchestrating' this version of the birth experience (Sears 2003, 5), and yet because many women are choosing what is tantamount to an improbable childbirth on the back of unrealistic knowledge and little relevant first-hand information concerning pregnancy and labour, these same women often feel deluded, disappointed or disheartened about the reality of the experience, which as we have been told can have implications for maternal bonding.

Although women can to some small extent determine their midwife and birthing partner, birthing venue and perhaps prepare themselves by taking breathing classes and learning about the stages of labour, 'when labor starts, the woman's intellect is her least valuable or accessible resource. Labor controls the woman, the woman does not control the labor' (Arnold 2003, 6). We find that 'the disjunction between our expectations of control and performance' (ibid., 6) and the reality of childbirth is one of the most frightening parts of the birthing ordeal (ibid., 6), which 'leads many new mothers to feel anger [and] shame [...] after the birth of their baby' (ibid., 6). Extant research on the childbirth experience tells us that a woman attending prenatal classes has 'no impact [...] on women's experience of pain, use of pain relief, extent of interventions, or level of satisfaction and emotional well-being' (Lumley and Brown cited in Maushart 1999, 75). Indeed, the most careful, considered and conscientious of mothers might be seen to be the most 'battle scarred, bewildered, and betrayed' by the reality of the childbirth experience (Maushart 1999, 64). Tina Miller discovered that the 'experience of giving birth [...] usually leads women to reflect that their lived experiences are different from their expectations and to question their "expert" preparation' (Miller 2005, 61). One woman tells us that 'now I just recount it, I say that it was awful and that I'm disillusioned, but *then* – a couple of days afterwards – I felt I'd been *tricked*, actually *tricked*, by the health visitor, by the books I'd read' (Oakley 1979, 109; italics in original). With such voices in mind, it has been suggested that 'the illusion that childbirth is an experience that women can shape and control is just that – an illusion' (Maushart 1999, 91).

In her work on pregnancy and new motherhood Naomi Wolf writes about her own birth experience and tells us that although she initially thought that her traumatic birthing story was a unique and isolated narrative, she soon realised this was not the case. Wolf tells us that 'I heard comparable ordinary traumas among many women I talked to – what I have come to call "ordinary bad births"' (Wolf 2002, 122). Women tend to feel confused, frustrated and angry at the differences between the 'good' birthing narrative and their own experiences, and this friction between rose-hued fiction and the darker reality carries through to their experiences of first seeing their new baby. Social norms and mores demand that women talk of the blissful moment of recognition when they first view and are allowed to hold their baby. Ann Oakley reminds us that 'holding the baby for the first time has for so long been the light at the end of the seemingly endless tunnel of pregnancy: the mental image that has sustained the mother through all sorts of trials and tribulations. It is this moment that symbolises the achievement of motherhood. The birth is over: mother and baby are born' (Oakley 1979, 115). However, rather than adhere to this emotional scene, Oakley seeks to debunk what she sees as another childbirthing cliché because 70 per cent of her informants confessed that they were 'not interested' on first holding their new baby (ibid., 117). Like their experiences of pregnancy, many women sense a discord between the imagined moment of holding their new child and the reality of that moment (ibid., 115).

Rather than chide or condemn these women for not conforming to appropriate maternal codes or mothering practices, Oakley goes on to discuss the understandable, and yet little-acknowledged, role of postnatal depression in such narratives. After all, when these women say that they are not interested in holding their newborn babies, what many of them are signalling 'is a deep-rooted anxiety state, expressing terror and panic, devotion [...]despair [and] helplessness' when faced with the reality of looking after a wholly dependent baby (ibid., 143). Oakley goes as far as to say that those women who do not experience such short-term postnatal depression should be looked on curiously and that we should perhaps 'express surprise at easy satisfaction with the maternal role (the experience of the minority) rather than at anxious despair (the fate of the majority)' (ibid., 143). Miller echoes this point when she tells us that the 'conflicting and sometimes overwhelming feelings of love, guilt, exhaustion, joy and fear are not uncommon experiences in the early weeks and months of becoming a mother. But they need to be understood, and made sense of, recognised and accepted as *normal* responses to early mothering experiences and motherhood' (Miller 2005, 61–2; italics in original).

The 'good' birth plan rarely matches up with the 'bad' birth experience, and as such, women are judging themselves, and other women, in relation to their childbirth ordeals. Rather than share their unrealistic plans or realistic stories to help inform other women about the painful reality of labour, we find that women uphold the 'good' mother myth from the outset, making sure that their version of events speaks of an informed, controlled and thus appropriate childbirth experience. Those mothers who silence themselves and present themselves in line with the ideology of the 'good' mother are helping to perpetuate and reproduce the very myth that they struggle to relate to. Miller makes this point when she tells us that 'presenting a self as a responsible mother involves self-governance around what can and cannot be voiced' (ibid., 89).

Although there exists a wealth of medical advice, celebrity pregnancy manuals, mothering websites and antenatal classes available to contemporary women, there continues to be a sense that women are unprepared for the reality of pregnancy, labour and the experience of seeing their new baby. Therefore, it becomes crucial to look at the ways in which pregnancy and childbirth are portrayed in reality television and the ways in which programmes such as *One Born Every Minute UK* can help, or otherwise, to prepare women for the experience of childbirth. After all, 'these media representations are likely the only opportunity most women have to watch an actual birth' (Morris and McInerney 2010, 134). Extant literature in the field of television studies tells us that women tend to watch these shows precisely to 'learn about childbirth', and as such, it is important that we understand the ways in which such popular texts construct, circulate and narrate the childbirth experience (ibid., 134).

Reality pregnancy and childbirth programmes are targeted at and watched by a young female audience. Indeed, a recent survey revealed 'that 68 percent of pregnant women in the United States watch reality-based programs on pregnancy and birth regularly [...] and of women who watch these shows, 72 percent of women pregnant for the first time and 34 percent of women who have been pregnant at least once before indicated that the shows "help me understand what it would be like to give birth"' (ibid., 134). Perhaps most importantly however is the understanding that while two-thirds of 'all pregnant women watch these reality shows' only one quarter 'of these women go to child-birth classes' (Elson, 2009). In short, these programmes are being asked to speak to and thus may be seen to be accountable for young women's expectations of labour and childbirth.

A Baby Story: The Cosy Reality of Pregnancy and Childbirth Television

A Baby Story is the popular and long-running daytime reality show depicting a carefully edited version of pregnancy and childbirth for the 18-to-34-year-old female demographic (Maher 2004, 197). The programme is marketed as 'Life Unscripted' by the TLC network, formerly the Learning Channel, and it is currently part of 'the most successful cable programming line-up on American daytime television' to date (Stephens 2004, 191). So successful are its ratings that even the highbrow British film magazine *Sight and Sound* has commented on the 'sensational' success of the show within its target demographic (cited in Stephens 2004, 191).

The programme is filmed, edited and narrated in such a way as to encourage audiences to believe that they are watching a home video of an everyday, ordinary married couple expecting a child. Audiences are asked to follow husband and wife as they 'review their relationship, their other children, and their decision to have this child [and] complete a couple or family activity preparing for the birth' (Stephens 2004, 202). Audiences are thus invested in the couple, their pregnancy and their birth story as we go on to watch as 'labour begins or is induced, the baby is born, and the programme concludes with the couple holding their (always) healthy child and discussing the joy that they've experienced in the days or weeks that have elapsed since the birth' (ibid., 202). The birth itself is always viewed in a medium shot of the hospital room and the camera maintains this respectful, critical distance.

Although the programme seeks to emphasise the normalcy of the couple involved, and the mundane nature of shopping for baby apparel, the show is clearly and consciously 'constructed around a precise format that culminates in a clichéd fairy-tale ending' for a white middle-class married couple who give birth to a healthy baby amidst loving looks, maternal bonding and consumer spending (ibid., 195). Indeed, the programme could and perhaps should be challenged for overlooking the 'complexities of gender, race and class in favour of a fantasy vision of some mythic past where gender norms were absolute, the nuclear family serenely solved individual and social ills, and consumption is the ultimate normalising rite' (ibid., 193). *A Baby Story* adheres to this same formula day after day, week after week, year after year, with interchangeable white middle-class married couples, interchangeable demonstrations of maternal bonding and interchangeable depictions of consumer spending, and as such, the sheer force of this routine might be said to slowly convince women in the audience that one prepares for childbirth by shopping for the unborn child, that all mothers are passive and uncomplaining and that all babies are not only perfectly healthy but are wanted by married middle-class parents (ibid., 203). Rebecca Stephens makes this point when she comments that 'the shows' sub-textual lullaby is that if we submit to the formula [...] we too can live in an Edenic world where every child is wanted and nostalgic 1950s family values (that only ever existing in our earlier TV dreams [...]) really will come true' (ibid., 207). Likewise, Jennifer Maher makes the point that part of the selection and editing process excludes those 'couples who fight, divorce, or are in any way ambivalent about or less than fully committed to parenthood' (Maher 2004, 203). She continues that 'there are no ambivalent parents here, just loving heterosexual couples with supportive families, money to spend on child-rearing accessories aplenty, and the apparent psychological preparedness to have their lives change with the new arrival' (ibid., 207).

A Baby Story claims 'to represent a range of births' (Morris and McInerney 2010, 135), and yet the show can be seen to depict a vast number of carefully chosen and heavily edited birthing experiences that ignore the birthing realities of single mothers, working-class parents, non-white couples, lesbian mothers, adoption or surrogacy. And although the programme routinely depicts stories of infertility, these 'stories are about heterosexual couples giving *biological* birth, regardless of the technologies that made that birth possible', and the couples in question do not deviate from those white, middle-class examples seen elsewhere in the show (Stephens 2004, 206; italics in original). The programme lacks diversity in its representations of birthing women, in relation to their economic status, marital situation and sexual preference, and as such, it fails to 'give women an accurate portrayal of how women typically experience birth in the United States' and, perhaps more worryingly, misrepresents 'evidence-based maternity practices' (Morris and McInerney 2010, 134). The show cannot be said to present the reality of childbirth for those women who are watching in an attempt to garner information about late pregnancy and labour in preparation for their own delivery. Rather, *A Baby Story* conforms to the 'good' childbirthing myth, which in turn prevents women from understanding the painful truth of childbirth, which goes some way towards creating disharmony between the image and reality of their own birth experiences.

Although audiences might expect and indeed find pleasure in the ways in which birth narratives are chosen and edited for the programme, it is perhaps surprising to find that a show that is marketed as 'Life Unscripted' is on occasion not only heavily edited but deliberately staged. One of the midwives involved in the show tells of an occasion where the film crew arrived too late at the hospital for the birth of a baby, but rather than look to a different couple for the show, they merely asked the woman to re-enact her delivery. The 'film crew had the new mother simulate the birth of the baby, lying flat on her back with the midwife poised at the bottom of the bed' (ibid., 140). Although the fact that the film crew asked the new mother to re-enact the delivery is perhaps shocking, the fact that she agreed to is even more so, and the fact that she was asked to perform the delivery on her back even though she had herself actually given birth to her baby in a squatting position is disturbing in relation to the programme's public commitment to the reality of the birthing experience.

Although one must assume that this particular new mother was compliant with her performance of childbirth, the programme is rarely seen to give control to pregnant and birthing mothers. Rather, women tend to be treated like young children; they are often blamed for the problems that occur in pregnancy and birth, and they are often spoken about as if they are not physically or mentally present (ibid., 136). The birth plan of the mother is often ignored or overlooked, especially when it demands a more natural and thus less interventionalist approach, and women are seldom shown taking control of their birth experience by pushing without professional instruction (ibid., 136). Women are encouraged to be quiet and compliant during the pushing stage of labour, and it is not unusual to hear a physician tell a birthing mother to 'have a baby in a nice *civilized* way [...] No screaming. No yelling' (ibid., 136; italics in original).

Theresa Morris and Katherine McInerney summarise the format of *A Baby Story* when they say that the programme portrays 'women as powerless, physicians in control, and technology as the saving grace for women's imperfect bodies' (ibid., 140). Moreover, even though medical interventions demand a woman's informed consent, the fact that women are seldom shown receiving such information or signing such forms gives the impression that the birthing mothers in the programme 'had no say in whether they would undergo interventions or not' (ibid., 136–7). *A Baby Story* encourages the medicalised and masculinised view of childbirth as the norm, and suggests that the female body is 'incapable of birthing a baby without medical intervention' (ibid., 134). The programme routinely depicts a number of medical interventions, including electronic foetal monitoring, inductions, augmentation, IV fluids for hydration, breaking the waters, anaesthesia and caesarean births, and it asks us to view such interventions as 'normal' procedures. These practices are not questioned by medical staff, the birthing mother or family members; rather, they seem to be presented as a natural part of childbirth (ibid., 137). In order to further direct audience readings, the voice-over narration often reminds us about the positive results of such medical interventions. We are told that the 'past ten years have brought dramatic improvements in obstetrics. Doctors now have an increased ability to manage the onset of labour and delivery. As a result inductions of labour happen more systematically with more successful outcomes' (ibid., 137). Success indeed. Extant literature on the show in question makes the point that although caesarean deliveries are common, both in the programme and contemporary society, the 'discussion of risks of caesarean surgery to women was not only largely absent in these episodes, but sometimes even misrepresented' (ibid., 138).

There are few examples of birthing experiences that demand no medical interventions, little acknowledgement of a woman's choice to have a vaginal birth after a previous caesarean and little evidence of a woman planning a vaginal breech delivery (ibid., 138). On the rare occasion where a birthing experience deviates from the medicalised, interventionist norm of the programme, 'these births were [...] marginalized by being presented in episodes titled "Alternative Practitioners", "Alternative Birth", "Birth Centers", and

"Unexpected Deliveries", making them seem like the "other" way to give birth' (ibid., 139). Vicki Elson makes this point in her recent documentary, when she tells us that childbirth is routinely medicalised in contemporary popular media culture, and 'those that were not medicalized were marginalized or presented as exotic' (Elson cited in Morris and McInerney 2010, 139). Furthermore, 'because only 5.7 percent of births in these episodes took place outside the hospital, the odds of a woman seeing one of these births on the shows were slim' (Morris and McInerney 2010, 139). These programmes present childbirth as painful, and presents pain medication 'as the only effective way to deal with it' (ibid., 137). Wolf makes the point that the 'pain of childbirth without an epidural was clearly unendurable, and modern drug intervention was the only humane solution' (Wolf 2002, 75). Indeed, the experience of labour is portrayed as 'easy and fun with pain medication' (Morris and McInerney 2010, 137). And for those women who chose to have a more natural and non-interventionalist birth, they 'were often represented not only as suffering through labor, but also as being "out of control" [and] hysterical' and thus not in line with the appropriate medicalised and masculinised 'good' birth experience (ibid., 137–8).

However, irrespective of the ways in which these women give birth, the outcome is always a healthy, happy mother and baby. Even when minor complications are revealed during the birthing process, they 'never resulted in actual serious injury to the women or babies but were used to create suspense and an ultimate happy ending' (ibid., 138). *A Baby Story* does not show or acknowledge foetal birth defects or stillbirth. Indeed, the commitment to health, harmony and happiness is expressed by the producers of the show when they tell us that 'negative outcomes [...] are not televised' (cited in Maher 2004, 203). In this way, the programme adheres to codes and conventions of existing pregnancy books and childcare magazines that fail to acknowledge or even allude to notions of death or disability for the child (Gregory 1994, 125).

Maternity Ward: The Difficult Reality of Pregnancy and Childbirth Television

While *A Baby Story* offers a rosy, cosy, romantic, safe and sanitised version of consumer-driven birthing experiences, *Maternity Ward* offers a starkly different, albeit no more realistic, version of pregnancy and the childbirth experience. *Maternity Ward* is a late-evening reality pregnancy and childbirth television programme that presents a rather more shocking and sensationalistic image of birthing mothers. Whereas *A Baby Story* is committed to the pregnancy and birthing experiences of happy, middle-class, white married couples who are devoted to their healthy new baby, *Maternity Ward* routinely focuses on poor, single, teenage, drug-addicted, homeless or non-white mothers who are seen to be indifferent and ambiguous rather than happy and contented at the prospect of motherhood.

Whereas *A Baby Story* asks audiences to spend time with, invest in and thus commit to the pregnant couples and their consumer-driven preparations for parenthood, *Maternity Ward* uses the pregnant bodies rather more interchangeably here. The programme presents pregnant women as 'generic bodies' that face 'difficult and life-threatening births', and because we are not encouraged to invest in a particular birthing story it allows the programme the opportunity to focus in close-up on a number of medical procedures ranging from caesarean sections to infant spinal surgery, without shying away from newborn disability and death (Maher 2004, 204–6). Jennifer Maher makes the point that if

> the viewers were introduced as in-depth to the parents of [*Maternity Ward*] as they are to the parents on *A Baby Story*, they'd learn some very uncomfortable things. They'd be forced to swallow the story of how a thirteen year old met the father of her child, what growing up in a series of foster homes means, or what an apartment available to someone working minimum wage with no health benefits looks like [...] So our information about the participants of [*Maternity Ward*] is kept at an emotional distance while their immediate medical circumstance produces enough sadness, worry, and tension to keep the viewer engaged: close enough for tsk-tsking, but far enough removed that no one gets too attached to folks who are, in one way or another, victims of a society gone haywire. (Ibid., 205)

Middle-class audiences are given only minimal and marginal details about the less privileged birthing mothers; rather, our attention is diverted to the personal details and familial minutia of the medical professionals who treat these often at risk 'generic' pregnant bodies. Each section of *Maternity Ward* begins with a drawn-out introduction to the medical team involved in the delivery, detailing their 'full names, personal histories, education, and reasons for choosing medicine' prior to seeing them working with the pregnant bodies (ibid., 205). While *A Baby Story* gives a voice, albeit heavily orchestrated and edited, to the birthing family, *Maternity Ward* gives that voice to the medical professionals, so we routinely see 'doctors ...talk about their own family bonds and how their surgical skill has everything to do with innate maternal or paternal feelings' (ibid., 205).

While *A Baby Story* finds its drama in the somewhat mundane experiences of birth and family life, *Maternity Ward* excels at exaggerating the fear, pain and danger of childbirth for dramatic effect. Programmes such as *Maternity Ward* present 'birth as unpredictable and potentially dangerous [and focus on] what can go wrong' during that ordeal (Morris and McInerney 2010, 135). They tend to show problems such as 'abnormal birth positions, hypertension and postpartum bleeding, labor and delivery triage, cervical cancer, bicornuate uterus, mothers in preterm labor, and diabetes [...] as though these problems are typical' (ibid., 135). Moreover, the programme 'gives the impression that simply being nonwhite and poor ups your chances for Down's syndrome, conjoined twins, congenital deformity of the limbs, spina bifada, and stillbirth' (Maher 2004, 205). Although it is easy to critique *A Baby Story* for its cosy, considered and carefully chosen childbirth narratives, this heavily dramatised version does little to present a more realistic image of contemporary childbirth. Programmes such as *Maternity Ward* exploit the potential fears and possible risks related to childbirth in order to find advertising revenue, because the dramatic action involved has proved popular with young middle-class audiences with disposable incomes (ibid., 205). However, rather than create fear, anxiety or tension in the middle-class female audience who are watching the show, the women being presented here are socially and sexually 'other', and as such, offer no sense of identification or investment for the woman in the audience.

One Born Every Minute UK

One Born Every Minute UK is a new British reality pregnancy and childbirth programme that focuses on the late-pregnancy and childbirth narratives of a number of women in a busy maternity unit at the Princess Anne Hospital in Southampton. *One Born Every Minute UK* regularly receives over 3 million viewers (MediaTel 2012), and the show has proved popular with critics, winning a British Academy Television Award for best documentary series in 2010. The series is referred to as 'fly-on-the-wall' in line with the documentary tradition because it is filmed by 40 small, fixed, remote-controlled cameras in the maternity unit, including in reception, the neonatal ward, the operating theatre and the birthing pool, which although not invisible are unobtrusive, as they seem to blend in with the other technological paraphernalia that adorns each room in the ward.

The programme features a number of birthing women each week, with sequences cutting between these deliveries. Much of the narrative focuses around the mundane activities and trivial conversations of soon-to-be mothers and their friends, families, partners and medical professionals as they wait for the final stages of labour. One young mother seems distressed that she 'forgot to put deodorant on this morning' (S2:E1), while another admits that she wished that she had 'shaved my legs' that day (S2:E11). This action is on occasion intercut with short talking heads with medical staff who discuss themes such as pain relief, the role of the midwife and the reality of neonatal care. There is the suggestion that the families seen in the programme are behaving normally, due to the fact that the birthing mother and their partners are involved in the birth of a child and have little time, space or energy to worry about performing for the cameras. Moreover, there is no voice-over narration or commentary; rather, details of a mother's name, age, number of existing children and partner are shown over the sequence being viewed, and as such, audiences are not being asked to form a particular idea or agenda about the birthing woman or her family. We are told that 'the subtle use of incidental music occasionally augments the action, but otherwise you're left to watch people going through this universal, at times mundane, yet utterly incredible experience, unprodded' (Raeside 2011). The *One Born Every Minute UK* website tells us that 'the show is focused on providing helpful insights into the realities of giving birth, especially in a hospital environment' (Channel 4 2011). This is not to say that the programme is without editing or cliff-hangers, but it is read by critical commentators and audiences alike as 'a refreshing take on a reality show portraying birth as the natural, wonderful, gut-wrenching experience it is' (Beda cited in Wilson 2010). Emine Saner applauds the programme for its 'educated and balanced view of childbirth', for its lack of shock tactics or sensationalism and for balancing difficult childbirths with the realistic 'tedium of mothers waiting for their waters to break' (Saner 2011).

Fixed Cameras, No Commentary and a More Balanced View of Childbirth

While *A Baby Story* is committed to the white, middle-class and happily married parent, and *Maternity Ward* presents an interchangeable number of poor, single, teenage, non-white mothers, *One Born Every Minute UK* offers a perhaps more believable balance between the two. The programme follows the white middle-class parents, but also the black lesbian mothers, childhood sweethearts now in their thirties, single mothers and teenage parents. And while *A Baby Story* refuses to allow anything but a healthy, happy ending for mother and baby, and *Maternity Ward* is committed to the more harrowing and brutal pain of dangerous deliveries and infant disability, *One Born Every Minute UK* can again be seen to present a more balanced view. After all, although the programme is committed to natural and 'normal' pregnancy and birthing narratives, the show does not shy away from birth stories that expose and explore the reality of IVF, multiple miscarriages and stillbirth. Indeed, the programme has been commended for its natural depiction of late pregnancy and childbirth by Sue Macdonald, the education manager of the Royal College of Midwives. Macdonald tells us that the programme gives an accurate portrayal of childbirth that can be both natural and in need of intervention. She goes on to say that the show can act as an educator for pregnant women because 'it does help women think about what it's going to be like and help them plan what they want for their birth' (Macdonald cited in Saner 2011).

Indeed, the role and representation of the midwife is of crucial importance in the programme, because irrespective of the social, sexual or economic status of the birthing mother, and irrespective of the woman's choice of birth plan, these predominantly female practitioners speak of respect, consideration and care for their patients. The head of midwifery at the Princess Anne Hospital tells us that 'I think that we have an incredibly privileged job – to be part of anybody's birth experience is just the best. I think if you ask any midwife, you never quite get over that miracle from one moment the mother being pregnant [...] to the moment that baby comes out [...] with a personality all its own the moment it's born, and the emotion in that room when the baby is born is just fantastic' (S1:E1). Likewise, the midwife coordinator is heard commenting that 'the midwife still holds the key to making it a special and memorable experience for the woman and her partner, it is a very powerful privilege [...] If you looked into any midwife's heart, you would see that what she really wants is to be able to help that woman and to empower her to give birth to a healthy baby' (S2:E7). In this same way, another midwife comments that 'in my training hospital we used to say that every patient in this house should be treated like an honoured guest [...] Florence Nightingale said that and I believe it – it is engraved upon my heart' (S2:E1).

It is the role of the midwife that distinguishes *One Born Every Minute UK* from its American predecessors. After all, the role of the midwife differs dramatically between Britain and North America, because 'while in the United States [...] midwives were hounded out of existence, in Britain they became state registered in 1902, and the amount of training required to practice as a midwife was steadily increased' (Cosslett 1994, 53–4). More recently the role of the midwife was enshrined in British government reports such as 'Changing Childbirth' (Department of Health 1993) and 'Maternity Matters' (Department of Health 2007). Therefore, although hospitalised childbirth continues to dominate the contemporary birthing agenda in both Britain and America, the midwife plays an important, significant and respected role in both the hospitalised and home birth experience in Britain, whereas the American birthing experience is dominated by male physicians who have specialised in obstetrics and gynaecology. Naomi Wolf tells us that American midwives 'have little power to influence what happens to delivering mothers in hospitals, officiating at only 10 per cent of hospital births – and even then only in a subordinate role' (Wolf 2002, 127).

That said, the role and responsibility of a team of caring professional midwives does not detract from the anxiety, fear and pain of childbirth, as demonstrated in the programme. First-time expectant mothers are routinely heard commenting on their fear of the unknown that is childbirth. While one comments that 'I'm scared of going into labour because I don't know what to expect' (S2:E3), another admits that 'the thought of being in excruciating pain is unbelievable, I am just terribly frightened by it' (S2:E5), while another tells her partner that it is the fear of losing control that 'absolutely petrifies me' (S2:E3). Even existing mothers who have had caesarean sections admit to this fear of the unknown in relation to a vaginal birth. For example, one mother says 'I don't know what it's like to do it properly, normally. I'm worried that I'm going to fail at it, it's one thing a woman's supposed to do and I won't be able to do it' (S1:E3). In this instance, fear of pain is less evident than a fear of failure, but both are understood as natural and expectant reactions that elicit sympathy and reassurance from medical staff.

These women go on to experience the reality of childbirth, and the vast majority of birthing mothers scream, cry or whimper at some point that they are unable to cope with the pain of the experience. One women says 'I can't – enough, enough, I can't do it anymore' (S1:E6); another comments that 'I can't do this anymore [...] I've had enough' (S1:E8); yet another is heard to say 'I want to have an epidural, I'm so scared, I can't do this [...] I am so frightened' (S2:E5); and another reacts to the pain by saying that 'I can't do it' (S2:E6). This experience continues as we hear one young woman say 'I can't do this' (S2:E7), another that 'I can't, it's so painful, I can't do it' (S2:E11) and another tells midwives to 'get him out – this is the worst experience of my life, its exhausting. Why didn't I get any pre-warning it was going to be so bad?' (S2:E7). A number of women are both crying out with pain while also apologising for these painful and panicked outbursts. One mother comments that 'I'm struggling, sorry, they are coming really really, really painful [*sic*]' (S1:E1), while another says that 'if I'm in proper established labour I want an epidural [...] Sorry, I've never had one before ... Sorry, I can't do this any longer' (S1:E1), and we hear a similar sentiment when one young mother cries that 'I don't want to have this baby anymore [...] As soon as I can I want the epidural [...] I can't do it, I'm not cut out for this [...] I really, really can't do this, I'm just not strong enough [...] I'm sorry' (S1:E2). The midwives are heard talking to camera about the reality of childbirth as a fearful and painful experience when they comment that 'labour, as the name says, is labour, and it is hard work and women only have one or two or three chances at it, so only two or three times in your life will you actually be pregnant and go through a labour and that still makes it a daunting and challenging time for you' (S2:E1). In short, childbirth is both frightening and painful, and although the programme does not shy away from the reality of this experience, it does not exaggerate these emotions for dramatic effect.

One Born Every Minute UK shows the medical staff in general and the midwives in particular to be committed to helping to actualise each birth plan, be it for a natural or more medicated birth experience. While some women are seen to forgo pain medication altogether, others choose to have a number of different pain-relief treatments. Although the medical team will not perform an intervention unless they have a specific reason to do so, the suggestion is, as one midwife says clearly, that 'what the lady says goes' (S1:E3). We are told by another that 'there are no hard and fast rules in this game – whatever is right at the time' (S2:E6), and audiences get a sense that these women are not judged or found wanting for their personal pain-relief decisions.

This response to pain relief is reassuring in a society which seems dominated by the notion that pain relief during childbirth is problematic for mother and baby. For example, in the bestselling *What to Expect When You're Expecting*, readers are told that

> if you feel you need some pain relief, don't be afraid to discuss it with your attendant. He or she may suggest waiting for 20 minutes or half an hour before actual administration – at which point you may have made so much progress that you won't need it, or you may have found renewed strength and no longer want it. (Eisenberg 1996, 294)

Abby Arnold makes the point that such discourses tell us that 'there is something to be afraid of in asking for pain relief […] That your attendant does not want you to have pain relief [and] that if you are strong you won't need it' (Arnold 2003, 6). However, while *What to Expect When You're Expecting* appears to suggest that asking for pain medication is a sign of weakness, *One Born Every Minute UK* seems to respect a woman's knowledge of her own body and legitimises her pain-relief decisions.

The programme routinely presents birthing women who although in pain and often scared are able to retain an element of control in the hospitalised environment, be it through the use of a birthing pool, breathing exercises or a more vocal performance. On one occasion when a midwife was seen trying to calm a scared and screaming woman, we hear the medical professional say that 'screaming is not going to make [the pain] any better' (S2:E1). However, the pregnant woman is not silenced and she makes it clear that the screaming does in fact 'make it feel better' (S2:E1). And although we are shown a number of midwives raising eyebrows at this particular instance of prolonged and vocal screaming, the mother admits, without shame or embarrassment, that 'I was very vocal; that helped me, and I would do it again. I don't care if people thought I was silly, they didn't feel the pain' (S2:E1). It has been suggested that asking birthing women to focus on their breathing techniques is popular in medicalised births because 'the method keeps the woman quiet by giving her a task to do, making being a "good" – uncomplaining, obedient, cooperative – patient the woman's primary goal' (Rothman 1982, 92). Wolf makes this point when she tells us that breathing techniques are 'used for institutional convenience, and to create docile patients, rather than to support more natural births' (Wolf 2002, 73). However, in this particular instance the new mother made it clear that being a 'good' patient was of less importance than following her natural vocal instincts. Moreover, the fact that the programme shows women viewing and signing their consent forms for caesarean sections, for example, goes further to give these women a semblance of informed agency and control over their childbirth experiences that is little seen elsewhere in the reality pregnancy and childbirth genre (S2:E10, S1:E8).

Although cultural commentators have acknowledged the ways in which *One Born Every Minute UK* offers a more natural, balanced and thus potentially realistic and authentic view of contemporary hospitalised childbirth practices and procedures, one might suggest that the programme should be applauded not merely for presenting the reality of 'normal' and 'healthy', albeit painful, labour, but also for acknowledging – and without dramatizing – issues such as infertility, lesbian mothering and the growing dependence on neonatal care units.

Revealing the Hidden Truths of Pregnancy and Childbirth

One Born Every Minute UK presents lesbian mothers who have conceived using donor insemination and heterosexual women who have used artificial insemination due to infertility, and at a time when other mainstream media outlets are ignoring, overlooking or offering misinformation about the reality of infertility, the inclusion of such childbirth narratives is meaningful. And although one might suggest that such narratives are merely another way to reinforce the patriarchal agenda, the stories being presented here speak less about medical intervention and more about caring both physically and emotionally for pregnant women who have, in several cases, undergone years of IVF treatment and several miscarriages before they deliver their baby.

Evidence suggests that undergoing IVF treatment is a physically grueling and emotionally agonising experience that often 'involves daily hormone injections and, depending on the reasons for infertility, surgery to retrieve eggs' (Menabawey 2010), and as such, it is significant that *One Born Every Minute UK* gives women a voice to talk about their experiences of assisted reproduction. One woman explains her growing pain at not being able to conceive naturally after four years of trying before having triplets through IVF (S2:E12). Another tells of a five-year struggle to become pregnant through IVF, but, after the birth of her baby, makes it clear that not only was the physical and emotional pain worth it, but that she would not hesitate to go through the experience again (S1:E4). Many women assume that when they decide to start a family then they will be able to do so naturally and quickly, without intervention. One woman makes this point when she tells us that 'I never thought I couldn't have children. Why would you think you couldn't have children? It's one of the most normal things' (S2:E12). However, 'conceiving a child is not like buying a new three-piece suite [because] demand and supply may not be easily equated' (Oakley 1979, 32). And although listening to women talk about their use of artificial insemination, the cycles of treatment that were unsuccessful and the tremendous burden that a successful pregnancy placed on them emotionally might make for uncomfortable or upsetting viewing, it is important that the programme in question acknowledge the reality of this pregnancy experience, not for dramatic narratives, but in order to inform and educate its female audience.

One Born Every Minute UK includes the birthing narratives of two lesbian couples: one where one partner has given birth to triplets (S1:E7) and another where both partners have at different times become pregnant through artificial donor insemination (S1:E8). Lesbian mothers came to public attention in the early 1970s when growing numbers of these women started to fight for custody of their children from earlier heterosexual marriages. Many of these women were facing custody challenges by former husbands, and as such, they tended to be 'constructed as being dangerous to their children because of their sexual orientation' (Ryan 2008, 36). However, there is a much more positive take of contemporary lesbian mothering, and many have suggested that lesbian mothers are 'exceptional parents' due to the fact that their children 'are the most considered and planned-for children on earth' (Martin cited in Esterberg 2008, 76). The visibility of lesbian mothers in the programme should not come as a surprise in and of itself; after all, statistics tend to show that one in ten women are lesbians and that 'between 20 and 30 percent of lesbians are mothers' (Arnup 1998, 59). Indeed, in both Britain and America, 'we are witnessing the early stages of a "gaby" boom, a situation wherein lesbian women [...] are opting into parenthood in increasing numbers' (Dunne 2000, 12).

What is fascinating here is the ways in which the medical staff treat the lesbian mothers – not merely with respect, compassion and patience, but as mothers. The midwives treat both the birth mother and the non-birth mother as mothers, and although this may not appear worthy of note, it becomes so if one is aware of the ways in which lesbian mothers tend to be spoken about in the wider society. Although the identity and language for the biological mother is fixed, the term used to identify the role of her partner is less clear; existing literature uses terms such as 'a "co-parent" [...] a "co-parent partner" [...] a "non-biological mother", a "non biological parent" [and] a "co-mother"' (Hequembourg and Farrell 1999, 542). The language used to describe a lesbian family structure becomes more complicated and confused when the members of a lesbian couple both give birth. And, according to Gillian Dunne's work on lesbian mothering, it is 'not unusual for both partners to have experienced biological motherhood as the result of donor insemination while in their relationship' (Dunne 2000, 21). The importance of language is significant if one considers that 'unlike the birth mother who has a biological claim to motherhood, the partner's claim to motherhood is socially constructed and depends on the validation of significant others: her partner, the children [and] her own kin' (Hequembourg and Farrell 1999, 542). Jane Bernstein and Laura Stephenson make the point that 'if you are not a "mommy" or a "daddy", you are unacknowledged in the public life of a child [...] At some point every parent wants to be recognized as the central figure in their child's world – by teachers, neighbours and, yes, total strangers' (Bernstein and Stephenson 1997, 12). Moreover, the non-biological mother has only recently been in a situation whereby she could legally legitimate her relationship to her child in Britain, and today lesbian 'comothers must still rely on the court's discretion in validating their claims to parenthood' in America (Hequembourg and Farrell 1999, 547). Second-parent adoption gives non-birth mothers 'tangible rights as a parent while [...] legitimat[ing] their relationship with their children. Subsequently, their parents often felt more willing to emotionally invest in their grandchildren' (ibid., 548). *One Born Every Minute UK* both acknowledges the role of the birth and non-birth lesbian mother and shows respect for the lived reality of that family unit, which is significant given the wider social and sexual context of the period.

The programme is open, honest and indeed candid about not only the emotional and physical ordeal of artificial insemination and lesbian mothering, but also the role and responsibility of the neonatal unit that cares for premature or otherwise-sick babies. And although staff tell us that 'no-one expects to turn up at our doors' (S1:E7), statistics remind us that one in every ten new 'babies will spend time being looked after by the staff of the neonatal unit', and that in many cases, the parents of these children 'must wait for weeks, sometimes months to find out when they can take their babies home' (S1:E7). Watching such small, vulnerable and weak babies in large plastic incubators with a number of drips, wires and monitors attached to their tiny frames is clearly painful for mothers, fathers and family members. And although the medical staff are trained to look after the physical needs of such babies, the programme makes it clear that these selfsame staff take the necessary time to support parents who are struggling with the reality of the situation.

The programme details not only the reality of working in this pressurised medical environment but also the ways in which new parents experience their time in the unit, and as such, audiences are able to witness a neonatal environment that is otherwise below the radar of contemporary media texts and maternal discourses. One paediatric doctor tells us that

> once the babies are delivered, that's usually the start of a very long process if they have been born a lot of weeks prematurely. They are very frail, they will need a lot of care until they are safe, ready and large enough to cope with the outside world and go home, and they will spend usually many weeks in the neonatal intensive care unit. (S2:E12)

Likewise, a neonatal nurse comments that 'a lot of babies are with us for the long haul, they are there for weeks and weeks [...] Some of the babies we have are pretty close to the edge sometimes – you know, not all babies make it out of there' (S1:E7). The medical staff clearly understand the pain, anguish and indeed the feelings of grief that overwhelm parents when their baby is rushed into the neonatal care unit. One neonatal consultant says that

> as a new mum, you want to hold your baby, touch your babies skin; you want to smell your baby, you want to feed your baby, and just do all of those things. But you have a plastic box between you and the baby in a space just surrounded by equipment, and it is noisy, there's bells and whistles and alarms going off all the time, and that can be quite overwhelming just from a sensory point of view. It's a really alien environment for most people. (S2:E12)

Parents say that they are fearful of and unprepared for the noise of the machines and that it is terrifying to try to hold their baby because of the sheer volume of wires that are attached to the newborns (S2:E12). Mothers admit that they are worried about changing the nappies on their baby, but also scared not to, just in case they are being judged by the medical staff for their lack of maternal engagement (S1:E7), and they confess that whilst they are grateful to medical staff for helping their babies, they are also sad, lonely and jealous as they watch other mothers with their babies and witness medical staff holding their own newborn (S1:E3).

One mother talks of spending the three months while her baby was in neonatal care waiting to hear that her vulnerable and 'fragile' baby had died, telling the medical team looking after her son that she does not want to extend his life artificially only for him to suffer further physical pain (S1:E7). Another mother tells us of how she apologises to her prematurely born daughter for the time that she is spending in the special-care unit, because 'I felt like I hadn't done my job, I didn't do what I was supposed to do. All I remember is apologising [...] because I felt like I had failed and it was very hard to come to terms with' (S1:E7). Indeed, the programme gives voice not only to those women who are currently watching their babies in neonatal care, but also to those who have lost their babies, and although these are upsetting and painful narratives, they are part of the childbirth experience, and as such, they should be acknowledged here.

Dramatic Action, Voice-Over Narration and Medicalised Childbirth in *One Born Every Minute USA*

One Born Every Minute USA, like its British predecessor, acknowledges the painful reality and unpredictability of childbirth, the social and sexual diversity of new mothers, and the role of artificial insemination and neonatal care. However, although the programme is ostensibly – as the title suggests – an American version of the British production, there are several differences between the two shows. Whereas the British title is seen to present a balanced and realistic view of childbirth, the American version seems more interested in generating soap opera-style narratives and dramatic action. While the British title rarely acknowledges the cameras, the American version routinely reminds us of their presence. While the British title views women waiting for hours and days for full labour with limited pain medication, the American version presents a much more interventionalist approach to childbirth. And while the British title seems to offer a believable, albeit edited, account of childbirth, the American version is peppered with recaps, cliff-hangers that flash forward to an upcoming labour and delivery, speeded-up sequences of staff movements, a heavy use of mood music and dramatic narration that foregrounds 'terrifying' (S1:E3), 'frightening' (S1:E4) and potentially 'fatal' (S1:E3) deliveries.

The British show begins with a voice-over that tells us that 'every minute of every hour of every day a baby is born in Britain. To find out what it feels like to bring life into the world, we put 40 cameras into a bustling maternity hospital, from the front desk to the operating theatre, from the birthing pool to neonatal, capturing new lives beginning and others changing forever', but no other voice-over narration exists in the programme (S1:E1). On the very rare occasion when information is needed in order to provide the relevant context for the viewing audience, a minimal intertitle appears. Alternatively, the American version is narrated by Hollywood actress Jamie Lee Curtis throughout, anchoring our reading of particular staff, new mothers and the wider family units. Narration such as 'ready or not, Riverside Hospital is always open for baby business' is neither informative, educational nor necessary; indeed, much of the commentary, be it concerning pregnant mothers or medical staff, is infantile, trite and clichéd. While the British version puts the mother's name, age and number of previous pregnancies on screen, the American version narrates such information using quippy commentaries such as 'Melissa has just checked in. She got a late start on her family and she is wasting no time – she is having her second baby in twelve months' (S1:E1). Moreover, the American programme ends by narrating the birth announcements of each couple. Although some audiences might find such narration useful, there is a sense that it encourages audiences to read, respond to and indeed rank some pregnancy and maternal practices as more or less acceptable than others.

Although there are clear differences in the choice of participants, the editing processes and the use of narration, the starkest distinctions between the two shows are less about stylistic or documentary conventions, and more about the labour and delivery practices that routinely take place on different sides of the Atlantic. The British version depicts a childbirth experience whereby most women attempt a natural delivery using gas and air, with some use of the epidural. Women are encouraged to stay active, move around and find a comfortable and workable position while waiting for their waters to break. The staff appear respectful of the birthing woman and her childbirth plans, and the midwives in particular deem it a privilege to work with these women. However, the American programme shows a rather different relationship between medical staff and the birthing woman. It is clear that labour and delivery nurses encourage the use of pain-relieving drugs and anaesthesia, irrespective of the birth plan of the woman in question. Naomi Wolf's writing appears relevant here, as the author quotes one independent midwife as saying that birth plans are 'not worth the paper' they are written on because 'nursing staff laugh at birth plans [...] They pass them around for entertainment [...] The joke is that you would believe that you have any power in the hospital to change the outcome' (Wolf 2002, 72). Wolf goes on to suggest that 'hospitals and obstetrical practices that deal with demanding clients [...] encourage couples to write such a plan, as it gives us a sense of consumer choice. We are not told outright that it is the hospital protocols that determine what will happen in the course of delivery, usually regardless of what the plan might say' (ibid., 72). Hospital protocol indeed. The vast majority of women are seen giving birth lying on their backs with their feet in stirrups, having had their waters broken and an epidural delivered.

While it is important for medical staff to appear accessible and approachable, some of the professionals depicted here appear over-familiar. There are jokes about female flatulence (S1:E4) and the use of a vasectomy (S1:E2), and when a nurse struggles to get a blood sample from an anxious mother she tells her that her veins 'suck' (S1:E2). When one birthing mother is scared about delivering a large baby, the professional advice here is 'well, you got to be careful about who you reproduce with – big daddy: big babies; that's what happens' (S1:E1). This is not to say that the medical staff are any less caring or capable in the American version of the show; indeed, many young nurses speak of the joy that comes from their work (S1:E4), but the relationship between mother and practitioner, and the tone used to speak to these new mothers, is starkly different. It is as if, as Tina Miller has suggested, the woman's awareness of her own body is regarded as less accurate or relevant when placed alongside biomedical ways of knowing (Miller 2005, 43). Indeed, the author has gone as far as to suggest that 'authoritative ways of knowing are hierarchical and have led to distinctions being made between those who are regarded as "expert" – the medical and health professionals, and those who are not – childbearing women' (ibid., 31). There is a sense that both programmes present a realistic, authentic and thus potentially educational view of childbirth in contemporary Britain and America, respectively, and that differences between birthing techniques and medical interventions speak about differences in birthing procedures rather than editing practices.

And yet, one thing that both shows have in common is the ways in which the new and expectant mothers seek to align themselves with the 'good' mother myth. While a number of partners and husbands appear ambiguous or ill at ease with the prospect of fatherhood, mothers are, without exception, overjoyed at their new maternal role, irrespective of their social, sexual or financial situations. In the British title one mother tells us that 'I do love being a mum – best thing I ever did, having those kids' (S2:E11), while yet another tells us that she felt 'instant love' on seeing her new baby (S2:E12). Similarly, a young new mother announces that 'I really love being a mum, [my daughter] has bought so much happiness [into my life]' (S2: E10). In this same way, the American version finds one mother announcing that motherhood 'is the most wonderful thing that has ever happened to me' (S1:E4), and anchors another birth by reminding us that although the mother's 'delivery was painful and terrifying [...] the result was a lifelong dream come true: a beautiful baby girl' (S1:E4).

Conclusion

This chapter has outlined the ways in which pregnancy and childbirth have become increasingly medicalised and thus masculinised in recent decades, and the ways in which many women struggle to adjust to the discord between their 'good' birth plan and the painful reality of their 'bad' birth experience. I have suggested that although early reality pregnancy and childbirth programming tended to present opposing extremes of the birth experience as either rosy and romantic or dangerous and debilitating, *One Born Every Minute UK* can be seen to offer a more realistic and thus potentially informative image of contemporary hospitalised childbirth. What is worth noting of course is that even though medical interventions have made pregnancy and childbirth safer for mother and baby, and in many cases medical advancements have created previously unexplored forms of reproduction, contemporary society still seems unwilling or unable to change existing childcare practices whereby women take sole responsibility for the physical, emotional and intellectual development of their children, in line with the 'good' mother myth.

Reality pregnancy and childbirth television has proved phenomenally popular with female audiences, and indeed programmes such as *One Born Every Minute UK* have garnered both critical and commercial success on both sides of the Atlantic. As such, we should not be surprised to find that reality television producers are looking to other pregnancy and birthing formats to find future audiences. However, we should be surprised to hear that Endemol, the makers of *Big Brother* (2000–), have launched the concept for a new reality pregnancy and childbirth programme entitled *Make Me A Mum*. The premise of the show is that 1,000 men vie for the chance to father a child. *Make Me A Mum* would whittle down candidates until two men are left, who would then compete against each other to father a child. The future mother will be asked to choose the man who she believes would make the better father – judged on personality and attractiveness – while another man will be chosen on the basis of genetic compatibility and sperm quality. The 'sperm race' would be filmed in order to see which of the two finalists reach the woman's egg first. And although the concept has been criticised and condemned by pro-life groups, ethicists, broadcasters and parliamentarians alike, such controversy does not necessarily mean that the programme will never make it to air.

Chapter 9
CONCLUSION

Media texts are, in the main, genre texts with predictable codes, conventions, features and norms, and television productions are no exception (Burton 2010, 27). Genre texts such as those interrogated here, be it soap opera, situation comedy or teen drama, all follow pre-existing patterns, known formulas and a safe framework in order to satisfy audience desires for predictability and security. That said, although such texts are grounded in a predictable repertoire of elements and pre-existing tropes, there is also room for what Steve Neale views as 'difference, variation and change' (Neale 2003, 171) in terms of the minutia of the characters, themes, settings, costumes, props, lighting, music, dialogue, visual style, plots and narratives (McQueen 1998, 27). In this way genres provide audience pleasure because they encourage viewers to both anticipate the 'horizons of expectations' (Jauss cited in Neale 2003, 171) and the predictable framework whilst awaiting unexpected twists on pre-existing codes and conventions. Graeme Burton makes this point when he tells us that audiences are 'brought to want to consume the text because they want to revisit the emotional turmoil of a battle scene or of a love affair [or, I would add, a common representation of motherhood and the maternal role]. They also give a kind of power to the reader, the power to predict some of the meanings that the text will propose' (Burton 2010, 31).

Some genres go in and out of favour with audiences while others merge, fluctuate and develop. In terms of television, soap operas and situation comedies have long proved popular with audiences on both sides of the Atlantic since transferring from commercial radio, new genres such as the dramedy have been seen to merge existing genre classifications while others such as celebrity reality programming develop out of earlier examples of a genre committed to camera surveillance and first-person observation. However, irrespective of the history or fluidity of television genres, much contemporary popular programming remains genre-based, seeking to guarantee viewers by way of 'exploitation and variation of commercially successful formulas' (Grant 2003, xv). And yet although genre texts are said to cater to the demands and expectations of the audience, these texts can also be seen to 'satisfy the market interests of media institutions' (Burton 2010, 27) in general and the market interests of the television industry in particular; after all, such texts provide a way of organising the expensive and volatile business of television production because the material is predictable and budgets are known. In short, genres help to minimise risk and 'predict expenditure' (Branston and Stafford 2010, 79) at a time when the number of broadcasting channels are growing and the demand for genre material increasing.

Extant literature on the notion of genre makes it clear that those routine codes, repetitive features and predictable norms that make up genre texts are recognised by industry, audience and advertisers alike. We are told that the 'classification of texts is not just the province of academic specialists, it is a fundamental aspect of the way texts of all kinds are understood' (Neale 2008, 3). That said, what may be less known or understood is the ideological function of such texts. Genre productions are understood as ideological texts due to the fact that they help to construct and circulate specific ideologies pertaining to the importance of heterosexuality, the institution of marriage and traditional gender roles that foreground the maternal role. And although much research exists to account for the hybridity, fluidity and relative flexibility of existing genre classifications (Turner 2008, 8–9), these texts continue to naturalise social, sexual and familial roles and 'endorse ideas about social, economic, and political power' (Burton 2010, 37).

With this in mind, representations of motherhood and motherwork have the power and scope to foreground culturally accepted familial relations and provide 'common sense' understandings about appropriate, inappropriate, acceptable and other maternal behaviours for a contemporary audience. As such, it is crucial that we examine those representations of motherhood and motherwork that dominate contemporary popular programming, and consider the ways in which these depictions relate to the wider social, sexual, political and economic context. And although little research exists to account for the myriad representations of motherhood, motherwork and the maternal role seen in contemporary television, this book has begun to explore, unmask and account for the ways in which motherhood is being constructed, circulated and interrogated in both fictional and factual programming, and the ways in which such representations can be understood in relation to the ideology of intensive mothering and the 'good' mother myth that is said to dominate the contemporary period.

The soap opera has long been associated with the problematic rather than perfect family unit (Modleski 2008, 32) and this is related to the fact that the genre has been historically linked to and continues to be watched by the working and lower-middle-class female audience (Geraghty 2005, 318). The ways in which this set of programmes presents an ostensibly self-serving rather than serene image of motherhood might speak to the reality of an audience who are struggling to uphold or maintain a romanticised image of the 'good' mother, be it due to social, sexual or economic forces, and it is this figure of maternal struggle and strength that continues to be a mainstay of the genre. The situation comedy has long been associated with a liberal feminist agenda, with issues such as divorce, abortion and infidelity being of crucial importance to the history of both British and American comedy texts (Rabinovitz 1995, 145). The genre is successful in presenting a potentially controversial stance on a range of social, sexual, familial and political issues due to its commitment to humour, comedy and narrative resolution. The ways in which the sitcom currently presents the working mother as a harried, hurried and chaotic figure must be understood as one more way in which the genre is both exploiting the reality of the social period while also containing the potential threat of that situation. The teen drama can be seen to borrow codes and conventions, although not the humble locations, of the long-running soap opera and situation comedy; after all, the genre has a clear commitment to the emotional reality of the teen experience and is keen to present the disharmony and dysfunction of the family unit (McQueen 1998, 58). Teen dramas in general and the glossy American productions in particular tend to demonise the mother of the piece as a toxic rather than taming influence on the younger generation (Feasey 2012). Indeed, mothers in these texts are not marginally failing to conform to the 'good' mother myth, or struggling to present themselves within the ideology of intensive motherhood, but something altogether more destructive. Although this might appeal to a sense of freedom and liberation for the young adult audience, the fact that fathers are not presented in this same way makes it clear that these programmes are less interested in challenging the adult agenda and more interested in interrogating the role and responsibilities of the mother figure here, in line with the soap opera and situation comedy genre. The dramedy appears committed to the representation of the family and the emotional commitment demanded of that unit. Irrespective of whether it takes a teen, single or married mother as its starting point, the genre demands that the viewer witness the physical and emotional efforts involved in maintaining a stable family. This is not to say that mothers are either universally unhappy or in crisis, but rather, they are shown having to work at constructing and maintaining their family unit, which in itself points to the maternal efforts and motherwork practices demanded by but seldom mentioned in relation to the ideology of intensive mothering.

Reality parenting television has its roots in makeover programming, and the discussion concerning 'postfeminist symbolic violence' that exists in relation to the fashion, style and sartorial makeover (McRobbie 2004) can also be seen to relate to the representation of the maternal figure here, whereby women in the audience are encouraged to both sympathise with and critically judge women on screen for what are presented as their unacceptable parenting practices. Indeed, any audience sympathy or empathy is 'intricately bound up with moral judgements of value' (Skeggs, Thumim and Wood 2008b, 145). The reality parenting genre upholds the 'good' mother myth while simultaneously debunking the improbable and impossible ideal, which can be seen to speak to the woman in the audience who although aware of the unrealistic nature of the 'good' mother continues to try and thus routinely fails to conform to that same romanticised ideal (Ryan 2007). Celebrity reality programming has its roots in reality parenting television, with the genre keen to point to the 'ordinariness' of the woman, wife and mother in question, irrespective of wealth, celebrity status or lifestyle. What is interesting about this new and growing set of programmes is the ways in which the lived reality of the women in question seldom lives up to the idealised image of motherhood that dominates the contemporary cultural climate. These women tend in the main to have access to the leisure time and financial resources that underpin the ideology of intensive mothering which in turn acts as the foundation for the 'good' mother, and yet these women present an image of motherhood that refuses to adhere to this strict, fixed and rigid ideal. The point here, then, is that these women have the resources at their disposal but choose to negotiate the romanticised ideal, which might be seen to give comfort to a generation of working-class women who struggle to emulate an impossible maternal role. Reality pregnancy and childbirth television must be seen as an extension of the aforementioned genres of reality programming, and like these other reality texts, this genre gives a voice, albeit edited and framed, to the maternal figure to speak of their pregnancy and birth experiences. Although one might suggest that these reality texts are exploitative in their treatment of ordinary women or encouraging exhibitionism in a generation of future female celebrities, what is undeniable here is that these women are speaking about both their maternal role and motherwork practices, which goes someway to both uphold but very slowly break through the 'good' mother myth.

Each genre outlined here has its own repertoire of elements, thematic codes and narrative conventions, and yet they appear to form a televisual consensus in the ways in which they present mothers struggling to construct and maintain the ideology of intensive mothering and the 'good' mother myth. The mothers presented in this volume tend to be white, working, heterosexual women, and many of these mothers are devoted to their children, consider their maternal role to be a privilege and want to create happy and harmonious families. However, the fact that many of these women are single, sexual, scared, struggling to maintain authority in the home and finding little satisfaction in the routines of domestic life demonstrates their removal from the ideology of appropriate or acceptable intensive mothering. With this in mind, one might choose to critique such texts for seeking to deride and dismiss motherhood, motherwork and the maternal role. However, rather than condemn such seemingly problematic figures for their inability to adhere to maternal ideals, these expectant, new and existing mothers should be applauded for debunking the improbable and unattainable 'good' mother myth in favour of 'good enough' and achievable maternal practices. After all, the sheer volume, scope and reach of such struggling maternal figures goes some way towards revealing the unrealisable myth of the 'good' mother archetype that dominates the cultural context of such texts. That said, although these popular television programmes can be seen to expose the 'good' mother myth and present a broad and varied number of mothers who shatter the romanticised image of the selfless, satisfied stay-at-home maternal care-giver, it is worth noting that these genres continue to do so while simultaneously upholding this maternal ideal.

Although I have suggested that the aforementioned genres form a televisual consensus in their portrayal of the 'good enough' rather than idealised mother, it is worth noting that audiences will of course read the myriad of maternal practices in different, diverse and distinct ways. Audiences might choose to read certain genres as reflecting the lived experience of motherhood in contemporary society, understanding others as an explorative and reflective space in which to think through and contextualise their own maternal identities, and others still as empowering sites of social change. Alternatively, audiences might read specific programmes as depicting aspirational and inspirational examples of motherhood, understanding others as ideological texts that normalise a traditional conservative agenda, and others still as cautionary tales for future, new and existing mothers. While some audiences view these programmes as open texts that encourage disparate, diverse and different points of maternal identification, others will decide that these productions are limiting such viewing practices.

What is clear, however, is that irrespective of genre fluctuation or diverse reading practices, these programmes remain popular with female audiences, be they non-mothers, future mothers, expecting, new or existing mothers, and as such, it would be enlightening to discover the ways in which these women respond to, invest in and take umbrage with representations of mothers, the maternal role and motherwork on the small screen. It is therefore important that future research looks to understand the ways in which women from the television audience read such texts and relate them to their lived experiences, exploring and unmasking the ways in which these women adopt moral positions, present emotive and personal responses, and derive pleasure, empowerment, escapist-fantasy, displeasure and frustration from popular depictions of motherhood, as well as considering the ways in which such responses inform their own maternal thoughts and practices. Research from within the fields of motherhood studies, media criticism and feminist theory must draw on a number of empirical research methods such as those employed by Skeggs, Thumim and Wood (2008a) in order to shed light on and offer critical insight into the varied and diverse ways in which female audiences read and respond to popular representations of motherhood on the small screen, and the ways in which their own social and domestic context informs their viewing positions.

What is so crucially important about empirical audience research of course is its 'capacity for "surprises" that can be revealed about the social dynamics of textual meaning' (Wood and Taylor 2008, 147). My point here then is that while researchers might look to interrogate and unmask what they deem to be crucial, significant, timely or relevant representations in their wider social and sexual context, the ways in which audiences read and respond to these texts may in some instances speak to the researchers hypothesis, but they may also read and respond to existing representations in ways previously unclear to or not considered by the researcher, and it is this range of voices that must be heard.

In this way, future research could offer a significant contribution to the work of seminal theorists such as Ien Ang, whose detailed audience project on the ways in which female viewers responded to *Dallas* (1978–91) pointed to the politics of pleasure in the glamorous and melodramatic American soap opera (Ang 1996); Dorothy Hobson, whose work on British soap opera highlighted the role of sociality and sociability within and beyond female viewing practices (Hobson 1982); Ann Gray, whose work foregrounds the role and relevance of gender in television viewing habits (Gray 1992); Helen Wood's work on the ways in which the television talk-show audience formed their opinions and expressed their (dis)appreciation of the genre based on their sense of 'connection' with the talk-show host and their ability to empathise or relate to the topic under discussion (Wood 2009); and more recently Beverley Skeggs, Nancy Thumim and Helen Wood's work on 'emotional labour' and the 'uncomfortable' ways in which empathy was expressed towards reality-parenting participants, and the ways in which the feelings of 'sadness' and 'sorrow' that were expressed were bound up with a recognition of their own lived experiences (Skeggs, Thumim and Wood 2008b).

Skeggs, Thumim and Wood have recently employed audience-studies methods in order to interrogate the ways in which a diverse range of women living in four different South London locations responded to reality parenting television. The point here is that 'the women's lives under such scrutiny on programs like *Wife Swap* and *Supernanny* evoke a moral framework in which female audiences are impelled to locate themselves as well as others, revealing the current pressures and politics of class and gender as they are firmly ensconced within modes of neoliberal citizenship' (Wood and Taylor 2008, 148). The theorists tell us that there are clear distinctions between middle and working-class female viewers, not just in terms of the starkly different ways in which they find pleasure, frustration, empathy or camaraderie in these reality texts, but more importantly in terms of the different ways in which individuals are able to articulate their responses to the genre in question. After all, the ability to explore, critique and be self-reflexive all depends on 'access to resources and concomitant forms of capital that are classed, raced and gendered' (Skeggs, Thumim and Wood 2008a, 3).

Although an examination of class formations and cultural distinctions has long been of interest to the field of sociology and feminist media scholarship (Press 1991, Gray 1992, Thomas 1995, Skeggs 1997, Skeggs 2003, Dines and Humez 2002), little contemporary work has sought to explore the role and relevance of class in audience accounts of television. And yet 'despite the claims of much poststructuralist theory, class is still very much with us, if in new and always changing forms' (Morley cited in Skeggs, Thumim and Wood 2008a, 2). With this in mind, Skeggs, Thumim and Wood utilised a diverse range of audience methods in order to encourage both working and middle-class women to engage with reality parenting texts. The research team relied on sociological interviews, the 'text-in-action' method (which involves watching a particular television title with the respondent and detailing their responses at the time of viewing) and focus-group discussions. The 'text-in-action' research event sought to 'capture the dynamic interaction between viewer and television programme as an event taking place in a particular moment in time, rather than as in traditional reception research where data is only gathered after viewing' (Skeggs, Thumim and Wood 2008a, 11). The aim here was to encourage not just those confident, professional, white, middle-class women to engage in a critical discussion of the genre but to allow those working-class women who were ill at-ease during the interview and focus-group stages of the research process to present their own voice during the less demanding and yet entirely candid 'text-in-action' approach. After all,

> the unfamiliar research encounter was made less daunting since the television programme provided a focus, relegating the researcher to the background. This opportunity allowed some women, who had difficulties in directly articulating their responses to 'reality' television in the interview stage a space to 'perform' their viewing relationship in a less self-conscious way. (Ibid., 11)

In short, their 'methodological design enabled different kinds of knowledge to be displayed, and offered a more transparent account of that process than is often rendered in research' (ibid., 24). And it was this range of empirical techniques that led them to conclude that their working-class participants refused to be attached to the category of class, while their middle-class counterparts rejected associations 'to that which is a cultural display of working-class (low) taste' (ibid., 9). On the back of this research, it would be crucial to discover not only the ways in which notions of class inform audience interests and reading practices, but also the role of sexuality, disability, ethnicity, age and marital status.

The reality of mothering will always be more fluid and fluctuating than those representations of motherhood and motherwork that are presented in popular television programming; for example, images of disabled mothers and notions of racial diversity are seldom seen on the small screen. However, it remains clear that existing representations have the power to define the boundaries of appropriate and acceptable mothering practices, and as such, it is crucial that we continue to explore the ways in which these representations present the maternal role across schedules, genres and programme titles. What I hope is that theorists from within the fields of feminist television criticism and motherhood studies use this book as a starting point for further research concerning the representation of motherhood in popular television and as a foundation for a broad range of empirical audience research that asks expecting, new and experienced mothers to account for their pleasures and frustrations, or what has been understood elsewhere as the 'emotional labour' (Skeggs, Thumim and Wood 2008b) associated with and invested in such representations. Furthermore, I would hope that future research will take into account not only an examination of those genres and titles seen here, but also consider the relevance of those not included, such as daytime television, children's programming, science fiction and fantasy texts, and police, crime, medical, legal and political dramas, as they could prove invaluable for future considerations of the depiction of motherhood on contemporary popular television.

Genre classifications may be fluid and in flux, and so too empirical audience methods are shifting and developing; yet this does not detract from the importance of examining both the representations of motherhood and the ways in which women respond to such representations. After all, television has historically been and continues to be 'bound up with the very serious cultural politics of our time' (Wood and Taylor 2008, 149).

BIBLIOGRAPHY

Abercrombie, Nicholas (1997), *Television and Society*, Cambridge: Polity Press.
Addison, Heather (2009), 'Modernizing Mother: The Maternal Figure in Early Hollywood', in *Motherhood Misconceived: Representing the Maternal in U.S. Films*, edited by Heather Addison, Mary Kate Goodwin-Kelly and Elaine Roth, Albany: State University of New York Press, pp. 63–80.
Allen, Robert C. (2012), 'Soap Opera', The Museum of Broadcast Communications. Available at: http://www.museum.tv/eotvsection.php?entrycode=soapopera (accessed 4 January 2012).
American Pregnancy Association (2012), 'Miscarriage'. Available at: http://www.americanpregnancy.org/pregnancycomplications/miscarriage.html (accessed 11 January 2012).
Andrews, Maggie (1998), '*Butterflies* and Caustic Asides: Housewives, Comedy and the Feminist Movement', in *Because I Tell a Joke or Two: Comedy, Politics and Social Difference*, edited by Stephen Wagg, New York: Routledge, pp. 50–64.
Ang, Ien (1996), *Watching Dallas: Soap Opera and the Melodramatic Imagination*, London: Routledge.
Anger, Dorothy (1999), *Other Worlds: Society Seen through Soap Opera*, Peterborough: Broadview Press.
Arnold, Abby (2003), 'The Rhetoric of Motherhood', *The Mothers Movement Online*, pp. 1–9. Available at: http://www.mothersmovement.org/features/rhetoric_motherhood/rhetoric_motherhood.htm (accessed 10 August 2010).
Arnup, Katherine (1998), 'Does the Word Lesbian Mean Anything to You? Lesbians Raising Daughters', in *Redefining Motherhood: Changing Identities and Patterns*, edited by Sharon Abbey and Andrea O'Reilly, Toronto: Second Story Press, pp. 59–68.
Arthurs, Jane (2003), '*Sex and the City* and Consumer Culture: Remediating Postfeminist Television Drama', *Feminist Media Studies*, 3:1, pp. 83–98.
Aubrun, Axel and Grady, Joseph (2000), 'Aliens in Our Living Room: How TV Shapes Our Understandings of Teens', The Frameworks Institute.
Badinter, Elizabeth (1980), *Mother Love: Myth and Reality*, New York: MacMillan.
Banks, Miranda (2004), 'A Boy For All Planets: *Roswell, Smallville* and the Teen Male Melodrama', in *Teen TV: Genre, Consumption and Identity*, edited by Glyn Davis and Kay Dickinson, London: BFI, pp. 17–28.
Barb (2012) http://www.barb.co.uk/report/weeklyTopProgrammes/? *Broadcasters' Audience Research Board*. Available at: *http://www.barb.co.uk/report/weeklyTopProgrammes/?* (accessed 4 October 2012).
Bassin, Donna; Honey, Margaret and Kaplan, Meryle Mahrer (1994), 'Introduction', in *Representations of Motherhood*, edited by Donna Bassin et al., London: Yale University Press, pp. 1–25.

Bathrick, Serafina (2003), '*The Mary Tyler Moore Show*: Women at Home and at Work', in *Critiquing the Sitcom: A Reader*, edited by Joanne Morreale, New York: Syracuse University Press, pp.155–86.

BBC News (2004), 'New Mums Want Celebrity Figures'. Available at: http://news.bbc.co.uk/1/hi/health/3890589.stm (accessed 10 August 2011).

———. (2007a), 'Jordan Crowned Mum of the Year'. Available at: http://news.bbc.co.uk/1/hi/entertainment/6454103.stm (accessed 10 August 2011).

———. (2007b), 'Pregnant Katona admits to Smoking'. Available at: http://news.bbc.co.uk/1/hi/entertainment/7080507.stm (accessed 22 September 2011).

———. (2010), 'Caution Over Abortion Rate Fall'. Available at: http://news.bbc.co.uk/1/hi/health/8702839.stm (accessed 9 February 2012).

Beech, Beverley Lawrence (2004), 'NICE Guidelines for Caesarean Section', *AIMS* [Association for Improvements in the Maternity Services] *Journal*, 2004, 16:2. Available at: http://www.aims.org.uk/Journal/Vol16No2/csGuidelines.htm (accessed 10 August 2011).

Belkin, Lisa (2003), 'The Opt Out Revolution', *The New York Times*. Available at: http://www.nytimes.com/2003/10/26/magazine/26WOMEN.html (accessed 10 August 2011).

Bell, Emma (2008), 'From Bad Girl to Mad Girl: British Female Celebrity, Reality Products and the Pathologization of Pop-Feminism', *Genders*, 48. Available at: http://www.genders.org/g48/g48_bell.html (accessed 10 August 2010).

Benfer, Amy (2000), 'Knocked Up Like Me', Salon.com. Available at: http://www.salon.com/life/feature/2000/11/02/gilmore_girls (accessed 10 August 2011).

Berila, Beth (2007), 'Savvy Women, Old Boys' School Politics, and *The West Wing*', in *Geek Chick: Smart Women in Popular Culture*, edited by Sherrie A. Innes, London: Routledge, pp. 153–70.

Bernstein, Jane and Laura Stephenson (1997), 'Dykes, Donors & Dry Ice: Alternative Insemination', in *Lesbian Parenting: Living with Pride and Prejudice*, edited by Katherine Arnup, Charlottetown: Gynergy Books, pp. 3–15.

Berryman, Julia (1994), 'Perspectives on Later Motherhood', in *Motherhood: Meanings, Practices and Ideologies*, edited by Ann Phoenix, Anne Woollett and Eva Lloyd, London: Sage, pp. 103–22.

Bonifazi, Wendy (2003), 'Midlife Motherhood: Late Expectations?', NurseWeek. Available at: http://www2.nursingspectrum.com/articles/print.html?AID=10792 (accessed 10 August 2011).

Borisoff, Deborah (2005), 'Transforming Motherhood: "We've Come a Long Way", Maybe', *Review of Communication*, 5:1, pp. 1–11.

Bortolaia Silva, Elizabeth (1996), 'Introduction', in *Good Enough Mothering?: Feminist Perspectives on Lone Motherhood*, edited by Elizabeth Bortolaia Silva, London: Routledge, pp. 1–9.

Bowers, Sharon (2006), 'I Bet You Were a Cheerleader', in *Welcome to Wisteria Lane: On America's Favorite Desperate Housewives*, edited by Leah Wilson, Texas: Benbella Books, pp. 93–104.

Braithwaite, Andrea (2008), 'That Girl of Yours, She's Pretty Hardboiled, Huh? Detecting Feminism in *Veronica Mars*', in *Teen Television: Essays on Programming and Fandom*, edited by Sharon Marie Ross and Louise Ellen Stein, London: McFarland & Company, Inc., pp. 132–49.

Brancato, Jim (2007), 'Domesticating Politics: The Representation of Wives and Mothers in American Reality Television', *Film & History: An Interdisciplinary Journal of Film and Television*, 37:3, pp.49–56.

Branston, Gill and Roy Stafford (2010), *The Media Student's Book*, 5th ed. London: Routledge.
Bronars, Stephen and Jeff Grogger (1994), 'The Economic Consequences of Unwed Motherhood: Using Twin Births as a Natural Experiment', *The American Economic Review*, 84:5, pp. 1141–56.
Brown, Jane, Jeanne Steele and Kim Walsh-Childers, (2002), 'Introduction and Overview', in *Sexual Teens, Sexual Media: Investigating Media's Influence on Adolescent Sexuality*, edited by Jane Brown, Jeanne Steele and Kim Walsh-Childers, London: Routledge, pp. 1–24.
Brown, Mary Ellen (1990), 'Consumption and Resistance – The Problem of Pleasure', in *Television and Women's Culture: The Politics of the Popular*, edited by Mary Ellen Brown, London: Sage.
———. (1994), *Soap Opera and Women's Talk: The Pleasures of Resistance*, London: Sage.
Brunsdon, Charlotte (1997), *Screen Tastes: Soap Opera to Satellite Dishes*, London: Routledge.
———. (2000), *The Feminist, the Housewife, and the Soap Opera*, Oxford: Clarendon Press.
Buckman, Peter (1984), *All For Love: A Study in Soap Opera*, London: Secker & Warburg.
Burton, Graeme (2010), *Media and Society: Critical Perspectives*, 2nd ed., Maidenhead: Open University Press.
Büskens, Petra (2004), 'From Perfect Housewife to Fishnet Stockings and Not Quite Back Again: One Mother's Story of Leaving Home', in *Mother Outlaws: Theories and Practices of Empowered Mothering*, edited by Andrea O'Reilly, Toronto: Women's Press, pp. 105–22.
———. (2005), 'When Eve Left the Garden: A Modern Tale about Mothers Who Leave Their Families', in *Motherhood: Power and Oppression*, edited by Marie Porter, Patricia Short and Andrea O'Reilly, Toronto: Women's Press, pp. 265–84.
Casey, Bernadette et al., (2002), *Television Studies: The Key Concepts*, London: Routledge.
CDC National Vital Statistics Reports (2009), 'National Vital Statistics Reports: Births', 57:7, pp. 1–102, Available at: http://www.cdc.gov/nchs/products/nvsr.htm (accessed 30 August 2011).
Channel 4 (2011), '*One Born Every Minute*: Insights into the Realities of Birth'. Available at: http://lifebegins.channel4.com/ (accessed 10 August 2011).
Chappell, Marisa (2005), 'If It Takes A Village, Why Am I Doing This Alone? Motherhood and Citizenship in Modern America', *Journal of Women's History*, 17:4, pp. 134–41.
Chase, Susan and Mary Rogers (2001), *Mothers and Children: Feminist Analysis and Personal Narratives*, New Jersey: Rutgars University Press.
Chatton, Barbara (2001), 'Picture Books for Preschool Children: Exploring Gender Issues with Three-and Four-Year Olds', in *Beauty, Brains and Brawn: The Construction of Gender in Children's Literature*, edited by Susan Lehr, Portsmouth, NH: Heinemann, pp. 57–78.
Cheng, Shu-Ju Ada (2007), 'Right to Mothering: Motherhood as a Transborder Concern in the Age of Globalization', in *Maternal Theory: Essential Readings*, edited by Andrea O'Reilly, Toronto: Demeter Press, pp. 640–648.
Clark, Hilary (2008), 'Confessions of a Celebrity Mom: Brooke Shields's *Down Came the Rain: My Journey Through Postpartum Depression*', *Canadian Review of American Studies*, 38:3, pp. 449–61.
Cobb, Shelley (2008), 'Mother of the Year: Kathy Hilton, Lynne Spears, Dina Lohan and Bad Celebrity Motherhood', *Genders*, 48. Available at: http://www.genders.org/g48/g48_cobb.html (accessed 10 August 2011).
Coleman, Lindsay (2008), 'Food Fights: Food and its Consumption as a Narrative Device', in *Gilmore Girls and the Politics of Identity*, edited by Ritch Calvin, London: McFarland & Company, pp. 175–92.

Collett, Jessica (2005), What Kind of Mother am I? Impression Management and the Social Construction of Motherhood, *Symbolic Interaction*, 28:3, pp. 327–47.

Cooper, Baba (1987), 'The Radical Potential in Lesbian Mothering of Daughters', in *Politics of the Heart: A Lesbian Parenting Anthology*, edited by Sandra Pollock and Jeanne Vaughn, New York: Firebrand Books, pp. 233–40.

Cosslett, Tess (1994), *Women Writing Childbirth: Modern Discourses of Motherhood*, Manchester: Manchester University Press.

Crompton, Sarah (2012), '*Outnumbered* [...] Review: Love and Laughter in the Modern World' Available at: http://www.telegraph.co.uk/culture/tvandradio/bbc/8741308/Outnumbered-and-The-Inbetweeners-review-love-and-laughter-in-the-modern-world.html (accessed 4 January 2012).

Cummings, Dolan (2002) 'Introduction', in *Reality TV: How Real is Real*, edited by Dolan Cummings et al., London: Hodder & Stoughton, pp. xi–xvii

Dally, Ann (1982), *Inventing Motherhood: The Consequences of an Ideal*, London: Burnett Books.

Davies, Jude and Carol Smith (1998), 'Race, Gender, and the America Mother: Political Speech and the Maternity Episodes of *I Love Lucy* and *Murphy Brown*', *American Studies*, 39:2, pp. 33–63.

Davis-Floyd, Robbie (1992), *Birth as an American Rite of Passage*, Berkeley: University of California Press.

Davis, Glyn and Kay Dickinson (2004), 'Introduction', in *Teen TV: Genre, Consumption and Identity*, edited by Glyn Davis and Kay Dickinson, London: BFI, pp. 1–16.

Dayna, B. Royal (2010), 'Jon & Kate Plus the State: Why Congress Should Protect Children in Reality Programming', *Akro Law Review*, 43:435. Available at: http://papers.ssrn.com/sol3/papers.cfm?abstract_id=1452986 (accessed 23 January 2012).

Department of Health (1993), 'Changing Childbirth' cited in 'Changing Childbirth: Development Projects Summary Report' (1998). Available at: http://www.dh.gov.uk/en/Publicationsandstatistics/Publications/PublicationsPolicyAndGuidance/DH_4005211 (accessed 11 December 2011).

———. (2011), 'Abortion Statistics, England and Wales: 2010'. Available at: http://www.dh.gov.uk/en/Publicationsandstatistics/Publications/PublicationsStatistics/DH_126769 (accessed 4 January 2012).

———. (2007), 'Maternity Matters: Choice, Access and Continuity of Care in a Safe Service'. Available at: http://www.dh.gov.uk/en/Publicationsandstatistics/Publications/PublicationsPolicyAndGuidance/DH_073312 (accessed 11 December 2011).

Devine, Darren (2008), 'Modern Mothers Feel "Yummy Mummy" Pressure', *Western Mail*. Available at: http://www.walesonline.co.uk/news/wales-news/2008/02/28/modern-mothers-feel-yummy-mummy-pressure-91466-20533241/ (accessed 10 August 2011).

Dines, Gail and Jean Humez (eds) (2002), *Gender, Race and Class in Media: A Text Reader*, London: Sage.

Discovery Health (2011), 'It's *Runway Moms!*'. Available at: http://health.discovery.com/convergence/runway-moms/about.html (accessed 10 August 2011).

Dow, Bonnie (1996), *Prime-Time Feminism: Television, Media Culture, and the Women's Movement Since 1970*, Philadelphia: University of Pennsylvania Press.

Dow, Bonnie (1990), 'Hegemony, Feminist Criticism and *The Mary Tyler Moore Show*', *Critical Studies in Mass Communication*, 7, pp. 261–74.

Downe, Pamela (2004), 'Stepping on Maternal Ground: Reflections of Becoming an "Other Mother"', in *Mother Matters: Motherhood as Discourse and Practice*, edited by Andrea O'Reilly, Toronto: Demeter Press, pp. 165–78.

Douglas, Susan (1995), *Where the Girls Are Growing up Female with the Media*, New York: Times Books.
Douglas, Susan and Meredith Michaels (2005), *The Mommy Myth: The Idealization of Motherhood and How it Has Undermined All Women*, London: Free Press.
Dovey, Jon (2002), 'Reality TV', in *The Television Genre Book*, edited by Glen Creeber, London: BFI, pp. 134–7.
Dunne, Gillian (2000), 'Opting into Motherhood: Lesbians Blurring the Boundaries and Transforming the Meaning of Parenthood and Kinship', *Gender & Society*, 14:1, pp. 11–35.
Dworkin, Shari and Faye Linda Wachs (2004), 'Getting Your Body Back: Postindustrial Fit Motherhood in *Shape Fit Pregnancy* Magazine', *Gender & Society*, 18:5, pp. 610–624.
Ehrensaft, Diane (1983), 'When Women and Men Mother', in *Mothering: Essays in Feminist Theory*, edited by Joyce Trebilcot, New Jersey: Rowman & Allanheld, pp. 41–61.
Eisenberg, Arlene, Heidi Murkoff and Sandee Hathaway, (1996), *What to Expect When You're Expecting*, 2nd ed., New York: Workman Publishing Company.
Elson, Vicki (2009), *Laboring Under an Illusion: Mass Media Childbirth vs. The Real Thing*, DVD.
Erickson, Ann Burke (2008), 'Drats! Foiled Again: A Contrast in Definitions', in *Gilmore Girls and the Politics of Identity*, edited by Ritch Calvin, London: McFarland & Company, pp. 63–79.
Esterberg, Kristin (2008), 'Planned Parenthood: The Construction of Motherhood in Lesbian Mother Advice Books', in *Feminist Mothering*, edited by Andrea O'Reilly, New York: State University of New York Press, pp. 75–88.
Fairclough, Kirsty (2004), 'Women's Work? *Wife Swap* and the Reality Problem', *Feminist Media Studies*, 4:3, pp. 344–7.
Feasey, Rebecca (2006), 'Watching *Charmed*: Why Teen Television Appeals to Women', *Journal of Popular Film and Television*, 34:1, pp. 2–9.
_____. (2008), *Masculinity and Popular Television*, Edinburgh: Edinburgh University Press.
_____. (2012), 'Absent, Ineffectual and Intoxicated Mothers: Representing the Maternal in Teen Television', *Feminist Media Studies*, 1:12, pp. 155–9.
Ferguson, Ann (1983), 'On Conceiving Motherhood and Sexuality: A Feminist Materialist Approach', in *Mothering: Essays in Feminist Theory*, edited by Joyce Trebilcot, New Jersey: Rowman & Allanheld, pp. 153–84.
Ferguson, Alease and Toni King (2008), 'Going Down for the Third Time', in *Mothering in the Third Wave*, edited by Amber Kinser, Toronto: Demeter Press, pp. 166–85.
Ferguson Galit (2010), 'The Family on Reality Television: Who's Shaming Whom?' *Television & New Media*, 11:2, pp. 87–104.
Feuer, Jane (2002), 'Situation Comedy, Part 2', in *The Television Genre Book*, edited by Glen Creeber, London: BFI, pp. 67–70.
Feuer, Jane (1986), 'Narrative Form in American Network Television', in *High Theory/Low Culture: Analysing Popular Television and Film*, edited by Colin McCabe, New York: St. Martin's Press, pp. 101–14.
First, Elsa (1994), 'Mothering, Hate, and Winnicott' in *Representations of Motherhood*, edited by Donna Bassin, Margaret Honey and Meryle Mahrer Kaplan, London: Yale University Press, pp. 147–61.
Fiske, John (2003), *Television Culture*, London: Routledge.
Fleegal, Stacia (2008), 'Like Mother-Daughter, Like Daughter-Mother: Constructs of Motherhood in Three Generations', in *Gilmore Girls and the Politics of Identity*, edited by Ritch Calvin, London: McFarland & Company, pp. 143–58.

Flynn, Emily (2005), 'Nanny to the Rescue', *Newsweek*, 17 January, pp. 48–50.
Fox, Bonnie (1998), 'Motherhood, Changing Relationships and the Reproduction of Gender Inequality', in *Redefining Motherhood: Changing Identities and Patterns*, edited by Sharon Abbey and Andrea O'Reilly, Toronto: Second Story Press, pp. 159–74.
Friedan, Betty (1963), *The Feminine Mystique*, London: Penguin.
Gailey, Elizabeth Atwood (2007), 'Self-Made Women: Cosmetic Surgery Shows and the Construction of Female Psychopathology', in *Makeover Television: Realities Remodelled*, edited by Dana Heller, London: I.B. Tauris, pp. 107–18.
Gallagher, Margaret et al., (2005), 'Who Makes the News? Global Media Monitoring Project 2005'. Available at: http://www.whomakesthenews.org/reports/2005-global-report.html (accessed 7 December 2011).
Ganeshasundaram, Raguragavan and Nadine Henley (2009), 'Reality Television (*Supernanny*): A Social Marketing "Place" Strategy', *Journal of Consumer Marketing*, 26:5, pp. 311–19.
Gannon, Louise (2005), 'Sarah Jessica Parker: My Style Icon: Kate Moss', *Grazia*, 12 September, pp. 12–16.
Gatrell, Caroline (2008), *Embodying Women's Work*, Maidenhead: Open University Press.
Geraghty, Christine (2005), 'The Study of Soap Opera', in *A Companion to Television*, edited by Janet Wasko, London: Wiley-Blackwell, pp. 308–23.
Geraghty, Christine (1999), *Women and Soap Opera: A Study of Prime Time Soaps*, Cambridge: Polity Press.
Gill, Rosalind (2006), *Gender and the Media*, Cambridge: Polity.
Gingerbread (2011), 'Gingerbread Fact File: Myths and Labels Abound about Single Parents…'. Available at: http://www.gingerbread.org.uk/content.aspx?CategoryID=365 (accessed 10 August 2011).
Goc, Nicola (2007), 'Monstrous Mothers and the Media', in *Monsters and the Monstrous: Myths and Metaphors of Enduring Evil*, edited by Scott Niall, New York: Rodopi, pp. 149–66.
González, Libertad (2006), 'The Effect of Benefits on Single Motherhood in Europe', Institute for the Study of Labor. Available at: http://papers.ssrn.com/sol3/papers.cfm?abstract_id=892363 (accessed 10 August 2012).
González, Marta (2010), *The Art of Motherhood*, Los Angeles: J. Paul Getty Museum.
Goodman, Judith (2008), *The Myths Behind Marriage and Motherhood: Understanding the Source of Women's Anger*, Women and Addiction Counseling and Educational Services.
Google Analytics (2011), 'Mumsnet'. Available at: http://www.google.com/analytics/ (accessed 1 July 2011).
Gore, Ariel and Bee Lavender (2001), *Breeder: Real-Life Stories from the New Generation of Mothers*, Seattle: Seal Press.
Gorman, Bill (2008), 'Top CW Primetime Shows, September 1–7', TVbytheNumbers. Zap2It.com. Available at: http://tvbythenumbers.zap2it.com/2008/09/10/top-cw-primetime-shows-september-1-7/5026/ (accessed 4 January 2012).
Grandparents Plus (2012), 'Home', GrandparentsPlus.org. Available at: http://www.grandparentsplus.org.uk/ (accessed 5 January 2012).
Grant, Barry Keith (2003), 'Introduction', in *Film Genre Reader III*, edited by Barry Keith Grant, Austin: University of Texas Press
Gray, Ann (1992), *Video Playtime: The Gendering of a Leisure Technology*, London: Routledge.
Green, Fiona (2004), 'Feminist Mothers: Successfully Negotiating the Tensions between Motherhood as "Institution" and "Experience"', in *Mother Outlaws: Theories and Practices of Empowered Mothering*, edited by Andrea O'Reilly, Toronto: Women's Press, pp. 31–42.

_____. (2007), '*Supernanny*: Disciplining Mothers through a Narrative of Domesticity', *Storytelling*, 6:2, pp. 99–109. Available at: http://lion.chadwyck.co.uk (accessed 10 August 2011).
Gregory, Susan (1994), 'Challenging Motherhood: Mothers and their Deaf Children', in *Motherhood: Meanings, Practices and Ideologies*, edited by Ann Phoenix, Anne Woollett and Eva Lloyd, London: Sage, pp. 123–42.
Groskop, Viv (2009), 'What is the Truth Behind Sarah Jessica Parker's use of a Surrogate?', *Guardian.co.uk*. Available at: http://www.guardian.co.uk/lifeandstyle/2009/apr/30/sarah-jessica-parker-twins-surrogate (accessed 10 August 2011).
Guttmacher Institute (2011), 'Facts on Induced Abortion in the United States'. Available at: http://www.guttmacher.org/pubs/fb_induced_abortion.html (accessed 10 August 2011).
Hadfield, Lucy, Naomi Rudoe and Jo Sanderson-Mann (2007), 'Motherhood, Choice and the British Media: A Time to Reflect', *Gender and Education*, 19:2, pp. 225–63.
Haffner, Debra (1995), *Facing Facts: Sexual Health for America's Adolescents*, New York: SIECUS.
Hains, Rebecca (2007), 'Inventing the Teenage Girl: The Construction of Female Identity in Nickelodeon's *My Life as a Teenage Robot*', *Popular Communication*, 5:3, pp. 191–213.
Hall, Ann and Mardia Bishop (2009), 'Introduction', in *Mommy Angst: Motherhood in America Popular Culture*, edited by Ann Hall and Mardia Bishop, Oxford: Praeger, pp. vii–xvii.
Hall, Pamela Courtenay (1998), 'Mothering Mythology in the Late Twentieth Century: Science, Gender Lore, and Celebratory Narrative', *Canadian Woman Studies*, 18:2–3, pp. 59–63.
Hamamoto, Darrell (1991), *Nervous Laughter: Television Situation Comedy and Liberal Democratic Ideology*, New York: Praeger.
Hart-Davis, (2010), 'One Generation wants to Appear Younger, the Other to Seem Older. So when did Mothers and Daughters Start Looking Like Sisters?', *Mail Online*, Available at: http://www.dailymail.co.uk/femail/article-1284828/One-genera tion-wants-appear-younger-older-So-did-mothers-daughters-start-looking-like-sisters. html (accessed 10 August 2011).
Hartley, John (2002), 'Situation Comedy, Part 1', in *The Television Genre Book*, edited by Glen Creeber, London: BFI, pp. 65–7.
Haupt, Melanie (2008), 'Wheat Balls, Gravalax, Pop Tarts: Mothering and Power', in *Gilmore Girls and the Politics of Identity*, edited by Ritch Calvin, London: McFarland & Company, pp. 114–26.
Held, Virginia (1983), 'The Obligations of Mothers and Fathers', in *Mothering: Essays in Feminist Theory*, edited by Joyce Trebilcot, New Jersey: Rowman & Allanheld, pp. 7–20.
Hequembourg, Amy and Farrell, Michael (1999), 'Lesbian Motherhood: Negotiating Marginal-Mainstream Identities', *Gender & Society*, 13:4, pp. 540–557.
Hobson, Dorothy (1982), *Crossroads: The Drama of Soap Opera*, London: Methuen.
_____. (2003), *Soap Opera*, Cambridge: Polity Press.
Holgate, Mark (2003), 'Girl's World', *Vogue* (UK), October, pp. 344–9 and 405.
Hollows, Joanne (2000), *Feminism, Femininity and Popular Culture*, Manchester: Manchester University Press.
_____. (2003), 'Feeling Like a Domestic Goddess: Postfeminism and Cooking', *European Journal of Cultural Studies*, 6:2, pp.179–202.
_____. (2008), *Domestic Cultures*, Maidenhead: Open University Press.

hooks, bell (2007), 'Revolutionary Parenting', in *Maternal Theory: Essential Readings*, edited by Andrea O'Reilly, Toronto: Demeter Press, pp. 145–56.

Horowitz, Rachael (2005), 'Mary, Roseanne, and Carrie: Television and Fictional Feminism', *Michigan Journal of History*. Available at: http://www.umich.edu/~historyj/issues.html (accessed 10 August 2011).

Horwitz, Erika (2004), 'Resistance as a Site of Empowerment: The Journey Away from Maternal Sacrifice', in *Mother Outlaws: Theories and Practices of Empowered Mothering*, edited by Andrea O'Reilly, Toronto: Women's Press, pp. 43–58.

Jensen, Tracey (2010), '"What Kind of Mum are you at the Moment?" *Supernanny* and the Psychologising of Classed Embodiment', *Subjectivity*, 3, pp. 170–92.

Jensen, Tracey and Imogen Tyler (2011), 'Call for Papers - Austerity Parenting: New Economies of Parent-Citizenship Call For Papers, Special Issue of *Studies in the Maternal*'. Available at: https://www.jiscmail.ac.uk/cgi-bin/webadmin?A2=meccsa;de2dfb16.1110 (accessed 14 October 2011).

Jermyn, Deborah (2008), 'Still Something Else Besides a Mother? Negotiating Celebrity Motherhood in Sarah Jessica Parker's Star Story', *Social Semiotics*, 18:2, pp. 163–76.

———. (2010), *Prime Suspect*, London: BFI.

Jones, Tanya (2006), 'Oh Baby! Motherhood and the Media', *Noise to Signal*. Available at: http://www.noisetosignal.org/tv/2006/06/oh-baby-motherhood-and-the-media.php (accessed 10 August 2011).

Joyrich, Lynne (1996), *Re-viewing Reception: Television, Gender and Postmodern Culture*, Bloomington: Indiana University Press.

Juffer, Jane (2007), 'Domestic Intellectuals: Freedom and the Single Mom', in *Maternal Theory: Essential Readings*, edited by Andrea O'Reilly, Toronto: Demeter Press, pp. 726–55.

———. (2006), *Single Mother: The Emergence of the Domestic Intellectual*, New York: New York University Press.

Kanner, Bernice (2002), 'From *Father Knows Best* to *The Simpsons* – On TV, Parenting has Lost its Halo', in *Taking Parenting Public: The Case for a New Social Movement*, edited by Sylvia Ann Hewlett, Nancy Rankin and Cornel West, Oxford: Rowman & Littlefield, pp. 45–58.

Kendrick, Beth (2006), 'Growing up Wisteria', in *Welcome to Wisteria Lane: On America's Favorite Desperate Housewives*, edited by Leah Wilson, Texas: Benbella Books, pp. 29–36.

Kenner, Julie (2006), 'Sex and the Television Suburbs', in *Welcome to Wisteria Lane: On America's Favorite Desperate Housewives*, edited by Leah Wilson, Texas: Benbella Books, pp. 51–8.

Kerrigan, Susan and Phillip McIntyre (2010), 'The Creative Treatment of Actuality: Rationalizing and Reconceptualizing the Notion of Creativity for Documentary Practice', *Journal of Media Practice*, 11:2, pp. 111–30.

Khanapure, Amita and Bewley, Susan (2007), 'Ageing Motherhood: Private Grief and Public Health Concern', *South African Journal of Obstetrics and Gynaecology*, 13:1, pp. 20–22.

Kinnick, Katherine (2009), 'Media Morality Tales and the Politics of Motherhood', in *Mommy Angst: Motherhood in America Popular Culture*, edited by Ann Hall and Mardia Bishop, Oxford: Praeger, pp. 1–28.

Kinser, Amber (2010), *Motherhood and Feminism*, Berkeley, California: Seal Press.

Klass, Mylene (2008), *My Bump and Me: From Morning Sickness to Motherhood – An Honest Diary of My Pregnancy*, London: Virgin Books.

Knowles, Jo (2005), '*Desperate Housewives*', TheFWord.org. Available at: http://www.thefword.org.uk/reviews/2005/06/desperate_house (accessed 10 August 2011).

Kutulas, Judy (1998), 'Do I Look Like a Chick? Men, Women, and Babies on Sitcom Maternity Stories', *American Studies*, 39:2, pp. 13–32.
_____. (2005), 'Who Rules the Roost? Family Dynamics from the Cleavers to the Osbournes', in *The Sitcom Reader: America Viewed and Skewed*, edited by Mary Dalton and Laura Linder, Albany: State University of New York Press, pp. 49–60.
La Ferla, Ruth (2002), 'Sexy Singles Make way for Glamour Moms', NYTimes.com. Available at: http://www.nytimes.com/2002/11/10/style/noticed-sexy-singles-make-way-for-glamour-moms.html?src=pm (accessed 10 August 2011).
Lancioni, Judith (2006), 'Murder and Mayhem on Wisteria Lane: A Study of Genre and Cultural Context in *Desperate Housewives*', in *Reading Desperate Housewives: Beyond the White Picket Fence*, edited by Janet McCabe and Kim Akass, London: I.B. Tauris, pp. 129–43.
Landay, Lori (2005), '*I Love Lucy*: Television and Gender in Postwar Domestic Ideology', in *The Sitcom Reader: America Viewed and Skewed*, edited by Mary Dalton and Laura Linder, Albany: State University of New York Press, pp. 87–98.
Lichtenstein, Therese (1994), 'Images of the Maternal: An Interview with Barbara Kruger', in *Representations of Motherhood*, edited by Donna Bassin, Margaret Honey and Meryle Mahrer Kaplan, London: Yale University Press, pp. 198–203.
Liebes, Tamar and Livingstone, Sonia (1992), 'Mothers and Lovers: Managing Women's Role Conflicts in American and British Soap Operas', in *Comparatively Speaking: Communication and Culture Across Space and Time* (Sage Annual Reviews of Communication Research), edited by Jay Blumer, Jack McLeod and Karl Erik Rosengren, London: Sage, pp. 94–120.
Macaulay, Sean (2010), 'Jo Frost Interview', TheTelegraph.co.uk. Available at: http://www.telegraph.co.uk/family/7051886/Jo-Frost-interview.html (accessed 10 August 2011).
MacBain, Tiffany Aldrich and Mahato, Mita (2008), 'Got MILF? Losing Lorelai in Season Seven', in *Gilmore Girls and the Politics of Identity*, edited by Ritch Calvin, London: McFarland & Company, pp. 96–113.
Madill, Anna and Rebecca Goldmeier (2003), '*EastEnders*: Texts of Female Desire and Community', *International Journal of Cultural Studies* 6:4, pp. 471–94.
Maher, Jennifer (2004), 'What do Women Watch? Tuning in to the Compulsory Heterosexuality Channel', in *Reality TV: Remaking Television Culture*, edited by Susan Murray and Laurie Ouellette, London: New York University Press, pp. 197–213.
Marshall, David (2006), 'Introduction to Part Six: It Takes Effort to be Famous', in *The Celebrity Culture Reader*, edited by David Marshall, London: Routledge, pp. 647–8.
Martens, Lydia (2009), *Motherhoods, Markets and Consumption* (seminar series), Economic and Social Research Council, Available at: http://www.lums.lancs.ac.uk/mmc/motherhood-consumption-transition.htm (accessed 30 August 2011).
Matheson, Sarah (2007), 'The Cultural Politics of *Wife Swap*: Taste, Lifestyle Media, and the American Family', *Film & History: An Interdisciplinary Journal of Film and Television Studies*, 37:2, pp. 33–47.
Maushart, Susan (1999), *The Mask of Motherhood: How Becoming a Mother Changes Everything and Why We Pretend it Doesn't*, London: Pandora.
_____. (2007), 'Faking Motherhood: The Mask Revealed', in *Maternal Theory: Essential Readings*, edited by Andrea O'Reilly, Toronto: Demeter Press, pp. 460–481.
McKinley, Graham (1997), *Beverly Hills 90210: Television, Gender and Identity*, Philadelphia: Philadelphia University Press.
McQueen, David (1998), *Television: A Media Student's Guide*, London: Arnold.
McRobbie, Angela (2009), *The Aftermath of Feminism: Gender, Culture and Social Change*, London: Sage.

_____. (2004), 'Notes on *What Not To Wear* and Post-Feminist Symbolic Violence', *The Sociological Review Special Issue: Feminism After Bourdieu*, 52:2, pp. 97–109.

_____. (2006), 'Yummy Mummies Leave a Bad Taste for Young Women', TheGuardian.co.uk. Available at: http://www.guardian.co.uk/world/2006/mar/02/gender.comment (accessed 10 August 2011).

MediaTel (2012). Available at: http://mediatel.co.uk/ (accessed 10 May 2012).

Menabawey, Mohamed (2010), 'How Could a Woman Who's Been Through IVF Abort Her Baby', *Mail Online*. Available at: http://www.dailymail.co.uk/femail/article-1284831/How-COULD-woman-whos-IVF-abort-baby.html (accessed 10 August 2011).

Midgley, Carol (2007), 'No Kidding', TheTimes.co.uk. Available at: http://women.timesonline.co.uk/tol/life_and_style/women/families/article2341758.ece (accessed 10 August 2011).

Millar, Fiona (2007), 'For the Sake of the Children', *British Journalism Review*, 18:1, pp. 45–9.

Miller, Tina (2005), *Making Sense of Motherhood: A Narrative Approach*, Cambridge: Cambridge University Press.

Millman, Joyce (2000), 'The Parent Trap', Salon.com. Available at: http://www.salon.com/entertainment/col/mill/2000/11/14/gilmore_girls/index.html (accessed 10 August 2011).

Mills, Brett (2005), *Television Sitcom*, London: BFI.

Miner, Madonne (1996), 'Like a Natural Woman: Nature, Technology, and Birthing Bodies in *Murphy Brown*', *Frontiers*, 16:1, pp. 1–18. Available at: http://www.jstor.org/pss/3346915 (accessed 10 August 2011).

_____. (2009), 'Not Exactly According to the Rules: Pregnancy and Motherhood in *Sugar & Spice*', in *Motherhood Misconceived: Representing the Maternal in U.S. Films*, edited by Heather Addison, Mary Kate Goodwin-Kelly and Elaine Roth, New York: State University of New York Press, pp. 43–62.

Modleski, Tania (2008), 'The Search for Tomorrow in Today's Soap Opera: Notes on a Feminine Narrative Form', in *Feminist Television Criticism*, 2nd ed., edited by Charlotte Brunsdon and Lynne Spiegel, Maidenhead: Open University Press, pp. 29–40.

Morreale, Joanne (2003), 'Television in the 1940s and 1950s', in *Critiquing the Sitcom: A Reader*, edited by Joanne Morreale, New York: Syracuse University Press, pp. 1–5.

_____. (2003), 'Television in the 1970s', in *Critiquing the Sitcom: A Reader*, edited by Joanne Morreale, New York: Syracuse University Press, pp. 151–3.

_____. (2003), 'Television in the 1980s', in *Critiquing the Sitcom: A Reader*, edited by Joanne Morreale, New York: Syracuse University Press, pp.209–11.

Morris, Theresa and McInerney, Katherine (2010), 'Media Representations of Pregnancy and Childbirth: An Analysis of Reality Television Programs in the United States', *Birth: Issues in Perinatal Care*, 37:2, pp. 134–40.

Moseley, Rachel (2002), 'The Teen Series', in *The Television Genre Book*, edited by Glen Creeber, London: BFI, pp. 41–3.

Mottarella, Karen et al., (2009), 'Exploration of "Good Mother" Stereotypes in the College Environment', *Sex Roles*, 60:3/4, pp. 223–31.

Mumford, Laura Stempel (1995a), *Love and Ideology in the Afternoon: Soap Opera, Women, and Television Genre*, Bloomington, Indianapolis: Indiana University Press.

_____. (1995b), 'Plotting Paternity: Looking for Dad on the Daytime Soaps', in *To Be Continued[…] Soap Opera Around the World*, edited by Robert C. Allen, London: Routledge, pp. 164–81.

Mumsnet (2012a), 'Money Matters', Mumsnet.com. Available at: http://www.mumsnet.com/family-money (accessed 5 January 2012).
———. (2012b), 'Style and Beauty', Mumsnet.com. Available at: http://www.mumsnet.com/ (accessed 5 January 2012).
———. (2012c), 'Lunchbox Tips and Ideas', Mumsnet.com. Available at: http://www.mumsnet.com/food/lunchbox-dos-and-donts (accessed 5 January 2012).
———. (2012d), 'Private School', Mumsnet.com. Available at: http://www.mumsnet.com/info/search?query=private+school (accessed 5 January 2012).
Munn, Penny (1994), 'Mothering More than One Child', in *Motherhood: Meanings, Practices and Ideologies*, edited by Ann Phoenix, Anne Woollett and Eva Lloyd, London: Sage, pp. 162–77.
Nanny Jo (2012), retrieved 10 August 2011, from http://jofrost.com/tv-shows/supernanny
Nathan, Sara and Mcconnell, Donna (2010), '"I Feel Let Down and Disappointed", Says Denise van Outen after being Axed from BBC Talent Show Due to Pregnancy', *Mail Online*. Available at: http://www.dailymail.co.uk/tvshowbiz/article-1251832/I-feel-let-disappointed-says-Denise-Van-Outen-axed-BBC-talent-pregnancy.html (accessed 22 September 2011).
Neale, Steve (2008), 'Studying Genre', in *The Television Genre Book*, 2nd ed., edited by Glen Creeber, London: BFI, pp. 3–5.
Neale, Steve (2003), 'Questions of Genre', in *Film Genre Reader III*, edited by Barry Keith Grant, Austin: University of Texas Press, pp. 159–86.
Neale, Steve and Krutnik, Frank (1995), *Popular Film and Television Comedy*, London: Routledge.
Nelson, Peter (1989), 'Roseanne Yay!', *Esquire*, 112:2, p. 98.
NHS (2011), 'Postnatal Depression', *NHS Choices*. Available at: http://www.nhs.uk/Conditions/Postnataldepression/Pages/Introduction.aspx (accessed 10 August 2011).
———. (2012), 'Miscarriage', *NHS Choices*. Available at: http://www.nhs.uk/conditions/miscarriage/Pages/Introduction.aspx (accessed 11 January 2012).
Nock, Steven (2000), 'The Divorce of Marriage and Parenthood', *Journal of Family Therapy*, 22, pp. 245–63.
Northglow (2008) 'Katie Price, *OK!'s* Celebrity Mum of the Year', CelebrityNorthglow.com. Available at: http://celebrity.northglow.com/category/jordan/ (accessed 1 October 2011).
Oakley, Ann (1979), *Becoming a Mother*, Oxford: Martin Robertson.
O'Donohoe, Stephanie (2006), 'Yummy Mummies: The Clamor of Glamour in Advertising to Mothers', *Advertising & Society Review*, 7:3. Available at: http://muse.jhu.edu/journals/asr/v007/7.3odonohoe.html (accessed 10 August 2011).
Office for National Statistics (2009), 'Population: Births and Fertility', *UK National Statistics*. Available at: http://www.statistics.gov.uk/hub/population/index.html (accessed 30 August 2011).
———. (2011), 'Conceptions in England and Wales 2009', *UK National Statistics*. Available at: http://www.ons.gov.uk/ons/search/index.html?newquery=Conceptions+in+England+and+Wales+2009 (accessed 5 January 2012).
Oldham, Jeanette (2003), 'Celebrity Mothers Set Bad Example', Scotsman.com. Available at: http://thescotsman.scotsman.com/celebrities/Celebrity-mothers-set-bad-example.2391114.jp (accessed 10 August 2011).
O'Malley, Lisa (2006), 'Does My Bump Look Big in This? Visualising the Pregnant Body', *Advertising & Society Review*, 7:3. Available at: http://muse.jhu.edu/journals/asr/v007/7.3omalley.html (accessed 10 August 2011).

O'Reilly, Abby (2007), 'Yummy-Mummy or Pramface?', TheFWord.org. Available at: http://www.thefword.org.uk/features/2007/07/the_thought_of (accessed 10 August 2011).

O'Reilly, Andrea (2008), 'Introduction', in *Feminist Mothering*, edited by Andrea O'Reilly, New York: State University of New York Press, pp. 1–24.

O'Reilly, Andrea (2004a), 'Introduction', in *From Motherhood to Mothering: The Legacy of Adrienne Rich's Of Woman Born*, edited by Andrea O'Reilly, New York: State University of New York Press, pp. 1–23.

———. (2004b), 'Introduction', in *Mother Outlaws: Theories and Practices of Empowered Mothering*, edited by Andrea O'Reilly, Toronto: Women's Press, pp. 1–30.

———. (2004c), 'Across the Divide: Contemporary Anglo-American Feminist Theory on the Mother-Daughter Relationship', in *Mother Outlaws: Theories and Practices of Empowered Mothering*, edited by Andrea O'Reilly, Toronto: Women's Press, pp. 243–62.

———. (2004d), 'Introduction', in *Mother Matters: Motherhood as Discourse and Practice: Essays From the Journal of The Association for Research on Mothering*, edited by Andrea O'Reilly, Toronto: Association for Research on Mothering, pp. 11–28.

O'Reilly, Andrea and Porter, Marie (2005), 'Introduction', in *Motherhood: Power and Oppression*, edited by Marie Porter, Patricia Short and Andrea O'Reilly, Toronto: Women's Press, pp. 1–24.

Pasquier, Dominique (1996), 'Teen Series' Reception: Television, Adolescence and Culture of Feelings', *Childhood: A Global Journal of Child Research*, 3:3, pp. 351–73.

Pearlman, Cindy and Jill Kramer (2007), *What They Know About…Parenting!: Celebrity Moms and Dads Give us Their Take on Having Kids*, London: Hay House.

Philips, Deborah (2000), 'Medicated Soap: The Woman Doctor in Television Medical Drama', in *Frames and Fictions on Television*, edited by Bruce Carson and Margaret Llewellyn-Jones, Exeter: Intellect, pp. 50–61.

Phoenix, Ann (1994), 'Mothers Under Twenty: Outside and Insider Views', in *Motherhood: Meanings, Practices and Ideologies*, edited by Ann Phoenix, Anne Woollett and Eva Lloyd, London: Sage, pp. 86–102.

Phoenix, Ann and Woollett, Anne (1994a), 'Introduction', in *Motherhood: Meanings, Practices and Ideologies*, edited by Ann Phoenix, Anne Woollett and Eva Lloyd, London: Sage, pp. 1–12.

Phoenix, Ann and Woollett, Anne (1994b), 'Motherhood: Social Construction, Politics and Psychology', in *Motherhood: Meanings, Practices and Ideologies* edited by Ann Phoenix, Anne Woollett and Eva Lloyd, London: Sage, pp. 13–27.

Pietsch, Nicole (2004), 'Un/titled: Constructions of Illegitimate Motherhood as Gender Insurrection', in *Mother Matters: Motherhood as Discourse and Practice*, edited by Andrea O'Reilly, Ontario: Association for Research on Mothering, pp. 65–78.

Pitt, Nicola (2008), 'Yummy Mummies: Angelina Jolie and Early 21st Century Representations of Mothering', paper presented at Re-Imagining Sociology: The annual conference of The Australian Sociological Association 2008, The University of Melbourne, Australia.

Plant, Rebecca Jo (2010), *Mom: The Transformation of Motherhood in Modern America*, Chicago: The University of Chicago Press.

Podnieks, Elizabeth and Andrea O'Reilly (2010), *Textual Mothers/Maternal Texts: Motherhood in Contemporary Women's Literatures*, Ontario: Wilfrid Laurier University Press.

Polatnick, Rivka (1983), 'Why Men Don't Rear Children: A Power Analysis', in *Mothering: Essays in Feminist Theory*, edited by Joyce Trebilcot, New Jersey: Rowman & Allanheld, pp. 21–40.

Poniewozik, James (2007), 'The 100 Best TV Shows of All-*TIME*', Time.com. Available at: http://www.time.com/time/specials/2007/article/0,28804,1651341_1659192_1652529,00.html. (accessed 10 August 2010).
Porter, Andrew (2011), 'Couples Should be Encouraged to Marry', Telegraph.co.uk. Available at: http://www.telegraph.co.uk/news/newstopics/politics/8310165/Couples-should-be-encouraged-to-marry-says-Iain-Duncan-Smith.html (accessed 10 August 2011).
Pozner, Jennifer (2004), 'The Unreal World: Why Women on Reality TV Have to Be Hot, Desperate and Dumb', *Ms. Magazine*. Available at: http://www.msmagazine.com/fall2004/unrealworld.asp (accessed 30 August 2011).
Press, Andrea (1991), *Women Watching Television: Gender, Class and Generation in the American Television Experience*, Philadelphia: University of Philadelphia Press.
Rabinovitz, Lauren (1995), 'Ms.-Representation: The Politics of the Feminist Sitcom', in *Television, History, and American Culture: Feminist Critical Essays*, edited by Mary Beth Haralovich and Lauren Rabinovitz, London: Duke University Press, pp. 144–67.
Raeside, Julia (2011), '*One Born Every Minute*: Labours of Love', Guardian.co.uk. Available at http://www.guardian.co.uk/tv-and-radio/tvandradioblog/2011/jan/10/one-born-every-minute (accessed 10 August 2010).
Rapp, Rayna (1994), 'The Power of "Positive" Diagnosis: Medical and Maternal Discourses on Amniocentesis', in *Representations of Motherhood*, edited by Donna Bassin, London: Yale University Press, pp. 204–19.
Reyes, (2012), 'Call for submissions: Other Mothers/Other Mothering' (*Demeter*). Available at: http://kalamu.posterous.com/pub-call-for-submissions-other-mothersother-m (5 January 2012).
Rich, Adrienne (1977), *Of Woman Born: Motherhood as Experience and Institution*, London: Virago.
Richardson, Diane (1993), *Women, Motherhood and Childrearing*, London: MacMillan.
Rogers, Deborah (1992), 'Rockabye Lady: Pregnancy as Punishment in Popular Culture', *Journal of American Studies*, 26:1, pp. 81–3.
Ross, Sharon Marie and Louisa Ellen Stein (2008a), 'Preface', in *Teen Television: Essays on Programming and Fandom*, edited by Sharon Marie Ross and Louise Ellen Stein, London: McFarland & Company, Inc., pp. 1–2.
_____. (2008b), 'Introduction: Watching Teen TV', in *Teen Television: Essays on Programming and Fandom*, edited by Sharon Marie Ross and Louise Ellen Stein, London: McFarland & Company, Inc., pp. 3–26.
Rothman, Barbara Katz (1982), *In Labor: Women and Power in the Birthplace*, London: Norton.
Roy, Kevin (2009), 'Demography: Unmarried Couples with Children Book Review', *Contemporary Sociology*, 38:1, pp. 35–6.
Ruddick, Sara (1980), 'Maternal Thinking', *Feminist Studies*, 6:2, pp. 342–67.
_____. (2007a), 'Preservative Love and Military Destruction: Some Reflections on Mothering and Peace', in *Maternal Theory: Essential Readings*, edited by Andrea O'Reilly, Toronto: Demeter Press, pp. 114–44.
_____. (2007b), 'Maternal Thinking', in *Maternal Theory: Essential Readings*, edited by Andrea O'Reilly, Toronto: Demeter Press, pp. 96–113.
Ryan, Kelly (2007), 'Bump Watch 2006: The Representation of Pregnancy in American Celebrity Magazines', paper presented at the Annual Meeting of the International Communication Association, San Francisco. Available at: http://www.allacademic.com//meta/p_mla_apa_research_citation/1/7/2/8/0/pages172807/p172807-1.php (accessed 10 August 2011).

Ryan, Maura (2008), 'An Open Letter to the Lesbians Who Have Mothered Before Me', in *Mothering in the Third Wave*, edited by Amber Kinser, Toronto: Demeter Press, pp. 31–7.

Saner, Emine (2011), 'How C4's *One Born Every Minute* Made Childbirth a Reality TV Hit', Guardian.co.uk. Available at: http://www.guardian.co.uk/lifeandstyle/2011/mar/22/one-born-every-minute-tv-c4-childbirth (accessed 10 August 2011).

Sargent, Carolyn and Grace Bascope (1997), 'Ways of Knowing about Birth in Three Cultures', in *Childbirth and Authoritative Knowledge: Cross-Cultural Perspectives*, edited by Robbie E. Davis-Floyd and Carolyn Sargent, Berkeley: University of California Press, pp. 183–208.

Sears, William and Martha, et al., (2003), *The Baby Book. Everything You Need to Know About Your Baby from Birth to Age Two*, 2nd ed., Boston: Little, Brown and Company.

Seiter, Ellen and Kreutzner, Gabriele (1991), 'Don't Treat us Like We're So Stupid and Naïve', in *Remote Control: Television, Audiences, and Cultural Power*, edited by Ellen Seiter et al., London: Routledge, pp. 223–47.

Shields, Brooke (2005), *Down Came the Rain: A Mother's Story of Depression and Recovery*, London: Michael Joseph.

Silbergleid, Robin (2009), 'Hip Mamas: *Gilmore Girls* and Ariel Gore', in *Mommy Angst: Motherhood in America Popular Culture*, edited by Ann Hall and Mardia Bishop, Oxford: Praeger, pp. 93–112.

Skeggs, Beverley (1997), *Formations of Class and Gender: Becoming Respectable*, London: Sage.

———. (2003), *Class, Self, Culture*, London: Routledge.

Skeggs, Beverley, Thumim, Nancy and Wood, Helen (2008a), 'Oh Goodness, I am Watching Reality TV: How Methods Make Class in Audience Research', *European Journal of Cultural Studies*, 11:1. Available at: http://eprints.gold.ac.uk/2217/ (accessed 12 May 2012).

———. (2008b), 'It's Just Sad: Affect, Judgement and Emotional Labour in Reality TV Viewing', in *Domesticity, Feminism and Popular Culture*, edited by Joanne Hollows and Stacy Gillis, London: Routledge, pp. 135–50.

Skipper, Alicia (2008), 'Good Girls, Bad Girls, and Motorcycles: Negotiating Feminism', in *Gilmore Girls and the Politics of Identity*, edited by Ritch Calvin, London: McFarland & Company, pp. 80–95.

Sky News (2005), 'Girls Idolise Abi', SkyNews.com. Available at: http://news.sky.com/skynews/article/0,,30000-13365755,00.html (accessed 12 June 2008).

Smart, Carol (1996), 'Deconstructing Motherhood', in *Good Enough Mothering?: Feminist Perspectives on Lone Motherhood*, edited by Elizabeth Bortolaia Silva, London: Routledge, pp. 37–57.

Smith, Liz (2006), 'Sarah Jessica's Secrets', *Good Housekeeping* (US), July, pp. 134–9.

Spangler, Lynn (2003), *Television Women From Lucy to Friends: Fifty Years of Sitcoms and Feminism*, London: Praeger.

Speier, Diane (2004), 'Becoming a Mother', in *Mother Matters: Motherhood as Discourse and Practice: Essays From the Journal of The Association for Research on Mothering*, edited by Andrea O'Reilly, Toronto: Association for Research on Mothering, pp. 141–53.

Stacey, Judith (1996), *In the Name of the Family: Rethinking Family Values in the Postmodern Age*, Boston: Beacon.

Stephens, Rebecca (2004), 'Socially Soothing Stories? Gender, Race and Class in TLC's *A Wedding Story* and *A Baby Story*', in *Understanding Reality Television*, edited by Su Holmes and Deborah Jermyn, London: Routledge, pp. 191–210.

Sullivan, Robert (2005), 'Pillow Talk', *Vogue* (US), September, pp. 701–11 and 794.
Supernanny (2010), retrieved 10 August 2011, from http://jofrost.com/tv-shows/supernanny
Sylvester, Sherri (1999), 'Teen TV, Reckless or Responsible?', *CNN.com*. Available at: http://edition.cnn.com/SHOWBIZ/TV/9904/29/responsible.teen.tv/ (accessed 10 August 2011).
Tagore, Chaya (2010), 'Not Alone', *Newgen*, Summer, pp. 23–4.
Tally, Margaret (2008), 'Reality Television and Contemporary Family Life: Make Over Television and the Question of Parenting', paper presented at the Annual Meeting of the American Sociological Association, Boston, pp. 1–30. Available at: http://www.allacademic.com/meta/p_mla_apa_research_citation/2/3/9/2/7/pages239270/p239270-1.php (accessed 10 August 2011).
Tardy, Rebecca (2000), 'But I Am a Good Mom: The Social Construction of Motherhood Through Health-Care Conversations', *Journal of Contemporary Ethnography*, 28, pp. 433–73.
Taylor, Ella (1989), *Prime-Time Families: Television Culture in Postwar America*, California: University of California Press.
The National Campaign (2012), 'National Data', The National Campaign to Prevent Teen and Unplanned Pregnancy. Available at: http://www.thenationalcampaign.org/national-data/default.aspx (accessed 5 January 2012).
The Social Issues Research Centre (2011), 'The Changing Face of Motherhood', Oxford: The Social Issues Research Centre. Available at: http://www.sirc.org/publik/changing_face_of_motherhood.shtml (accessed 18 October 2011).
Thomas, Carol (2007), 'The Baby and the Bath Water: Disabled Women and Motherhood in Social Context', in *Maternal Theory: Essential Readings*, edited by Andrea O'Reilly, Toronto: Demeter Press, pp. 500–519.
Thomas, Lyn (1995), 'In Love with Inspector Morse: Feminist Subculture and Quality Television', *Feminist Review*, 51, pp. 1–25.
Thomson, Rachel et al., (2008), *The Making of Modern Motherhood: Memories, Representations, Practices*, Maidenhead: The Open University. Available at: http://www.open.ac.uk/hsc/research/research-projects/making-of-modern-motherhood/making-of-modern-motherhood.php (accessed 30 August 2011).
Thorpe, Vanessa (2010), 'Big Gender Gap on the Small Screen: Men Outnumber Women on TV Two-to-One', Guardian.co.uk. Available at: http://www.guardian.co.uk/media/2010/mar/07/television-men-outnumber-women (accessed 30 August 2011).
Thurer, Shari (2007), 'The Myths of Motherhood' in *Maternal Theory: Essential Readings*, edited by Andrea O'Reilly, Toronto: Demeter Press, pp. 331–44.
Thurer, Shari (1994), *The Myths of Motherhood: How Culture Reinvents the Good Mother*, New York: Penguin.
Trebilcot, Joyce (1983), 'Introduction', in *Mothering: Essays in Feminist Theory*, edited by Joyce Trebilcot, New Jersey: Rowman & Allanheld, pp.1–6.
Tronto, Joan (2002), 'The "Nanny" Question in Feminism', *Hypatia*, 17:2, pp. 34–51.
Tropp, Laura (2006), 'Faking a Sonogram: Representations of Motherhood on *Sex and the City*', *The Journal of Popular Culture*, 39:5, pp. 861–77.
Tuchman, Gaye (1978), 'Introduction: The Symbolic Annihilation of Women by the Mass Media', in *Hearth and Home: Images of Women in the Mass Media*, edited by Gaye Tuchman, Arlene Kaplan Daniels, and James Benét, New York: Oxford University Press, pp. 3–37.

Turnbull, Sue (2008), 'They Stole Me, *The O.C.*, Masculinity, and the Strategies of Teen TV', in *Teen Television: Essays on Programming and Fandom*, edited by Sharon Marie Ross and Louise Ellen Stein, London: McFarland & Company, Inc., pp. 170–184.

Turner, Graeme (2008), 'Genre, Hybridity and Mutation', in *The Television Genre Book*, edited by Glen Creeber, London: BFI, pp. 8–9.

Tuttle Hansen (2007), 'A Sketch in Progress: Introducing Mother Without Child', in *Maternal Theory: Essential Readings*, edited by Andrea O'Reilly, Toronto: Demeter Press, pp. 431–59.

Tyler, Imogen (2001), 'Skin-tight: Celebrity, Pregnancy and Subjectivity', in *Thinking Through the Skin*, edited by Sarah Ahmed and Jackie Stacey, Routledge: London, pp. 69–83.

Tyler, Imogen and Bennett, Bruce (2010), 'Celebrity Chav: Fame, Femininity and Social Class', *European Journal of Cultural Studies*, 13:3 pp. 375–93.

U.S. Census Bureau (2009), 'American Community Survey'. Available at: http://factfinder.census.gov/home/saff/main.html?_lang=en (accessed 5 January 2012).

Valdivia, Angharad (1998), 'Clueless in Hollywood: Single Moms in Contemporary Family Movies', *Journal of Communication Inquiry*, 22:3, pp. 272–92.

Valeska, Lucia (1983), 'If All Else Fails, I'm Still a Mother', in *Mothering: Essays in Feminist Theory*, edited by Joyce Trebilcot, New Jersey: Rowman & Allanheld, pp. 70–80.

Van den Bulck, Hilde, Nele Simons and Baldwin Van Gorp, (2008), 'Let's Drink and Be Merry: The Framing of Alcohol in the Prime–Time American Youth Series *The O.C.*', *Journal of Studies on Alcohol & Drugs*, 69:6, pp. 933–40.

Van Meter, Jonathan (2004), 'Carrie Doesn't Live Here Anymore', *Marie Claire* (UK), June, pp. 82–8.

Vande Berg, Leah (2010), 'Dramedy', *The Museum of Broadcast Communications*. Available at: http://www.museum.tv/eotvsection.php?entrycode=dramedy (accessed 10 August 2011).

Vandenberg-Daves, Jodi (2004), 'Mama Bear as Domestic Micro Manager', in *Mother Matters: Motherhood as Discourse and Practice: Essays From the Journal of The Association for Research on Mothering*, edited by Andrea O'Reilly, Toronto: Association for Research on Mothering, pp. 111–24.

Vieten, Cassandra (2009), *Mindful Motherhood: Practical Tools for Staying Sane in Pregnancy and Your Child's First Year*, Oakland, CA: New Harbinger Publications.

Wall, Cara (2005), 'The Dark Secret of Stars Hollow', Salon.com, Available at: http://dir.salon.com/story/ent/tv/feature/2005/09/27/gilmore_porn/index.html (accessed 10 August 2011).

Warner, Judith (2007), 'The Motherhood Religion', in *Maternal Theory: Essential Readings*, edited by Andrea O'Reilly, Toronto: Demeter Press, pp. 705–25.

Wee, Valerie (2008), 'Teen Television and the WB Television Network', in *Teen Television: Essays on Programming and Fandom*, edited by Sharon Marie Ross and Louise Ellen Stein, London: McFarland & Company, Inc., pp. 43–60.

Wells, Paul (1998), 'Where Everybody Knows Your Name: Open Convictions in Closed Contexts in the American Situation Comedy', in *Because I Tell a Joke or Two: Comedy, Politics and Social Difference*, edited by Stephen Wagg, New York: Routledge, pp. 180–201.

Westman, Karin (2007), 'Beauty and the Geek: Changing Gender Stereotypes on the *Gilmore Girls*', in *Geek Chick: Smart Women in Popular Culture*, edited by Sherrie A. Innes, London: Routledge, pp. 11–30.

Whitbeck, Caroline (1983), 'The Maternal Instinct', in *Mothering: Essays in Feminist Theory*, edited by Joyce Trebilcot, New Jersey: Rowman and Allanhead, pp. 185–91.

Williams, Joan (2001), *Unbending Gender: Why Family and Work Conflict and What To Do About It*, Oxford: Oxford University Press.
Williams, Kristi, Sharon Sassler and Lisa Nicholson (2008), 'For Better or For Worse? The Consequences of Marriage and Cohabitation for Single Mothers', *Social Forces*, 86:4, pp. 1481–1511.
Williams, Zoe (2010), 'The Powerful Cynicism of Parenting TV', Guardian.co.uk. Available at: http://www.guardian.co.uk/tv-and-radio/tvandradioblog/2010/feb/09/cynicism-parenting-tv (accessed 10 August 2011).
Wilson, Benji (2010), '*One Born Every Minute*: Comments', Telegraph.co.uk. Available at: http://www.telegraph.co.uk/culture/tvandradio/7198234/One-Born-Every-Minute-Channel-4-review.html (accessed 10 August 2011).
Winnicott, Donald Woods (1973), *The Child, The Family, and the Outside World*, Harmondsworth: Penguin.
Wolf, Naomi (2002), *Misconceptions: Truth, Lies and the Unexpected on the Journey to Motherhood*, London: Vintage.
Woliver, Laura (1995), 'Reproductive Technologies, Surrogacy Arrangements, and the Politics of Motherhood', in *Mothers in Law: Feminist Theory and the Legal Regulation of Motherhood*, edited by Martha Albertson Fineman and Isabel Karpin, New York: Columbia University Press, pp. 346–60.
Wood, Helen and Lisa Taylor (2008), 'Feeling Sentimental about Television and Audiences', *Cinema Journal*, 47:3, pp. 144–51.
Wood, Helen (2009), *Talking with Television*, Urbana and Champaign: University of Illinois.
Wood, Michelle (2008), 'Celebrity Older Mothers: Does the Media Give Women a False Impression?', *British Journal of Midwifery*, 16:5, p. 326.
Woodward, Kath (2003), 'Representations of Motherhood', in *Gender, Identity and Reproduction: Social Perspectives*, edited by Sarah Earle and Gayle Letherby, London: Palgrave Macmillan, pp. 18–32.
Woollett, Anne (1994), 'The Mandate for Motherhood: Having Children – Accounts of Childless Women and Women with Reproductive Problems', in *Motherhood: Meanings, Practices and Ideologies*, edited by Ann Phoenix, Anne Woollett and Eva Lloyd, London: Sage, pp. 47–65.
Worthington, Marjorie (2009), 'The Motherless "Disney Princess": Marketing Mothers Out of the Picture', in *Mommy Angst: Motherhood in American Popular Culture*, edited by Ann Hall and Mardia Bishop, London: Praeger, pp. 29–46.

INDEX

The names of fictional characters are not inverted.

2point4 Children 41
8 Boys and Wanting a Girl 99, 101
90210 10, 55
10 Things I Hate About You 59

abortion 19, 36
Access Hollywood 130
Addicted to Surrogacy 102
adoptive mothers 17, 75, 170; *see also* biological mothers
Adrianna, in *90210* 61
advertisers 34
African-American single parents 37–8, 76–7; *see also* race
age at 'primigravida' 2
Aladdin 59
alcohol-abusing mothers 17, 57, 60, 61; *see also* Katona, Kerry
alienation 3
Ally McBeal 71–2
alternative practices of mothering 6
America, single parent families in 76
An American Family 98
American Society for Reproductive Medicine 102
Andy Griffith Show, The 30
Ang, Ien 17, 182
Angie Watts, in *EastEnders* 17
'anti-Donna Reed' 89
anxiety: 37, 99, 102, 151, 156
appearance: associated to maternal capabilities 127; beautiful 79, 89; celebrity mothers 121, 123, 126–7, 142, 145; overweight characters 39; pressure to maintain 128–9; of single mothers 74, 82; slender characters 3, 5, 40, 65, 73, 89
Aris, Rosemary 105
Arms, Suzanne 151–2
Arnaz, Desi 35
Arnold, Abby 63, 74, 154, 167
Ask Supernanny: What Every Parent Wants to Know (Frost) 110
audiences: of celebrity reality television 133, 134, 138; class relevance 183–4; of *Gilmore Girls* 81; of *90210* 60; personal interpretation of television 181; of pregnancy and childbirth programmes 157, 163; soap opera 16, 18, 178–9; studies of 182–3; of *Supernanny* 110–11; teen 54, 55; teen television 69

Baby Story, A 147, 157–61
Bachelor Father 56
bad mothers: in *Desperate Housewives* 72–4; on *Fast Food Baby* 100; intensive mothering standard 3; juxtaposed with good 4, 105; Katona as 143–4; Lorelai as 90; Price as 140–41; Roseanne as epitome of 39; of soap operas 26; *see also* 'good mother' myth; mothers
BAFTA award 19
Ball, Lucille 36
Bathrick, Serafina 32
BBC 97
Beauty and the Beast 59

Being Mum 99
Bell, Emma 142–3, 144
Benfer, Amy 73
Berebitsky, Julie 75
Bernstein, Jane 170
'Best Television Shows of All-*TIME*' 81
Beulah 30
Beverly Hills, 90210: as basis of *90210* 60; parental portrayal in 53, 57; profitability of 55; *see also 90210*; teen drama
Beyond the Break 57
Bianca Butcher, in *EastEnders* 24
biological mothers 8, 23–8, 63, 68, 76, 170; *see also* adoptive mothers
birth plans 173
Bishop, Mardia 107
Borisoff, Deborah 3
breastfeeding 62, 153, 155
Britain, lone parents in 76
British Academy Television Award 163
British Comedy Awards 42
British Soap Award 19
Brookside 17
Brown, Mary Ellen 16, 17, 21
Brunsdon, Charlotte 17–18, 72
Buckman, Peter 17
Buffy: The Vampire Slayer 55, 57–8
Bündchen, Gisele 121
Burton, Graeme 177
Butcher, Bianca, in *EastEnders* 24
Butcher, Janine, in *EastEnders* 20
Butterflies 37

caesarean sections 151–2, 160; *see also* childbirth
Casper 59
Celebrity Love Island 134
Celebrity Mother of the Year Award 138, 141, 143
celebrity reality television: Alicia Douvall 122, 133–7; Brooke Shields 130; Celebrity Mom-making machinery 130; celebrity mother profile 122–32; fertility 121, 131–2; Harvey Price 139; hierarchy of contemporary female celebrity 132–3; Georgia Howes 134–7; Kerry Katona 122, 133–4, 141–6; mothering and motherwork in 133–47; overview of 121–2; Sarah Jessica Parker 121, 126–7; Katie Price 122, 133–4, 137–41; stereotypes in 124; *see also* reality parenting programming
celibacy 74
Center for Disease Control 22
Chan, Janet 128
'Changing Childbirth' 165
Charmed 55, 56
Chatton, Barbara 58
child maintenance statistics 73
child rearing: demands of 63; interventions 100; as mothers' responsibility 107, 112–16, 175; parenting advice about 99–100; as personal vs. social issue 107–8, 116; 'pinnacle of parenting failure' 117; quality 100; as soap opera storyline 17, 25; as unmarked by gender 97; *see also* childcare; mothering practices; motherwork
child support statistics 73
childbirth: breathing techniques during 168; caesarean sections 151–2, 160; changing 'nature' of 147–53; discord following 156; fear of failure at 166; 'good' 154–5, 159, 161; interventionalist approach to 172; judgement about 156–7; marginalized 160–61; on *Maternity Ward* 163; medical team role in 147–8, 164–7; midwives role in 147–8, 164–7; a more balanced view of 164–8; on *Murphy Brown* 38; 'negative outcomes' of 161, 162, 164, 172; on *One Born Every Minute UK* 164–8; 'ordinary bad births' 156; pain of 154–5, 161; pain relief during 167; range of women's experiences 149; realistic portrayal of 28, 165; Stacey's on *EastEnders* 22; treatment of women during 159–60, 174; women's voices and 153–7

Childbirth Without Fear (Dick-Read) 152
childcare: communal 27; government funded 7; by grandparents 26; manuals 3–4, 110; routinised 111–12; web sites about 4–5, 50, 110; *see also* child rearing
child-free characters: 47, 84
children: caretakers of 63; health problems of related to maternal age 131; impact of parental marriage status change on 78; outcomes of 'good' vs. 'bad' mothers for 79; power of 44; social development of 106; unplanned 77, 89
children's literature 58
choice to not mother 48
Cinderella 58–9
Clark, Hilary 129
class (social) 3, 109–10, 158–9, 162–3, 183–4
Clifford, Max 142
Clueless 59
Colleen Sarkoissian, in *90210* 64–5
Collett, Jessica 137
competition between women 47, 49
conception: *see* pregnancy
Constance Tate-Duncan, in *90210* 61, 67–8
Coronation Street 16
Cosby Show, The 31
Cosslett, Tess 150
Cotton Wool Kids 101
Coupling 31
Courtship of Eddie's Father, The 56
Crawford, Cindy 121
Crossroads 16
cultural politics 184
Curtis, Jamie Lee 172
Cutting Edge: Bad Behaviour 98
CW network (US) 60

Dallas 24, 182
Dana Bowen, in *90210* 60, 68
Darcey, Lesley 104
Davis, Glyn 53
Dawson's Creek 53, 55, 56
Debbie Wilson, in *90210* 64–7
definitions 8

Degrassi: The Next Generation 57
demographics 1, 2, 48
Department of Health (UK) 19
Desperate Housewives 71, 72–3
Despicable Me 59
developmental psychology 45, 53–4
Dick van Dyke Show, The 30
Dickinson, Kay 53
Dick-Read, Grantly 152
Directors Guild of America 71
Dish Network 18
Disney 58–9
divorce, ill effects of 77–8
domestic drama: *see* soap opera
domestic help 44
domestic violence 35
Donna Reed Show, The 29, 30, 33, 89, 95–6
Donna Stone, in *The Donna Reed Show* 33
Douglas, Susan: on celebrity motherhood 122–5, 139–40; on expectations portrayed in media 3–4; on feminine mystique 34; on good mother masquerade 6; on intensive mothering 7; on postnatal depression 129
Douvall, Alicia 122, 133–7
Dovey, Jon 98
Down Came the Rain: A Mother's Story of Depression and Recovery (Shields) 130
Downe, Pamela 26
dramedy: defining single motherhood in society 75–8; exploiting maternal narrative 72; 'good' and 'bad' single mothers 79–80; history of genre 71–2; a myriad of mothers on Gilmore Girls 81–5; overview of 71; single, sexual and sisterly motherhood in 72–5; *see also Gilmore Girls*
drug addicts as mothers 57, 61
Dunne, Gillian 170

E4 (UK): 60, 81, 110
EastEnders: alcoholic adoptive mother on 17; Angie Watts in 17; awards won by 19; Bianca Butcher on

24; Butcher, Janine in 20; Carol (Bianca's mother) in 24–5; as genre example 10; Lola Pearce in 20, 22; mother–daughter bond in 25; nonconformist mother types on 22, 24; other-mothers in 26; overview of 18; paternity issues on 22; pregnancy outcomes on 19–20; realism of 24–5; Tanya Jessop in 23–4; teenage mothers on: 19–23
economic status 78
education 77, 78
eldercare 44
Elle (magazine) 127
Elsie Tanner, in *Coronation Street* 16
Elson, Vicki 161
Emily Gilmore, in *Gilmore Girls* 82, 91–5
'emotional labour' 107, 182, 184
empowerment: in Gilmore Girls 87; in images of motherhood 74; midwives providing 165; 'mother wars' inhibiting 51; parent programming as 111–12; soap operas as 16, 21, 24; of working-class motherhood image 40
Enchanted 59
Entertainment Tonight 130
Erickson, Ann 86
Experience of Childbirth, The (Kitzinger) 152
extra-marital affairs 37, 64–5, 73
Extreme Parental Guidance 99, 110

factual television: *Baby Story, A* 147, 157–61; changing 'nature' of childbirth 147–53; class (social) in 158–9, 162–3; dramatic effect in 162–3; fantasy vision portrayed in 158–9; 'generic bodies' in 162; 'good mother' myth in 174; hidden truths of pregnancy and childbirth 168–72; *Make Me A Mum* 175; *Maternity Ward* 147, 161–3; medical interventions in 160; midwives on 164–7; a more balanced view of childbirth 164–8; 'negative outcomes' of childbirth 161, 162,
164, 172; neonatal units on 170–72; *One Born Every Minute UK* 147, 157, 163–74; *One Born Every Minute USA* 172–4; over-familiarity on 173–4; role of medical team in 162, 164, 173; women's voices and childbirth 153–7; *see also* childbirth; pregnancy
Fairclough, Kirsty 107
Family Friendly Programming Forum 80–81
family position 21, 44
Family Television Award 81
Family Ties 31, 40
family unit: alternative 50, 72, 159, 164, 169–70; contemporary 26; dysfunctional 50; as foundation of situation comedy 30; loyalty portrayed in 66; *see also* nuclear family unit
Fast Food Baby 100
Father Knows Best 33
fathers: lack of attention to 38; on reality parenting shows 101, 107, 113; single 59; on teen dramas 179; who leave their children 104; *see also* men; paternity
feminine mystique 33, 34, 38, 51
'feminist mothering' 23
Ferguson, Ann 78
Ferguson, Galit 107, 109
fertility 168
fertility technologies 101, 131–2, 149, 168–9
Feuer, Jane 31
'fictional realism' 14
financial recompense, lack of 6, 26
First, Elsa 117
Fleegal, Stacia 95
Fly Away Home 59
Flynn, Emily 119
'formatted documentary' 99
foster-mothering 17
Four Sons versus Four Daughters 101
Fox network 55
Friedan, Betty 38
Friends 31, 84
Frost, Jo, in *Supernanny* 110–19
frustration 3

Full House 31
future research needs 181–4

'gaby' boom 169
Gailey, Elizabeth 128
Gatrell, Caroline 140
gender: childrearing and 97; 'disappointment' 101; essentialist notion of 39; imbalance in the home 43; roles in *Wife Swap* 107; rules of 'good mothers' 4, 90
genre productions 178
Geraghty, Christine 17
Getting Even with Dad 59
Ghost Dad 59
Gidget 56
Gilmore Girls: domestic indifference in 90–91; as dramedy 71–2; Emily and mother–daughter dynamic 91–5; myriad of mothers on 81–5; othermothers and community effort in 91; programme overview 80–81; sex and conversation in 87–90; sisterly bond in 85–7
Glamour (magazine) 126
Glamour Models 10, 133–4
Glamour Models, Mum and Me 122, 133–4
Glee 55, 56–7
Goldbergs, The 30
'good enough mothering' 9, 11, 114, 181
Good Housekeeping (magazine) 127
'good mother' myth: celebrities as archetypal models of 124–6; celebrity aesthetic ideal link to 127–9; conditions leading to myth of 7–8; in contemporary media 3, 11; cultural changes about 92, 96; Debbie Wilson, in *90210* and 65; defined 2–4; Douvall upholding 126; Emily Gilmore's version of 92, 94; exploitation of role of 36; in factual television 174; failure of in *90210* 65; fertility linked to 132; gender rules of 4; juxtaposed with 'bad mother' 4, 105; lack of power of 64; mask or masquerade of 6, 10, 115, 130, 141, 143; on Mumsnet 4; nonconformists of 140–41, 143; oppression and 115; Parker upholding 126; propagating conservative agenda 107–8; reaffirmation of 22, 99; single mothers and 79; soap opera challenging stereotype of 13–28; standards of 3, 5; in *Wife Swap* 108; working mothers and 108; *see also* intensive mothering; motherhood
Gossip Girl 55
government practices impacting mothers 5, 7, 111–12
Graham, Lauren 80–81
grandmothers, childrearing by 26
Grandparents Plus 26
Grant, Sheila, in *Brookside* 17
Gray, Ann 182
Grazia (magazine) 126, 127
Green, Fiona 27, 109, 115, 117
Growing Pains 40

Haffner, Debra 53–4
Half Ton Mum 97, 100–101
Hall, Ann 107
Harpers Bazaar (magazine) 123
Hart-Davis, Alice 74–5
health risks 131–2, 151–2, 160
Heartbreak High 56
Heinz-Knowles, Katharine 57
Hellcats 57
Help Me Love My Baby 101
'heroine television' 72
'Hi Honey, I'm Home' 30
Hobson, Dorothy 14, 17, 23, 182
Hochschild, Arlie 79
Hollows, Joanne 16
'home', as created 107
Home and Away 17
'Home Sweet Home' embroidery 32
Hooperman 71
Horowitz, Rachel 40
housewife role 8, 17, 36, 38, 41
How to Get the Best from Your Children (Frost) 110
Howes, Georgia 134–7

I Love Lucy 30, 34–6
I'm Pregnant and... 22

industrialisation 7
infidelity 37, 64–5, 73;
    see also marriage
informed consent 160, 168
institution of motherhood 8
intensive mothering 3; aberration of 7; Mumsnet's promotion of 5; in *Outnumbered* 49; 'powerful Trojan horse' of 124; in reality television 118; working mothers failure at 6; *see also* 'good mother' myth; motherhood
IVF treatment 131–2, 168–9; *see also* fertility technologies

Jackie Taylor, in *90210* 61, 67
Janine Butcher, in *EastEnders* 20
Jennifer Clark, in *90210* 61–2, 68
Jensen, Tracey 109, 116
Jermyn, Debra 127
Jessop, Tanya, in *EastEnders* 23–4
Jo Frost's Confident Baby Care 110
Joey 29
Jones, Tanya 106
Jordan: *see* Price, Katie
Joyrich, Lynne 32
judgement: about childbirth 156–7; of celebrity mothers 140–41, 142; challenge to celebrity-mother profile 133; class as factor in 109; of mothers by children's success 137; of mothers by mothers 48; of mothers in media environment 2; of motherwork 100; narration as encouraging 173; in parenting television 99, 113, 116–17; of self against idealized images 34, 118, 128–9; standards used in 105, 139–40; *see also* mothers; scrutiny of women
June Cleaver, in *Leave it to Beaver* 33

Kanner, Bernice 34
Kate and Allie 31
Katie (formerly *What Katie Did Next*) 10, 122, 133–4
Katona, Kerry 122, 133–4, 141–6
Kendrick, Beth 86

Kerry Katona: The Next Chapter 10, 133–4
Kinnick, Katherine 4, 90
Kinser, Amber 8–9, 33
Kitzinger, Sheila 3, 150–51, 152
Kutulas, Judy 34

Laurel Cooper, in *90210* 61
Leave it to Beaver 29, 30, 33, 34
lesbian mothers 169–70
Lichtenstein, Therese 40
Liebes, Tamar 18, 23, 27
'Life Unscripted' 157–8, 159
Little Mermaid, The 59
Livingstone, Sonia 18, 23, 27
Lola Pearce, in *EastEnders* 20, 22
Lorelai Gilmore, in *Gilmore Girls* 80–83, 85–95
Lucy Ricardo, in *I Love Lucy* 34–5

MacDonald, Sue 164–5
Maher, Jennifer 158, 162
Make Me A Mum 175
makeover reality programming 98–9, 128
Mama 30
Many Loves of Dobie Gillis, The 54
Margaret Anderson, *Father Knows Best* 33
Marie Claire (magazine) 126
marriage: benefits of 77; decreased prospects of 89; power dynamic 65; relationship in *90210* 66; 'single mothering' within and outside of 79; single mothers and 77–8; *see also* infidelity
Married… With Children 31
Mary Richards, in *Mary Tyler Moore Show* 36
Mary Tyler Moore Show, The 30
maternal instinct: assumptions about 103; attitude about in *Wifeswap* 107; child bonding and 102; in *Outnumbered* 50; questioning of 118; reflection of child in mother and 137; variability of 62
'maternal practice' 63
'Maternity Matters' 165
Maternity Ward 147, 161–3

Matheson, Sarah 34
matriarchs 15
Maude 29, 30, 36
Maushart, Susan 6, 153–4
May, Elaine Tyler 36
McInerney, Katherine 150, 160
McRobbie, Angela 114, 123
media pressure 4, 5
medical team role 162, 164, 173; *see also* midwives
Meg Mortimer, in *Crossroads* 16
men 1, 15, 65; *see also* fathers
mental illness: anxiety 37, 99, 102, 151, 156; celebrity 130, 142, 145; during motherhood 129–30; in *My Fake Baby* 104; in *My Monkey Baby* 103; portrayals of 61; postnatal depression 105, 129–30, 156
Michaels, Meredith: on celebrity motherhood 122–5, 139–40; on expectations portrayed in media 3–4; on good mother masquerade 6; on intensive mothering 7; on postnatal depression 129
midwives 147–8, 164–7; *see also* medical team role
Miller, Tina 63, 155, 156–7, 174
Millman, Joyce 56
Mills, Brett 31, 46
Miranda Hobbs, in *Sex in the City* 84
Misbehaving Mums to Be 100
miscarriage 20–21, 72, 138, 152
Modleski, Tania 14, 17, 18
'Mommie Dearest' 61
'mommy track' 41, 46
'Money Matters' (on Mumsnet) 4
Moonlighting 71, 72
Moore, Demi 121
Moore, Jane 104–6
Morris, Theresa 150, 160
mortality rates, maternal 131, 148
Moseley, Rachel 54
Mother Rabbit 58
mother 'wars' 48–50
mother–daughter relationships: in *90210* 65–6; in *Buffy: The Vampire Slayer* 57–8; in *Desperate Housewives* 74; in *EastEnders* 25; in *Gilmore Girls* 80–83,
85–95; in *Glamour Models, Mum and Me* 134–7; of Kerry Katona 145
motherhood: alternative role model of 39–40; claiming redemption through 144; as 'connecting force' 23; cultural practice of 7, 63; desire for portrayed 39; devaluation of 47; double shift of 64; empowering images of 74; essentialist notions of 63, 106, 108, 117; in feminist scholarship 2; historical construction of 63, 75; impact of representations of 178; intimate bond of 63; for low-income women 75; maternal feelings and instinct 62; maternal myths and reality 100–106; mental health during 129–30; negative feelings of 5; patriarchal institution of 8; problematic in teen drama 60; professionalization of 119; rendered pathological 128; soap opera and 16–18; social construction of 2, 63, 75, 170
mothering practices: advice on 3–4; alternative 6; in celebrity reality television 133–47; communal 27; dangerous 111; first-hand experience at 100; historical overview of 7; imperfection of 50; judgement of 48; 'maternal practice' 63; model for second and third time 45; patriarchal 112; personal 8; skills and resources for 63; *see also* child rearing; *Supernanny*
mothers: absence of in Disney productions 59; adoptive 17, 75, 170; bad single 79–80; biological 8, 23–8, 63, 68, 76, 170; contradiction in portrayal of 11, 68; lack of supports to 116; lesbian 169–70; maternal thinking of 117; paradox posed by celebrity 125; as root cause of behavioural problems 113; stay-at-home 6–7, 33, 47, 48, 50, 64, 72–3, 92, 108–9, 181; stepmothering 48; stigma of 'failed femininity' of 128; studies 67; 'symbolic annihilation' of 58;

as toxic influences 179; types of 17, 22, 24; unattainable celebrity image of 123, 125–6; as valued in eighteenth century 147–8; work as incompatible with 8; work-centric model of 84; working model of 23; working mothers 6, 7, 50, 82–4, 108; workloads of 114–15, 118, 140; *see also* bad mothers; 'good mother' myth; intensive mothering; judgement; *individual programme characters*
'mothers and lovers' 18
mother–son relationships 139
motherwork: in celebrity reality television 133–47; devaluation of 47; emotional connectedness in 63; impact of representations of 178; judgement of 100; on *Outnumbered* 42–5; personal experience of 8, 118
Mrs Dale's Diary 16
Mrs Kim, in *Gilmore Girls* 83
Mullender, Audrey 105
Mum and Me 10
Mumford, Laura Stempel 17, 20
Mums Who Leave Their Kids 104–6
Mumsnet 4–5, 50
Munn, Penny 44–5
Murphy Brown 29, 37–9, 46
My Fake Baby 104
My Family 31, 41, 44
My Girl 59
My Monkey Baby 103
My Three Sons 30, 56
My Wife and Kids 41

Nanny 911 99
narrative devices: of situation comedies 29–30; of soap operas 17, 19–21, 25
National Childbirth Trust 86
Neale, Steve 177
neonatal units 170–72
New York Times 38
Newgen (magazine) 86
Next Chapter, The 122
non-mother and mother divide 47
Northern Exposure 71, 72

nuclear family unit: challenged 39, 83; contemporary American politics and 38; dark side of patriarchal 64; development of 7; in *I Love Lucy* 36; as oppressive 8–9; shift to 'family of woman' 76; in situation comedies 31–4, 41, 44; in *Supernanny* 112
'nurturing nature' vs. biology 63

Oakley, Ann 153, 156
O.C., The 55, 56, 57
Octomom, My Monkey Baby 99
Octomom: Me and My 14 Kids 97, 102
O'Donohoe, Stephanie 128
OK! (magazine) 138, 141, 142
One Born Every Minute UK 10, 147, 157, 163–72
One Born Every Minute USA 10, 147, 172–4
One Day at a Time 31
One Tree Hill 55
oppression 115, 150
O'Reilly, Abby 123, 126
O'Reilly, Andrea 8, 25, 105
other-mothering 26–8, 91
Outnumbered 10, 29, 32, 41–50

pain relief 167, 173
Paltrow, Gwyneth 121
'parental Cosmo girl' 74
Parenthood 72
Parenting (magazine) 128
parenting advice 99–100
parenting documentaries 97–8
Parker, Sarah Jessica 121, 126–7
Party of Five 53, 55, 56
Pasquier, Dominique 56
paternity 20–22; *see also* fathers
patriarchal society: anxiety in 37; benefited by 'good mother myth' 6; childbirth in 150; father's role valued by 21; *I Love Lucy* in 35; maintaining 58; view of motherhood refuted 24
patriarchal unit: *see* nuclear family unit
Pávlovic, Annie 105
Pearce, Lola, in *EastEnders* 20, 22
People's Choice Awards 81

personal realm, expressed in public sphere 15
Phyllis 30, 36
'pinnacle of parenting failure' 117
Playboy 138
political vs. personal issues 15, 46, 108
politics and family 38, 73, 75
Popular 57
Porter, Marie 105
'post-family' television 72
postnatal depression 105, 129–30, 156
postwar redomestication program 124
Potter, Beatrix 58
poverty 77, 89
Powell, Nick 119
pregnancy: celebrity 121–2; celebrity style-guide for 127; first on television 35–6; in mature women 127, 131–2, 159; *Misbehaving Mums to Be* 100; in soap operas 19–20; statistics on 22; by surrogate mothers 102–3, 127; teen 33, 76; *see also* factual television
pre-industrial society 7
Press, Andrea 72
Price, Harvey 139
Price, Katie 122, 133–4, 137–41
'The Problem that Has No Name' 37
'professional motherhood': *see* intensive mothering
public policy impacting mothers 46, 75, 77
public sphere, personal realm expressed in 15

Quayle, Dan 37–8

race 77, 89; *see also* African-American single parents
Rachael Green, in *Friends* 84
Rapp, Rayna 151
reality parenting programming: class, gender and 106–10; emotional displays in 107; focus on working class 109; formal characteristics of 98; gender roles in *Wife Swap* 107; history of genre 97–100; makeover reality parenting 106–7, 116; makeover reality programming 98–9; maternal myths and reality of motherhood 100–106; middle-class standards in 109, 115; overview of 97; self-improvement reality programming 98–9; unrealistic assumptions of 108–9; *see also Supernanny*; *individual programmes*
Rehab 134
religion, agenda of 73
reproductive technologies 101, 131–2, 149, 168–9
research needs 181–4
Rhoda 36–7
Ria Parkinson, in *Butterflies* 37
Rich, Adrienne 150
Rory Gilmore, in *Gilmore Girls* 80, 82–7
Roseanne 29, 31, 39–41
Roseanne Conner, in *Roseanne* 39–40
Ross, Sharon 54
Roswell High 55, 56
Royal Television Society Programme Award 19, 42
Ruddick, Sara 62, 63, 106, 117
Runway Moms 130

Saner, Emine 164
Schiffer, Claudia 121
scrutiny of women 2, 122; *see also* judgement
second-wave feminists 8–9, 14, 17, 62; *see also* feminists
self-improvement reality programming 98–9
Sex and the City 84
sexuality 74, 75, 90
Sheila Grant, in *Brookside* 17
Sherry Tinsdale, in *Gilmore Girls* 84
Shields, Brooke 130
siblings 44–5
Sight and Sound (magazine) 158
Simpsons, The 31
single fathers 59
single mothers: African-American 37–8; 'bad' 79; by-choice 81; criterion for 'good' 79; defining of in society 75–8; in *Desperate Housewives* 73–5; differences between 79; as focus

in *Parenthood* 72; marriages of 77–8; Murphy Brown as 37–9; negative outcomes of 89; within and outside of marriage 79; positive presentation of 85–91; poverty of 77, 89; public assistance to 75; under representation of on television 73; routes to becoming 76

situation comedy: family and social change in 32; family importance in 30–32; genre limitations 46; genre repertoire 41, 179; history of genre 29–30; maternal routine and motherwork in 42–5; *Outnumbered* 41–2; pregnancy and motherhood in 32–41; women, work and mother 'wars' 45–50

Six Feet Under 72
Skeggs, Beverley 107, 115, 119, 182–3
Skipper, Alicia 73
Sleepless in Seattle 59
Smallville 56
Snow White and the Seven Dwarfs 58
soap opera: abortion, miscarriage and impending motherhood 19–23; awards 19; birth and biological mothers on 23–6; character types in 15; characteristics of 14–15; feminist television theorists on 15, 16; history of genre 13–14; motherhood and 16–18; narrative devices of 17, 19–21; other-mothers and 26–8; overview of 13; as 'social barometer' 14; women and 14–16; *see also EastEnders*
Soap Opera Digest 21
social change 13–14, 181
social construction of motherhood 2, 63, 75, 170
social development, of children 106
social inequality 58
social justice 100
Sookie St. James, in *Gilmore Girls* 83–4
Spain, child gender choice in 101
Spangler, Lynn 35
Spears, Britney 121, 123
Speier, Diane 50

Stein, Louise Ellen 54
stepchildren 78
Stephens, Rebecca 158
Stephenson, Laura 170
stepmothering 48
St. Trinian's 59
Sugar and Spice 59
Suleman, Nadya 102
'super-mom' myth 40
Supernanny: incompetent, incapable and ineffectual mothers in 112–19; negative maternal depictions in 99; as positive and empowering programming 111–12; *see also* reality parenting programming
Supernanny UK 10
Supernanny USA 10
surrogate mothers 102–3, 127
Susan Mayer, in *Desperate Housewives* 73–5
Sylvester, Sherri 56
'symbolic annihilation' 58

Tabitha, in *90210* 60
Tanner, Elsie, in *Coronation Street* 16
Tanya Jessop, in *EastEnders* 23–4
Teen Choice Award 67, 81
teen drama: debates about category of 55; genre trope 56, 179; history of genre 54–6; imperfect but available motherhood in 65–7; ineffective and absent parents in 56–9; parental types portrayed in 53, 56–7; power, patriarchy and single shift in 64–5; problematic motherhood in 60; *see also 90210*
teen pregnancy 33, 76, 81–2
teenagers 53–4, 134–5
Television and Radio Industries Club Award 19
television criticism by feminists 18
television theorists: on soap operas 14–15, 16, 18
'text-in-action' method 183
Thumim, Nancy 107, 115, 119, 182–3
Thurer, Shari 5, 33–4
'time famine' 115
Tinkerbell and the Great Fairy Rescue 59

Too Old to be a Mum 97
Tracy Clark, in *90210* 60–61, 65
Tuchman, Gaye 58
Turnbull, Sue 54

'unmarried mother': *see* single mothers
U.S., single parent families in 76
USA Today 38

Valdivia, Angharad 59, 73, 74, 79
values, impact of television on 9
Vanity Fair (magazine) 121
Veronica Mars 57

Wall, Cara 89
Watts, Angie, in *EastEnders* 17
web sites, about childcare 4–5, 50, 110
Wee, Valerie 55
Weeds 71, 72
welfare reforms 77
What They Know About…Parenting!: Celebrity Moms and Dads Give us Their Take on Having Kids 122
What to Expect When You're Expecting (Eisenberg) 167
Whitbeck, Caroline 20
Who's the Boss? 31
Wife Swap 107–8
Will and Grace 31
Williams, Renee 100–101
Williams, Zoe 99, 109

Wolf, Naomi: on American midwives 165; on birth plans 173; on birthing experience 155–6, 161; on breathing techniques 168; on caesarean section revenues 152
women: competition between 47, 49; low-income 75; as moral guardians 112; pathologizing of 114; patriarchal conclusions about 107; in primetime television 15; representations of on television 1–2, 11, 15; reproductive labour of valued variably 140; in situation comedies 33; soap opera and 14–16, 17; in unequal power dynamic 65; in workforce 5, 7
women's movement focus 32
Wood, Helen 107, 115, 119, 182–3
Woollett, Anne 132
work 8, 45–7
working mothers 6, 7, 50; *see also* individual television characters
working-class characters 39–40
workplace, being pushed out of 46
World News Tonight 38
World War II 7
World's Oldest Mums, The 101
Worthington, Marjorie 59

Young Artist Awards 81
'yummy mummy': *see* celebrity reality television

www.ingramcontent.com/pod-product-compliance
Lightning Source LLC
Chambersburg PA
CBHW031710230426
43668CB00006B/169